Advances in Contemporary Psychoanalytic Field Theory

Field theory is a powerful and growing paradigm within psychoanalysis, but has previously been split between various schools of thought with little overlap. In this book, a distinguished group of contributors from across all perspectives on field theory examine its uniting factors and set out future developments and directions for the paradigm within psychoanalysis.

Advances in Psychoanalytic Field Theory represents the work developed for the first international meeting of the International Field Theory Association. Founded in 2015 to offer a community for those interested in psychoanalytic field theory and promote its understanding and further development, IFTA recognizes all models of psychoanalytic field theory and seeks to foster communication among psychoanalysts working in different models, languages and parts of the world.

At the first ever meeting of IFTA, an international group of psychoanalysts participated in a roundtable discussion of the different contemporary models of psychoanalytic field theory. Each participant wrote a paper in advance of the meeting, all of which were shared among the group beforehand and then discussed. These are presented as the chapters in this volume, while a thirteenth member offers a unifying overview of all of the papers. Each chapter provides new, contemporary ways of approaching field theory.

Key excerpts from the roundtable discussion are also featured throughout to give a flavour of the collaborative efforts of the participants. The book's aim is to generate mutual understanding of the different models of field theory, their underlying concepts and their heuristic principles. Drawing on insights from literature, critical theory and philosophy as well as psychoanalysis, the book sets out a programme for the future of field theory.

Advances in Psychoanalytic Field Theory will appeal to psychoanalysts and mental-healthcare practitioners as well as academics from the fields of philosophy, psychology and literature.

S. Montana Katz, **Roosevelt Cassorla** and **Giuseppe Civitarese** are psychoanalysts and the Founding Directors of the International Field Theory Association.

Psychoanalytic field theory book series

The Routledge Psychoanalytic Field Theory book series was initiated in 2015 as a new sub-series of the Psychoanalytic Inquiry book series. The series publishes books on subjects relevant to the continuing development of psychoanalytic field theory. The emphasis of this series is on contemporary work that includes a vision of the future for psychoanalytic field theory.

Since the middle of the twentieth century, various forms of psychoanalytic field theory have emerged in different parts of the world with different objectives, heuristic principles and clinical techniques. Taken together, they form a family of psychoanalytic perspectives that employs a concept of a bi-personal psychoanalytic field. The Psychoanalytic Field Theory book series seeks to represent this pluralism in its publications. Books on field theory in all its diverse forms are of interest in this series, and both theoretical works and discussions of clinical technique will be published in the future.

The series editors are especially interested in manuscripts that actively promote the understanding and further expansion of psychoanalytic field theory. Part of the mission of the series is to foster communication among psychoanalysts working in different models, in different languages and in different parts of the world.

Books available in this series:

Vol. 1 Contemporary Psychoanalytic Field Theory
Stories, dreams, and metaphor
S. Montana Katz

Vol. 2 Advances in Contemporary Psychoanalytic Field Theory
Concept and future development
S. Montana Katz, Roosevelt Cassorla and Giuseppe Civitarese

Advances in Contemporary Psychoanalytic Field Theory

Concept and future development

Edited by S. Montana Katz, Roosevelt Cassorla and Giuseppe Civitarese

LONDON AND NEW YORK

First published 2017
by Routledge
2 Park Square, Milton Park, Abingdon, Oxon OX14 4RN

and by Routledge
711 Third Avenue, New York, NY 10017

Routledge is an imprint of the Taylor & Francis Group, an informa business

© 2017 selection and editorial matter, S. Montana Katz, Roosevelt Cassorla and Giuseppe Civitarese; individual chapters, the contributors

The right of the editors to be identified as the authors of the editorial material, and of the authors for their individual chapters, has been asserted in accordance with sections 77 and 78 of the Copyright, Designs and Patents Act 1988.

All rights reserved. No part of this book may be reprinted or reproduced or utilized in any form or by any electronic, mechanical, or other means, now known or hereafter invented, including photocopying and recording, or in any information storage or retrieval system, without permission in writing from the publishers.

Trademark notice: Product or corporate names may be trademarks or registered trademarks, and are used only for identification and explanation without intent to infringe.

British Library Cataloguing in Publication Data
A catalogue record for this book is available from the British Library

Library of Congress Cataloging in Publication Data
Names: Katz, Montana, editor. | Cassorla, Roosevelt M. S. (Roosevelt Moises Smeke), editor. | Civitarese, Giuseppe, 1958- editor.
Title: Advances in contemporary psychoanalytic field theory: concept and future development/edited by S. Montana Katz, Roosevelt Cassorla and Giuseppe Civitarese. Description: Abingdon, Oxon; New York, NY: Routledge, 2017. |
Series: Psychoanalytic field theory book series; 2 | Includes bibliographical references and index.
Identifiers: LCCN 2016017220| ISBN 9781138884625 (hardback: alk. paper) | ISBN 9781138884632 (pbk.:alk. paper) | ISBN 9781315715971 (e-book :alk. paper)
Subjects: LCSH: Psychoanalysis. | Field theory (Social psychology)
Classification: LCC BF175. A535 2017 | DDC 150.19/5—dc23
LC record available at https://lccn.loc.gov/2016017220

ISBN: 978-1-138-88462-5 (hbk)
ISBN: 978-1-138-88463-2 (pbk)
ISBN: 978-1-315-71597-1 (ebk)

Typeset in Times New Roman
by Keystroke, Neville Lodge, Tettenhall, Wolverhampton

Contents

List of contributors vii

1 **Introduction** 1
   S. MONTANA KATZ, ROOSEVELT CASSORLA and GIUSEPPE CIVITARESE

2 **The field evolves** 5
   ANTONINO FERRO

3 **Not all field theories are the same: the impact of listening perspectives and models of transference** 13
   JAMES L. FOSSHAGE

4 **Dialectics of transferential interpretation and analytic field** 31
   BEATRIZ DE LEÓN DE BERNARDI

5 **About the theory of the analytic field** 45
   ELSA RAPPOPORT DE AISEMBERG

6 **Notes on transformations in hallucinosis** 57
   GIUSEPPE CIVITARESE

7 **Psychoanalytic field theory: good for all analysts** 67
   MARTIN A. SILVERMAN

8 **Dreams and non-dreams: a study on the field of dreaming** 91
   ROOSEVELT CASSORLA

9	Analytic field theory: a dialogical approach, a pluralistic perspective, and the attempt at a new definition MARCO CONCI	113
10	The third model of contemporary psychoanalytic field theory S. MONTANA KATZ	139
11	The analytic field as a resonator and instrument for revealing the presence of other fields CLAUDIO NERI	163
12	Emergent properties of the interpersonal field DONNEL STERN	175
13	Field theories and process theories JUAN TUBERT-OKLANDER	191
14	Commentary on field theory presentations JOSEPH LICHTENBERG	201
	Index	205

Contributors

Elsa Rappoport de Aisemberg is a member and training analyst of the Argentine Psychoanalytic Association; former vice-president of the Argentine Psychoanalytic Association; member of the IPA New Groups for the Sponsoring Committee of Asunción; past chair of Scientific Colloquiums and advisor for the Scientific Department of the Argentine Psychoanalytic Association; and chair of the Research Group on Psychosomatics at the Argentine Psychoanalytic Association. She has worked closely with Willy and Madeleine Baranger for many years, sharing their ideas on the analytic field. She is the author of many papers and publications on sexuality and gender, psychosomatics, art and psychoanalysis and theoretical and clinical approaches of the analytic field in psychoanalytic journals and books in many languages. She is co-editor and co-author of *Psychosomatics Today: A Psychoanalytic Perspective* (2010) and editor and co-author of *El cuerpo en escena* [The body at the scene] (2013).

Roosevelt Cassorla is a medical doctor working as a psychoanalyst in private practice in Campinas, Brazil, and training analyst of the Brazilian Psychoanalytic Society of São Paulo and of the Psychoanalytic Study Group of Campinas. He is a supervisor and teacher at both societies and Secretary of Education Monitoring and Qualification of the Campinas Study Group. He has worked as a full professor at the Psychiatry and Psychological Medicine Department and coordinator of the doctoral postgraduate course in Mental Health at the State University of Campinas, where he is currently a visiting professor. He works with psychiatry residents as a psychotherapy supervisor. He is a member of the editorial board of the *International Journal of*

Psychoanalysis, Psychoanalytical Quarterly (Spanish) and other psychoanalytical journals. He has edited three books on suicide and death and is the author of a number of book chapters and papers on psychological medicine and psychoanalysis, mainly on technical aspects with difficult patients. He has contributed to *Unrepresented States and the Construction of the Meaning* (2013) and *Wilfred Bion Tradition* (2015). His most recent book is *The Psychoanalyst, the Dreaming Theater and the Clinic of Enactment* (2015). He has been awarded various prizes, such as the Parthenope Bion Talamo Prize in 2009 and the IPA Prize for best paper on symbolization in 2013. He is coordinator of the Latin American Psychoanalytic Federation working party Microscopy of the Analytical Session, and a consultant for the *International Psychoanalytical Association Encyclopedic Dictionary*.

Giuseppe Civitarese, MD, Ph.D. is a training and supervising analyst in the Italian Psychoanalytic Society (SPI), and a member of both the American Psychoanalytic Association (APsaA) and the International Psychoanalytic Association (IPA). He lives, and is in private practice, in Pavia, Italy. Currently he is the editor of the *Rivista di Psicoanalisi*, the official journal of the Italian Psychoanalytic Society. He has published several books, including: *The Intimate Room: Theory and Technique of the Analytic Field* (2010); *The Violence of Emotions: Bion and Post-Bionian Psychoanalysis* (2012); *The Necessary Dream: New Theories and Techniques of Interpretation in Psychoanalysis* (2014); *Losing Your Head: Abjection, Aesthetic Conflict and Psychoanalytic Criticism* (2015); *The Analytic Field and its Transformations* (2015); and *Truth and the Unconscious* (2016). He has also co-edited *L'ipocondria e il dubbio: L'approccio psicoanalitico* [Hypochondria and doubt: the psychoanalytic approach] (2011); *Le parole e i sogni* [The words and the dreams] (2015); and *The Bion Tradition: Lines of Development – Evolution of Theory and Practice over the Decades* (2015).

Marco Conci, MD is an Italian psychiatrist and psychoanalyst living and working in Munich, Germany, since 1997. He is a full member of the German, Italian and International psychoanalytic associations. In 1991 he was editor of the Italian edition of Freud's letters to E. Silberstein, and won the International Federation of Psychoanalytic Societies' Joseph Barnett Candidates Award for a paper on the topic that year. He is the author of *Sullivan Revisited: Life and Work*, which has been published in Italian (2000), German (2005), English (second edition 2012) and Spanish (2012). He has been co-editor-in-chief of the *International Forum of Psychoanalysis* since 2007, and a member of the editorial board since 1994. He is also on the editorial boards of *Contemporary Psychoanalsyis*, *Psychoanalysis and History* and *Rivista di psicoanalisi*. In 2006 he received the Oesterreichisce Kreuz fuer Wissenschaft und Kunst from the Austrian President for his work as a historian of psychoanalysis (awarded in celebration of the 150th anniversary of Freud's birth).

Beatriz de León de Bernardi is a Uruguayan psychoanalyst and a member and training analyst of the Uruguayan Psychoanalytic Association (APU). She is a past President of the APU, a former editor of the *Uruguayan Journal of Psychoanalysis* and a former representative for Latin America on the International Psychoanalytical Association Board. She is currently an editorial board member of the *International Journal of Psychoanalysis*. She has published papers and books in several languages on psychoanalytic topics, mainly about the patient–analyst interaction and the analyst's contribution to the analytic process, the notion of countertransference in Latin America, and the thought of Madeleine and Willy Baranger. She has also researched and published about implicit theories in psychoanalytic practice. She received the Award of the Latin American Psychoanalytical Federation in 1992 and the Training Today Award in 2009.

Antonino Ferro is a training analyst for the Italian Psychoanalytic Society and a member of IPA and APsaA. He has published several books that have been translated into many languages, including *Mind Works*, *Avoiding Emotions, Living Emotions* and *Supervision in Psychoanalysis: The São Paulo Seminars*. In 2007 he received the Mary S. Sigourney Award. He was European editor of the *International Journal of Psychoanalysis* until September 2008, is a member of both CAPSA (the Analytic Practice and Scientific Activities Committee) and the EPF Program Committee, and became chair of the Sponsoring Committee of the Turkish Provisional Society of Psychoanalysis in 2007. In 2009 he was elected "Chair for Europe" at the 47th IPA Congress in Mexico City. Since April 2012 he has been a consultant associate editor of the *International Journal of Psychoanalysis*, and he is current President of the Italian Psychoanalytic Society.

James L. Fosshage, Ph.D. is Founding President of the International Association for Psychoanalytic Self Psychology and advisory board member at the International Association for Psychoanalysis and Psychotherapy. He is a co-founder, board director and faculty member of the National Institute for the Psychotherapies (New York); founding faculty member of the Institute for the Psychoanalytic Study of Subjectivity (New York); and Clinical Professor of Psychology for New York University's postdoctoral programme in Psychotherapy and Psychoanalysis. Author of over a hundred psychoanalytic articles and eight books, he has focused on the implicit/explicit motivational and organizing processes traversing dreams, transference, countertransference, listening perspectives and therapeutic action. He maintains a private practice in New York City and Tenafly, NJ. (His website is: www.jamesfosshage.net.)

S. Montana Katz, Ph.D., LP is a practising psychoanalyst in New York. She is a training and supervising analyst and senior faculty member at the National Psychological Association for Psychoanalysis, and is on the editorial boards of the *Psychoanalytic Review* and *Psychoanalytic Inquiry*. She is co-editor of the Routledge Psychoanalytic Field Theory book series and a founding co-director of the International Field Theory Association. She is the editor of *Metaphor and Fields: Common Ground, Common Language and the Future of Psychoanalysis* (2013) and author of *Contemporary Psychoanalytic Field Theory: Stories, Dreams, and Metaphor* (2016).

Joseph Lichtenberg, MD is a practising psychoanalyst in Washington, DC. He received his psychiatric training at Spring Grove State Hospital and the Sheppard and Enoch Pratt Hospital, where he served as Clinical Director. He has written articles about psychoses, psychosomatic illnesses, psychoanalytic theory, attachment theory, technique and applied psychoanalysis. In 1976, as an adjunct professor, he taught a course on biographies written by psychoanalysts at the Humanities Center of the Johns Hopkins University College of Arts and Sciences. He is the chairman of an ongoing workshop/seminar on creativity, a member of the Washington Center for Psychoanalysis, past president of both the Baltimore Psychoanalytic Society and the International Association of Psychoanalytic Self Psychology, and a supervising analyst at the Institute for the Psychoanalytic Study of Subjectivity (New York). He is also editor-in-chief of *Psychoanalytic Inquiry* and Routledge's Psychoanalytic Inquiry book series. He presented a plenary address at the December 1996 meeting of the American Psychoanalytic Association. He is an Emeritus Clinical Professor of Psychiatry at Georgetown University, and a current member of the Program Committee of the American Psychoanalytic Association. He is a dounder, Director Emeritus and training and supervising analyst of the Institute of Contemporary Psychotherapy and Psychoanalysis (Washington, DC). He is the co-editor of *Reflections on Self Psychology* (1983), *Empathy I and II* (1984), and *Attachment and Sexuality* (2007). He is the author of *Psychoanalysis and Infant Research* (1983), *The Talking Cure* (1985), *Craft and Spirit: A Guide to the Exploratory Psychotherapies* (2005), *Sensuality and Sexuality across the Divide of Shame* (2008), *A Developmentalist's Approach to Research, Theory, and Therapy* (2015) and, with Frank Lachmann and James L. Fosshage, *Psychoanalysis and Motivation* (1989), *Self and Motivational Systems: Toward a Theory of Psychoanalytic Technique* (1992), *The Clinical Exchange: Techniques Derived from Self and Motivational Systems* (1996), *A Spirit of Inquiry: Communication in Psychoanalysis* (2002), *Psychoanalysis and Motivational Systems: A New Look* (2010) and *Enlivening the Self: The First Year, Clinical Enrichment, and The Wandering Mind* (2015). *Reading Joseph D. Lichtenberg: Psychoanalytic Theory, Research, and Clinical Practice*, edited by Linda Gunsberg and Sandra G. Hershberg, was published in 2015.

Claudio Neri, MD teaches at the Faculty of Medicine and Psychology, University of Rome "La Sapienza" and the Faculty of Psychology, Turin University. He is a training and teaching psychoanalyst of the Italian Psychoanalytic Society, a member of the London Institute of Group Analysis and a founder and faculty member of the International Organization of Group Analytic Psychotherapy in Melbourne. He is the author of *Group* (1998) and co-editor – with Malcolm Pines and Robert Friedman – of *Dreams in Group Psychotherapy* (2002).

Martin A. Silverman is a training and supervising analyst and supervising child analyst at the Institute for Psychoanalytic Education at NYU College of Medicine, and a training and supervising analyst at the Center for Psychoanalysis and Psychotherapy of New Jersey. He has also taught at a number of other psychoanalytic institutes as a visiting faculty member. He is associate editor and book review editor of

Psychoanalytic Quarterly and was formerly a contributing editor of *Psychoanalytic Inquiry* and *Psychoanalytic Books*. He has authored over seventy psychoanalytic papers and chapters, over eighty psychoanalytic book reviews and several books for children. He is a former Clinical Professor of Psychiatry at NYU College of Medicine, a past President of the Association for Child Psychoanalysis and a past President of the New Jersey Council of Child and Adolescent Psychiatry.

Donnel Stern, Ph.D. is a training and supervising analyst and a member of Faculty, William Alanson White Institute, New York City; Adjunct Clinical Professor, NYU postdoctoral programme in Psychoanalysis and Psychotherapy; editor and founder of Routledge's Psychoanalysis in a New Key book series; author of *Unformulated Experience: From Dissociation to Imagination in Psychoanalysis* (1997); *Partners in Thought: Working with Unformulated Experience, Dissociation, and Enactment* (2010); and *Relational Freedom: Emergent Properties of the Interpersonal Field* (2015).

Juan Tubert-Oklander, MD, Ph.D. was born, studied medicine and trained as a group therapist in Buenos Aires, Argentina. Since 1976 he has lived and worked in private practice in Mexico City, where he trained as a psychoanalyst. He is the author of numerous papers and book chapters, published in Spanish, English, Italian, French, Portuguese, Czech and Hebrew, the co-author, with Reyna Hernández-Tubert, of *Operative Groups: The Latin-American Approach to Group Analysis* (2004), and the author of *Theory of Psychoanalytic Practice: A Relational Process Approach* (2013) and *The One and the Many: Relational Psychoanalysis and Group Analysis* (2014). He is a full member of the Mexican Psychoanalytic Association, the Argentine Psychoanalytic Association and the Group-Analytic Society International, and is a training and supervising analyst at the Institute of the Mexican Psychoanalytic Association.

Chapter 1

Introduction

S. Montana Katz, Roosevelt Cassorla and
Giuseppe Civitarese

The International Field Theory Association (IFTA) was founded in 2015 to offer a community for those interested in psychoanalytic field theory and to promote the understanding and further development of psychoanalytic field theory. IFTA recognizes all models of psychoanalytic field theory and seeks to foster communication among psychoanalysts working in different models, in different languages, and in different parts of the world.

The first meeting of IFTA was held on July 21, 2015 in Cambridge, Massachusetts, at the Bard College Longy School of Music. This meeting was designed to begin to achieve the goals of the association. An international group of psychoanalysts was asked to participate in a roundtable discussion of the different contemporary models of psychoanalytic field theory. The group participants were: Elsa Rappoport de Aisemberg, Roosevelt Cassorla, Giuseppe Civitarese, Marco Conci, Beatriz de León de Bernardi, Antonino Ferro, James L. Fosshage, S. Montana Katz, Joseph Lichtenberg, Claudio Neri, Martin Silverman, Donnell Stern, and Juan Tubert-Oklander. Twelve of the participants wrote papers in advance of the meeting. These papers were then shared among the group prior to the meeting. At the meeting itself all of the papers were discussed by the group. The thirteenth member offered a discussion of the papers.

The papers and discussion presented in this volume are the papers that were written for the meeting. The meeting occupied a full day and was structured into four sessions of three papers each. The papers are ordered in this book according to the order in which they were discussed at the meeting. Brief excerpts from the discussion are also presented throughout the book to give a flavor of the collaborative effort of the participants. The emphasis of the discussion was to generate mutual understanding of the different models of field theory, their underlying concepts, and their heuristic principles. The meeting was videotaped, and extensive footage has been posted on the IFTA website (www.internationalfieldtheory association.com).

We would like to thank all of the participants for their efforts to make the meeting a highly stimulating and collegial exchange of ideas. In addition, the Academic Dean at Bard College at Simon's Rock, Anne O'Dwyer and the Bard College Longy School of Music staff were all helpful in the planning and operation of the meeting. Videographer Richard Lange devoted many hours of careful attention to producing an excellent videotaped documentation of the meeting. Our editor, Kate Hawes, at Routledge has been a source of encouragement throughout the process of creating this volume.

Freud compared the analytic interaction with the noble game of chess. That's too rationalistic for my taste. Nino Ferro compared it to a fencing match. That's better because it involves non-rational activity such as the body, reflexes, unthought reactions, but it is still ruled by strategical and purposive thinking. When things get moving in an analysis it's like dancing. Two people are dancing in such a way that it makes no sense to ask who is leading. What is leading is the music and the music is something different from the two people. It is a process, what Don Stern would call emergence. The emergence of something new, unbidden, unexpected, and uncontrollable by both. What both can do is either accept it or reject it; but if you accept it, you let yourself be carried away by it. Suddenly both analyst and patient find themselves knowing things they didn't know they knew and perhaps something they didn't know before.

Juan Tubert-Oklander

Chapter 2

The field evolves

Antonino Ferro

The analytic field is also the site of all the patient's and analyst's potential identities, which does not mean that all the potential identities must come to life or be integrated: sometimes it is appropriate for them to remain split off or to be buried within the strata of the field itself for the whole of the time in which this will be useful for the development of mental life.

For a narrative to develop, as Diderot remembered *àpropos Jacques the Fatalist*, there are so many possible stories that must be "put to sleep" so that the main story, "fruit" of the two co-narrators, can come to life and develop.

I have spoken elsewhere of how there are two "loci" of mental creativity in a Bionian metapsychology: the place where beta elements, carriers of all the sensoriality, are transformed via alpha function into pictograms (the sub-units of dream-thought in the waking state) and the place where the derived narrative in all its infinite variety, on a longer or shorter leash, moves away from or stays close to waking dream-thought within the field (Ferro 2002, 2009).

In Simenon's fine novel *Les Clients d'Avrenos*, the protagonist Nouchi tells how when she was a child on her way home from school, she would often observe from behind a fence her sister, only a few years older, giving herself to adult men in exchange for a few coins or chocolate. It was the poor Vienna of the early twentieth century. Then Nouchi becomes an *entraîneuse*—a hostess in a low-life bar—though she remains frigid.

I have purposely chosen the telling of a neutral episode so as to see the various models at work.

In a model based on historic reconstruction it is not hard to anticipate where it would take us: to the childhood traumatic experience, child sexuality, abuse, and then the acquaintance with pain.

A model centered on Nouchi's internal world could take us towards eroticized destructiveness and an attack on linking.

An intermediate field model could lead us to a reading like this: an infantile part remains as an observer of what happens in the field; that is, the analyst is relating to a more adult part of the patient, who gains warmth and comfort from this but remains nevertheless "cold" because the interpretative coupling has been premature. But I would like to open up a field understood in a totally different way. That is to say, we do not know it at all: we must merely postulate a field in development, but in doing so surrender all its predictability, or at least accept that what we are given to know is F0 (Field-0) while we wait for F1, F2 . . . Fn.

We cannot therefore postulate that the field will be decipherable except in the moment in time (0) at which it occurs, but this moment also gives birth to infinite other possible fields that will come to life and be selected by the movement of the potential multitude that is the "couple," and will be knowable only *après-coup* with the opening/closing of infinite possible fields, derivatives of infinite factors, many of which are unknown.

For a long time—too long a time—we thought interpretation was the engine of analysis, an oscillation between time and abstinence/presence and intervention.

The initial episode of which I spoke could in fact produce any number of possible stories.

This could be the starting point of an exercise using a range of writings with different outcomes. Or, equally, different directors could develop different films based on the same outline, the same plot. (Even if it is not clear what the role of "director" might be in the session or from what it might be constituted.)

From among all the hypotheticals I would prioritize the "atmospheric" factors of the session and the links formed by multiple and variable reveries with multiple and variable projective identifications.

There is more creativity in not hindering developments than there is in specifically initiating them.

In Sicilian dialect the term *"chiacco"* indicates a kind of noose made of rope suspended from wires, usually between opposite or adjacent balconies, for hanging out washing to dry. If something light—a sock or handkerchief—is hung from this it shows the strength of the wind. A patient in analysis tells me that his grandfather used to watch something hanging out to dry so he could see how windy the day was, though the wind was usually a gentle breeze rather than the Bora, the north-eastern gale which sometimes batters Palermo. From the "forecast" given by the movement of something hanging from the *"chiacco"* the grandfather would determine the day's risk of catching a cold or cough from the "change of air"—that is, the wind if he was outside, or the dreaded draught if he was indoors.

This could be seen as an anecdote about childhood and as the source of eventual hypochondriac anxieties. Or it could be seen as a warning present in the internal world; or, if seen in time 0 of the field, as the description of an alarm-signal for some emotional current possibly about to come to life. The description of a field in which possible differences in potential, in temperature, in heat could be dangerous because they would activate currents that will be difficult to control. In that case the emotions would be winds that could cause illness.

But if we move from time 0 towards time 1—and on to time "n"—we have no way of foreseeing what type of field will develop or what narratives will give meaning to the emotional lines of force that will have come to life. One exercise could be, having set this field to time 0, to describe its possible developments.

In fencing, and even in the very different kind that is dependent on marking thrusts with electrified jackets and weapons, there is still a basic set of terms—parries, circular parries, hits, feints, double feints, arrests, a "counter," "two counters," and so on—but it is the sum total of these that makes every fencing match—for the knowledgeable spectator—a unique, unrepeatable, and above all completely unpredictable experience, because it is the fruit of a combination of variables tending to infinity.

All this could also apply to the development of psychoanalysis, where every change could be experienced as a turbulence to be avoided, even though we cannot evolve without disturbing what we know.

The "analyst at work" ("analyst" and "patient" will henceforth always mean "analyst and patient at work in an appropriate setting") must dispense with, or rather mourn for, external reality, so as to enter into the deconcretized, deconstructed, and then, if possible, *redreamed* world, as suggested by Tom Ogden (2009) when he writes that the purpose of analysis is to help the patient to have the dreams he has been unable to have by himself, which have become symptoms that can be dissolved only if they are "dreamed."

The same idea, although formulated differently, is expressed by Jim Grotstein (2007), who holds that the human mind is at one and the same time an entity that is constantly processing stimuli and a defense against "O" (truth, ultimate reality, facts, beta elements). The same author goes on to say that all we can do is *transform* our perception, our experience of the truth ("O"), *into fiction*—that is, *mythicize* it. This is achieved by allowing "O" to pass through Column 2 of the Grid, which is the column not only of lies but also of dreams—and where "O" is concerned a dream is also a lie.

In Wisława Szymborska's fine poem "Conversation with a Stone," a man asks a stone for permission to go inside it, but the stone says "no," he will never be able to enter even if he is all seeing, because he lacks the sense outwardly of taking part. At the entrance to Column 2, the "fact," the "event," the "reality-based given," or the "stone" of the symptoms or of reality must encounter the analyst's sense of taking part, which, for me, is the capacity to share the patient's manifest story or "thing."

This will permit access to the interior of Row 2, where that "thing" will meet with the "lithotripter" represented by the analyst's capacity for deconstruction, deconcretization, and redreaming. (For the sake of simplicity, I shall often say "analyst and patient," but this will always imply the "analytic field" as something new and different from the sum of its component parts: what happens in Row 2 occurs substantially in a place in the field.)

After the sense of taking part (being in unison), a number of *active instruments* of subjective mythopoiesis come into play—namely, the alpha function and the various types of reverie (basic reverie, flash-type reverie, constructive reverie, transformation in dreaming, transformation in play, dreaming, and Ogden's talking-as-dreaming; see Ferro, 2007, 2009).

Besides these active instruments, we need certain "*basic atmospheres*" if transformations are to be possible. These arise from the alternation between negative capability and the preselected fact, between the autistic-contiguous position (ACP) and PS↔D, and between container and contained.

The principal aim of analysis (apart from the familiar elements of removing the veil of repression, the work of integrating split-off parts, insight, putting ego where id was, and so on) is to develop these active instruments and the atmospheres that are conducive to transformation. An initial approach to this description is to consider, for example, how a "person" in Row 2 becomes a "character" of the analysis—that is to say, an affective hologram arising out of what the field needs to express and what is mediated by the ongoing casting of characters (Ferro, 2013).

The librarian and the rifle

Dreaming the symptom

Luigi is a severely obsessional librarian. At our very first interview, he says he has a father with an aortic aneurysm and a paralyzed uncle. (This suggests two different forms of functioning in the patient—one incontinent and the other that immobilizes him, as in his obsessive rituals.) He goes on to tell me how he spends ages "cleaning," "sweeping," and tidying up the garden lawn, where animals sometimes dig "holes."

In this ritual-filled world (with the rituals practiced both at work and at bedtime) he seems to have one area of freedom: his hobby of hunting. He has to look after two dogs, clean his guns, and organize the various hunts. He goes on to describe his grandfather's terrible experience during the war when he found that his house had been destroyed by a bomber, killing his entire family. He then returns to the subject of his highly complex cleaning rituals. (Meanwhile, I cannot help associating the hunting with the bomber—the Italian word *"caccia"* means both—and the death of his whole family.)

In the next session he refers to Mario Tobino's famous book *Le libere donne di Magliano*, about women patients in a mental hospital (introducing the subject of madness?), and then mentions an inexplicable tic: whenever he feels tense, he raises his right shoulder and moves it backwards. He then launches into a long account in which the words "funeral" and "hunting (*caccia*) rifle" constantly recur.

At this point everything comes together in my mind, like a puzzle with previously scattered pieces. The raising and backward movement of the right shoulder is precisely the effect of a rifle's "recoil": Luigi is a kind of killer, who constantly eliminates anyone who makes him feel tense. We cannot see the rifle, but what remains is the recoil, the cleaning rituals after every crime, the holes dug in the garden so as not to leave any trace of the buried bodies. When the rage is at fever pitch, he takes off in his bomber (*caccia*) and kills everyone in sight.

So here we have the dream that I was able to dream on his behalf. We now need to observe the development of these themes together: we shall see the Quentin Tarantino function and shall then have to decide what to do with this Django Unchained, dressed as a well-raised librarian.

Having reached this point, I must now present an outline of my model, whose origins lie in the intersection of post-Bion and the post-Baranger field.

The upheaval wrought by Bion (1962, 1963, 1965, 1992) was comparable to the French Revolution: nothing has been the same since. Its cardinal point is that the unconscious is constantly in the throes of formation and transformation, and is secondary and subsequent to the relationship with the Other. Nameless anxieties, proto-sense impressions and proto-emotions, projected and evacuated into the Other's mind, are transformed into alpha-elements by the Other's function of digestion and metabolism, the Other being the caregiver, group of alpha-functions or analyst. (Perhaps I should say the field rather than the Other?) These entities are visual building blocks (pictograms)—although they could also be associated with all the other senses—which, when linked together, give rise to waking dream-thought. Alpha-elements will then be constantly repressed, laying the foundations of the capacity to remember, and hence to forget, and forming the "contact barrier," or boundary between conscious and unconscious.

All this is known. What is less familiar, although mentioned by both Ogden (2009) and Grotstein (2007), is that some beta-elements penetrate this barrier and escape the process of alphabetization. These—the quanta of proto-emotions and untransformed sense impressions—are in my opinion the principal focus of interest in analysis. It is these quanta that give rise to the tsunamis, whirlwinds, and gales of beta-elements, which, if not adequately transformed, lie at the root of the most severe pathologies.

References

Bion, W.R. (1962) *Learning from Experience*. Heinemann, London.
Bion, W.R. (1963) *Elements of Psycho-analysis*. Heinemann, London.
Bion, W.R. (1965) *Transformations*. Heinemann, London.
Bion, W.R. (1992) *Cogitations*. Karnac Books, London.
Diderot, D. (1962/1771) *Jacques le fataliste*. In *Oeuvres Romanesque*. Garnier, Paris.
Ferro, A. (2002) "Some implications of Bion's thought: The waking dream and narrative derivatives." *International Journal of Psychoanalysis*, 83, pp. 597–607.
Ferro, A. (2007) *Avoiding Emotions, Living Emotions*. Routledge/New Library, London and New York.

Ferro, A. (2009) "Transformations in dreaming and characters in the psychoanalytic field." *International Journal of Psychoanalysis*, 90, pp. 209–230 (keynote address to the 46th IPA Congress, Chicago).
Ferro, A. (ed.) (2013) *Psicoanalisi oggi*. Carocci Editore, Rome.
Grotstein, J.S. (2007) *"A Beam of Intense Darkness": Wilfred Bion's Legacy to Psychoanalysis*. Karnac, London.
Ogden, T. (2009) *Rediscovering Psychoanalysis*. Routledge/New Library, Abingdon and New York.
Szymborska, W. (1995/1962) "Conversation with a stone." In *View with a Grain of Sand: Selected Poems*. Harcourt Brace & Company, Orlando, FL.
Simenon, G. (1935) *Les Clients d'Avrenos*. Gallimard, Paris.

We are all interested in the field concept but then differ on everything else. The tools we use, how we conceptualize the process, and everything else. We should ask ourselves why do we need a field concept, what do we mean by the field? If it is only to introduce the subjectivity of the analyst, that is one thing. We mean something more specific: how the communication from unconscious to unconscious goes on. The field is just a metaphor to get to phenomena we will never know as they really are. It is very different if we use the field concept within the classical conceptualization of the unconscious or if we use the concept of the field within Bionian metapsychology. The idea of the unconscious is very different, totally different. We need to keep in mind what kind of model of the unconscious is at the center of the field concept.

Giuseppe Civitarese

Chapter 3

Not all field theories are the same

The impact of listening perspectives and models of transference

James L. Fosshage

While Freud (1915) was well aware that "our perceptions are subjectively conditioned and must not be regarded as identical with that which is perceived" (p. 171), his observations and theories were embedded in the positivistic science of his day and emphasized the analyst's objectivity and the patient's transference distortions of reality. In 1927 Heisenberg's Uncertainty Principle was based on a demonstration in quantum physics of the *observer effect*—that is, the act of observation affects that which is observed—initiating a revolutionary change in epistemological paradigms from positivistic to relativistic science, later termed from objectivism to constructivism.

When the Uncertainty Principle and observer effect were applied to psychoanalysis, the analyst could no longer be viewed as an objective observer; instead, he/she was an active participant in co-creating what Sullivan, borrowing from Kurt Lewin's (1935, 1951) field theory, called an interpersonal field. Based on Gestalt principles of perception in which the whole rather than the individual parts is perceived and interpreted, Lewin, from the 1930s to 1950s, developed *field theory*, a psychological theory that examines patterns of interaction between the individual and the total field, or environment. Stern (2013) has described in detail how Sullivan, from the 1920s to the 1940s, developed how "field theory was woven into his theory of interpersonal relations ... In Sullivan's frame of reference the psychotherapist cannot avoid creating, and then participating in, a field with the patient" (pp. 488, 489).

Within psychoanalysis the recognition that analyst and patient form an interpersonal field was subsequently elaborated in North America in intersubjectivity (Atwood and Stolorow, 1984; Stolorow, Brandchaft and Atwood, 1987) and relational (Mitchell, 1988) field theory that involves "the intersection of two subjectivities" (Atwood and Stolorow, 1984), a term that accentuates the subjectivity, in contrast to objectivity, of each participant. Each participant impacts the field perceptually (Piaget, 1954) and interactionally (Sullivan, 1940). The second paradigm change, thus, has been the shift from intrapsychic to relational field theory in understanding all psychological phenomena, including psychological development, pathogenesis, transference and therapeutic action.

More recently, relational field theories have expanded through the integration of nonlinear dynamic systems theory (e.g., Coburn, 2002; Fosshage, 1992; Ghent, 2002; Lichtenberg, 2002; Shane, Shane and Gales, 1998; Stolorow, 1997) and complexity theory (Coburn, 2013). Nonlinear dynamic systems theory is illuminating the intricate formative impact of experience that occurs within a context of multiple systems—individual, familial, peer community, cultural, national and world systems. The development of an individual person is a vastly complex, multivariable interactive process of genetic, neurobiological and environmental factors. Through its microscopic focus, systems theory reveals more fully the moment-to-moment fits and starts, progressions and regressions that occur in the overall process of development. Microscopic empirical process-based observations of cognitive/psychomotor development, for example, have illustrated how the emergence of certain cognitive/psychomotor functions, previously viewed as innate developments, spontaneously emerge as new properties within a system (Thelan and Smith, 1994). Simultaneously, a close view has identified the early presence of sophisticated cognitive functions thought to emerge much later. The questions still remain as to what genetic factors and capacities the newborn brings into the familial system and how they shape individual development and their systems throughout the lifespan, which Thelan and Smith (1994)—well-known developmental researchers and systems theorists—also note in the last chapter of their book.

It is axiomatic that psychoanalytic field theories share an emphasis on the formative influence of the relational fields within which we live throughout our lives. Yet, field theories vary considerably along a wide range of other dimensions, creating a marked variability in theory and clinical practice. For example, field theories differ in models of psychological development, pathogenesis, motivation, listening/experiencing perspectives, contribution of posited biological factors and capacities, clinical procedures, conceptualization of unconscious processes and therapeutic action. Montana Katz, first in her edited book (2013), and now in her current project of bringing together a number of field theorists, is clarifying both the commonalities and the diversity in our theories and clinical approaches.

Since I have written a good deal on listening/experiencing perspectives and transference, I have chosen to highlight the impact of models of listening/experiencing perspectives and models of transference on field theory and clinical practice. My thesis is that the analyst's selection of listening/experiencing perspective(s) and transference model profoundly shapes the field theory, clinical approach and the dyadic field of the analytic encounter.

Listening/experiencing perspectives

The paradigm changes from objectivism to constructivism and intrapsychic to relational field theory have required a new epistemology to address the issue of how psychoanalysts listen to and "observe" their patients. Sullivan (1940) addressed this question through conceptualizing the therapist as a "participant observer," emphasizing both the therapist's participation in the co-created encounter and the therapist's observation of the ongoing interplay.

Beginning in 1959, Kohut attempted to update psychoanalytic epistemology, focusing on its method of observation. Kohut recognized "the relativity of our perceptions of reality, . . . the framework of ordering concepts that shape our observations and explanations" (1982, p. 400), and that "the field that is observed, of necessity, includes the observer" (1984, p. 41). Understanding that the psychoanalytic field involves two subjectivities, neither one of which is "objective," Kohut (1959, 1982) deemed the patient's subjectivity to be the principal focus of the analytic endeavor. To gain entrance to the patient's experiential world, he formulated "the empathic mode of observation" that employs affect resonance and vicarious introspection to understand as best as we can from the vantage point of the patient's subjective experience or frame of reference. In his formulation of the empathic mode, Kohut attempted to bring the patient's subjective experience more directly to the forefront of clinical process that had heretofore been too commandeered by the analyst's presumed "objective" point of view. So central became the empathic mode that Kohut (1977) designated it as the method by which the field of psychoanalysis itself is defined (p. 302).

In 1992 I described the relativity of the empathic stance: "Although [the empathic] listening stance is designed 'to hear' as well as possible from within the vantage point of the analysand, this is clearly a relative matter, for what is heard is *always variably shaped by the analyst*" (p. 22; original emphasis). This is a constructivist perspective (Berger and Luckmann, 1967). All analytic listening, including empathic listening, passes through and is influenced by the analyst's subjectivity. I often use the term "listening/experiencing perspectives" to emphasize how all listening passes through our subjectivities for what else is there. In empathic listening the analyst attempts to infer her way as well as possible into the patient's subjective world (Lichtenberg, Lachmann and Fosshage, 2010).

All analysts variably use empathic listening in efforts to understand the analysand's "experiential world" (Stolorow, Atwood and Orange, 2002), a fundamental analytic task (Fosshage, 1992). Self psychologists (Kohut, 1982; Ornstein and Ornstein, 1985; and many others) and Schwaber (1981, 1997, 1998) have emphasized its *consistent usage* as the basis of analytic inquiry and understanding. Others have argued for additional listening perspectives (Lichtenberg, 1981; Gabbard, 1997; Goldberg, 1999; Smith, 1999). In addition to the empathic mode of listening, I have proposed two additional listening/experiencing perspectives that are required both to understand the patient more fully and to respond to a patient's inquiries of the analyst's experience (Fosshage, 1995, 1997, 2003, 2011). In my view, *all of us in our relationships as well as analysts, with or without awareness, experientially oscillate between the empathic, other-centered and analyst's self listening perspectives.*

The other-centered perspective refers to an analyst's experience of the analysand as "an other" in a relationship with the patient—what it feels like to be an other person in the interaction. When we experience an analysand as hostile, controlling, loving or manipulative, we are experiencing the analysand primarily from the vantage point of an other in a relationship with the analysand—what Bromberg (1989) calls the "target" of the patient's actions. This information about the analysand and the interaction potentially informs us about how the analysand impacts others, about the analysand's patterns of relating and about change in those interaction patterns. These interaction patterns, in addition, provide an entrée to an analysand's internal patterns of organization that have been established on the basis of lived experience, for patterns of organization and procedural interaction are intricately interrelated. For example, a person's expectancies tend to create confirming relational interactions. Racker's (1968) concordant and complementary countertransferences can be viewed as corresponding with analysts' experiences emanating from empathic and other-centered perspectives, respectively.

The empathic perspective advantageously positions the analyst to attend closely to how the analysand experiences his or her world, a process that implicitly acknowledges and validates the "reality" of the analysand's experience, contributing to a deep, safe sense of being "heard" and, correspondingly, a co-creation of reflective space. Empathic listening, however, is quite complex, for an analyst, in listening to an analysand's explicit and implicit verbal and non-verbal expressions, must hear (infer) the message (content) and the music (process). An analyst must differentiate between foreground and background features of an analysand's articulated experience. And an analyst must sense into and facilitate the emergence of the implicit—as yet unarticulated—intentions and meanings.

The other-centered perspective provides information about how others may experience the analysand and the analysand's patterns of interaction, facilitating understanding of what happens in the analysand's relationships. The disadvantage of other-centered listening/experiencing data is that the analyst's other-centered experience, when communicated, may be too distant from the analysand's experience for the analysand to be able meaningfully to appropriate. Moreover, analysts have traditionally used what I am calling other-centered experience to assess underlying (unconscious) motivations that have all too often superseded the analysand's expressed intentional experience. To assess intention or motivation on the basis of the interpersonal consequences of an analysand's actions (the analyst's other-centered experience) warrants considerable caution, for the interpersonal consequences might or might not reflect the analysand's intent. For example, hostile humor interpersonally feels aggressive and triggers aversion; yet, a person might be totally unaware of the aversiveness for the primary motivation may be to connect, and the procedure for connecting (a learned familial attachment pattern) is hostile jibing. Similarly, an analysand's intense tracking of the analyst can feel controlling and, yet, may be emanating primarily from underlying anxiety related to expectancies of abandonment (an anxious attachment pattern). While other-centered experience can reveal how the analysand impacts others, invaluable information about interaction patterns and relationships as well as evidence for related organizing patterns, empathic inquiry is required to assess what the primary conscious and unconscious motivations are from within the analysand's experiential world in order to weave together a complex picture of the analysand's "internal" and "external" experiential world.

The "analyst's self perspective" refers to when an analyst more centrally reflects on her own subjective experience attempting to understand one's contribution to an analytic interaction, especially at the moment of a rupture between patient and analyst. A patient might inquire about his experience of the analyst as angry, taken aback or upset with the patient and inquires about it. A relational analyst, in my view, would take the patient's experience seriously through attempting to understand who is contributing what to the patient's experience. To respond, the analyst must reflect more directly about resonances and triggers that were operating within her. Listening carefully to one's analysand might extend our awareness of previously unknown, unconscious resonances and communications.

As a general principle, to unravel a complex and difficult analysand–analyst interaction, in my view, if we start within an analysand's perspective and experience (for example, intentions, affects and expectancies), including relevant historical resonances, and work our way to the analysand's contribution to the interpersonal interaction, utilizing an analyst's other-centered data, we can sustain reflective processing for both analysand and analyst and arrive at the most comprehensive understanding of the analysand's internal organizations and contribution to relational experience that are palatable and digestible. In contrast, at the moment of especially difficult entanglements, the analyst must begin with the analyst's self perspective, reflecting on what triggers and resonances were activated in the analyst, and acknowledge the analyst's contribution to the interaction, before investigating the analysand's contribution. At these moments the analyst will not come off as defensive in focusing solely on the analysand. In other words, the analyst must acknowledge first her contribution to a rupture in order to create and protect the reflective space necessary to unravel who contributed what to that rupture.

Whether or not an analyst uses primarily one or all three of these listening/experiencing perspectives, in my view, will substantially impact the field theory, the analytic relational field and the analytic experience for both protagonists.

Transference models

Transference is arguably the most pivotal concept in psychoanalysis, for it addresses the patient's immediate feelings and fantasies toward the analyst, it houses an etiological theory as to the source of these feelings and fantasies, it posits a theory of therapeutic action and it encompasses a theory of clinical practice. Transference has evolved in various conceptualizations, understandings and definitions since Freud's (1895) initial formulation over a century ago. While models of transference can vary in any one of the above areas, creating an array of models, I believe that all transference theories at a structural level are represented by one of three fundamental models—the *displacement (classical)*, the *totalist* and the *organizing* models of transference. The transference model utilized, once again, powerfully shapes a field theory and its clinical approach.

Central in the conceptualization and evolution of these three basic models has been the ongoing, yet variable, integration of the two, previously addressed, paradigm changes in psychoanalysis—from objectivism to constructivism and from intrapsychic to relational field theory—that have occurred over the past sixty years. First, the change in epistemologies in psychoanalysis has had a profound impact theoretically and clinically. Initially emanating from an *objectivist epistemology*, transferences were viewed as *distortions of reality*; subsequently emanating from a *relativistic epistemology* (what Orange, 1995, has termed "perspectival realism"), transferences are now viewed as *constructions of "reality."* Second, when transferences, developmentally and currently within the analytic relationship, are viewed as emergent *principally from intrapsychic sources* or *from within relational fields*, these fundamentally different etiological explanations of transferences have a wide-ranging impact on understanding, interpretive explanations and the conceptualization of therapeutic action. My purpose here is to delineate the theoretical origin of the technical precept of *the singular, if not exclusive, focus on the transference in the analytic relationship*. The application of this principle during the psychoanalytic encounter, in my view, can easily lead to an overly analyst-centered focus (what I have referred to, on occasion, as "analyst-centric"; Fosshage, 1994) about which patients frequently complain. In addition, the analyst's overzealous application of the patient's material, especially the content, to the analyst and analytic relationship can disrupt the patient's articulated focus and/or abort a new, more progressive relational experience occurring in the analytic relationship.

Whether or not transference can be observed and effectively addressed outside the analytic relationship—called extratransference—has subsequently generated considerable debate. The long-held implicit and explicit clinical rule, what Wachtel (2008) refers to as the "default position" (p. 165), is that analysts should focus consistently on the transference as it is played out in the analytic relationship. It is commonly assumed, therefore, that if a psychoanalyst does not "bring" the transference into the analytic relationship, the analyst is "countertransferentially colluding with the transference."

The organizing model of transference has emerged over the past thirty-five years. This model, based on the integration of cognitive science, has redefined transference to refer to *patterned affective/cognitive/perceptual organizations of experience*. It provides the theoretical underpinnings of a new clinical principle: that is, to analyze transference when and where it is activated, whether inside or outside of the analytic relationship. Despite the contributions of cognitive science to the organizing model and application of this model to establish new clinical principles, psychoanalysts frequently adhere to clinical assumptions based on the original displacement model and, specifically, resort to the consistent emphasis to analyze the transference in the analytic relationship as a default position without regard to the patient's focus. For example, the patient describes feeling angry with a friend and the analyst begins to think that the patient is "really" angry with the analyst, unable to discuss this directly, and, therefore, talking "off-target."

A brief historical review

In his initial observations and formulations presented in the *Studies of Hysteria*, Freud (1895) noted on the basis of Breuer and Anna O. that patients make a "false connection" by transferring "on to the figure of the physician the distressing ideas which arise from the content of the analysis" (p. 302). Subsequently, Freud (1905) re-conceptualized this "false connection" as "transference" and distinguished two types: those that differ "from the model in no respect whatever except for the substitution," and those that take "advantage of some real peculiarity in the physician's person or circumstances," resulting not in "new impressions, but revised editions" (p. 116). In the first instance, the patient's transference *distorts* the "reality" of the analyst; in the second instance, the patient's transference draws on the analyst's idiosyncrasies to support the patient's view (Smith, 2003)—what became known colloquially as "the hook the patient hangs his hat on." This second distinction is remarkable in that it implicates the analyst's contribution, albeit limited and inadvertent, which became a forerunner to the future recognition based on field theory of the analyst's active participation and contribution to the transference.

The *classical* or *displacement* model, however, was formulated during the heyday of positivistic science and objectivism, and viewed transference principally as *intrapsychically generated distorted perceptions of the analyst*. Thus, clinically, it made sense for the analyst to remain anonymous, abstinent and a blank screen in order to reflect back to the patient his distorting displacements. Any introduction of the analyst's subjectivity would muddy the reflective lens; and any deviation from the maintenance of anonymity and abstinence was viewed as a countertransference problem or collusion with the patient's transference.

After initially viewing transference as a primary resistance to treatment, impeding the remembering of repressed material, Freud came to see it as a "most powerful ally" (1905, p. 117) in that *"every conflict has to be fought out in the sphere of transference"* (1912, p. 104; emphasis added) because "when all is said and done, it is impossible to destroy anyone *in absentia or in effigy*" (p. 108; original emphasis). Transference was conceptualized as specifically referencing its emergence toward the "physician" or analyst. The analysis of transference, thus, referred to the analytic relationship and became the central focus in psychoanalytic treatment. In other words, transference by definition referred to the analytic relationship, a conceptualization that was reinforced with Freud's concept of transference neurosis (1914, p. 154). The principal battleground of conflict, thus, is expressed in the *transference to the analyst* that became paramount for psychoanalytic treatment. When transference was detected outside the analytic relationship, a different term—extratransference—was used. It was assumed that the patient was defending against its emergence more directly in the analytic relationship, a defense that needed interpretation so that it could be brought back into the analytic relationship. Not to do so was viewed as the analyst's countertransferential collusion with the resistance to the transference.

The *totalist* model developed by Gill (1982, 1984) far more broadly defined transference as the patient's experience of the analyst and analytic relationship, further opening the door to recognizing the analyst's and not only the patient's contributions. Not only did Gill (1984) maintain the centrality of the analysis of transference, but he argued that four of the five intrinsic criteria defining psychoanalysis involved transference—namely, "the centrality of the analysis of transference, a neutral analyst, the induction of a regressive transference neurosis and the resolution of that neurosis by techniques of interpretation alone, or at least mainly by interpretation" (p. 161). Taken to task for his argument that transference in the analytic relationship should always be the focus of analysis, Gill (1984) "retreated from saying 'always,'" but reasserted "that what should . . . get first attention is the meaning the associations have for the transference" (p. 492)—that is, for the analytic relationship. In 1994, I pointed out that if we use the totalist model, we need to determine *whether the content or process of communicating* with the analyst carries the transferential meaning in order to avoid the clinically disruptive conundrum of always ascribing the content of a patient's communication to the analytic relationship.

Integrating cognitive science, and specifically Piaget's (1954) work, a host of authors (Wachtel, 1980; Hoffman, 1983, 1991; Stolorow and Lachmann, 1984/1985; Fosshage, 1994; Lichtenberg, Lachmann and Fosshage, 1996; Stern, 1997) subsequently contributed to the emergent *organizing model of transference* that refers to the primary organizing patterns with which the analysand constructs and assimilates his or her experiential world. Organizing patterns are cognitive/affective patterns established on the basis of lived experience that are variously used in constructing and negotiating one's life experience. Once established, they function in a given context in the following ways:

1. activation of expectancies;
2. selective attention to cues that correspond with the expectancies;
3. attribution of meanings that are in keeping with the expectancies; and
4. interacting in such a way as to confirm the expectancies.

(Fosshage, 1994)

While we call it transference when an organizing pattern is activated within the analytic relationship, the model of organizing patterns has broadened the relational fields in which organizing patterns operate.

Organizing patterns are activated and deactivated in relationships at large, legitimizing the analyst's focus on the context in which a pattern is activated, be it in the analytic relationship or an outside relationship. This model of cognitive/affective patterned organizing activity, thus, does not prioritize focus on the analytic relationship and expands the range of coverage to include all of a patient's relational experience. In contrast to the displacement model, it is never assumed that the subject of a patient's narrative or dream is the analyst. Rather, we focus on and illuminate an organizing pattern with whomever and whenever it is activated, whether it is with the analyst or with an outside person. If an analysand is troubled by an experience with a friend, the analysand wants to understand that experience, not to have the focus shifted back to the analyst.

While this might seem self-evident and even a matter of common sense, the default position of focusing on the transference in the analytic relationship is all too often looming. Analytic candidates will at times sheepishly and guiltily admit, "I'm not sure this is psychoanalysis because I didn't address the transference. Maybe the patient was really unconsciously talking about me." Or the patient describes feeling angry with a friend and the analyst begins to think that the patient is "really" angry with the analyst and defensively talking "off-target." Lingering default assumptions from the displacement model in these instances undermine the observations and instincts of a good clinician, interfering with the attuned listening and understanding that is the stuff of good clinical work. When an organizing theme is, at a particular moment, active in an outside relationship it might or might not be active in the analytic relationship. For example, when a patient is describing a shame-ridden abusive experience, he or she most likely is experiencing the analyst at that moment not as an abuser but as a trusted safe person with whom he or she can be vulnerable and open. To focus on the latter would interrupt the patient's articulated focus. In our complexity we typically have a number of experiences and cognitive/affective/perceptual organizations occurring implicitly and explicitly at the same time. While the organizing model of transference helps us to address this complexity, default clinical procedures can easily disrupt understanding of this complexity, clinical procedures that are not in keeping with the more recently developed organizing model of transference and require explicit declarative focus in order to change.

Clinical vignette

I present the following clinical vignette to illustrate the analyst's rapid oscillating use of three listening perspectives. It also illustrates when the action does directly involve the analyst.

A number of years ago, I began psychoanalytic treatment with an extremely sensitive, perceptive and reactive woman in her thirties. She was quite labile in mood and prone to fragile self-states. Easily feeling impinged upon, she experienced natural light in my office as painfully too bright, so, at her request, I regularly adjusted the blinds. Both of her parents had been remarkably absent, with her mother often feeling overwhelmed. She had a prolonged incestuous relationship with an extremely sadistic older brother. When she would cry out to her mother for protection, her mother would push her away with "Leave me alone, you're killing me." She felt that her previous analyst had saved her life. He had been her first real care-taker. His move to another city unfortunately aborted a long treatment and forced her to find another analyst.

During a session toward the end of the first month that I wish to present here, I experienced the room as uncomfortably warm. Silently, I went to the window to adjust the ventilation. At the following session my analysand related how upset she was with me for getting up in the middle of the session, when she was talking, to stare out the window. Taken aback by what, to me (*judgment from the analyst's self perspective*), was a very idiosyncratic, hurtful perception, and knowing that our capacity to share humor often helped her to regain reflective perspective, I, in a somewhat humorous, self-mocking vein, said, "The mark of a good analyst—get up in the middle of a session and stare out the window." This proved to be a misjudgment, for she was far too hurt with her particular framing of the event to join in with the joke. Instead, she felt invalidated, and perhaps even ridiculed. Recapturing my *empathic stance*, I inquired about her experience when I had gone to the window. She had felt that I was uninterested in what she was saying. With concern, I reflected that her feeling that I went to stare out the window while she was talking and seemed uninterested in her was understandably quite hurtful to her (what Lichtenberg, Lachmann and I (1992) call "wearing the attributions of the transference"). She appeared to feel better that I had heard, understood and validated her experience (*using the empathic perspective*); yet, she was still consumed by the injury and her particular organization of the event—

that is, that I had gone to stare out the window while she was telling me something important.

In my view, my analysand needed to become reflectively aware of this particular pattern of organizing events, along with its historical origins, in order to regain her self-equilibrium more fully and gradually to be able to maintain a reflective perspective when this pattern was activated in the future. To that end, I inquired toward the end of the session if she would like to hear about my experience as to what prompted me to go to the window (*analyst's self perspective*). Possibly the discrepancy of our experiences, I thought, would be useful in illuminating her view of the self-involved, uninterested and rejecting other and offering an alternative perspective. She declined.

At the next session, two days later, she told me that she had not wanted to hear my point of view at the previous session and poignantly remarked, "Jim, do me a favor. When I come into the room, just check your subjectivity at the door." In this instance, I winced at feeling controlled and negated (*other-centered experience*) and thought of how previously I and others had experienced her as controlling. While others from an other-centered perspective might have experienced her as sadistic, certainly in the light of her considerable sado-masochistic experience with her brother, I did not experience her delivery as sadistic. Instead, I experienced in her delivery the seriousness of her request and at the same time a note of recognition on her part about the extremity of her statement to the point of an almost humorous absurdity that was non-verbally recognized, I believe, by both of us. This mutual recognition enabled me "to hold" my *other-centered experience* and to respond primarily from within an *empathic perspective*. I warmly smiled and told her, also with an implicit touch of lightness and humor, "I will try my best, although it could prove difficult on occasion." She heard that I grasped her point that her subjectivity needed to take priority at that moment, while simultaneously letting her know (which she, I believe, already knew) that this was not entirely doable.

With relaxation on her part and increased reflective space, we then proceeded to focus on her experience and how precarious she felt my interest in her was. Within a few moments, it dawned on me what was occurring when she felt overwhelmed by my subjectivity (*an empathic perspective combined simultaneously with my other-centered experience* of feeling like the intrusive other), and I said in a gentle manner, "I think that I just got it. I think I understand that when I do something suddenly, like go to the window, or bring my subjective viewpoint in here, that it feels like I am taking up *all* the space in here, that there is *no* room for *you*, for *your* thoughts and desires, and I sense that you must have felt just that way with your very sadistic brother." I had acknowledged my contribution to her experience, noted that it had activated a primary experiential (organizing) pattern and had related its resonance to its historical origins. She notably relaxed, acknowledging that she thought I was right. Our empathic understanding had deepened immeasurably over my initial understanding of her feeling hurt and rejected by me.

Shortly afterward, she smiled and said, "Now, you can let me know what was happening for you at the window." Feeling seen and understood, she could now let in my subjectivity (*the analyst's self perspective*) without feeling threatened that I would treat her as her brother had. Her warm and open delivery triggered an empathic perspective within me and simultaneously prevented activation of an other-centered perspective (for example, a feeling of being controlled). Once again the analysand's delivery was a primary factor in eliciting the analyst's listening perspective. An analysand's openness and vulnerability, as was the case here, usually elicit an empathic perspective in the analyst. I then explained that I had been uncomfortably warm, had assumed that she was too, for she tended to be warmer than myself, and, thinking that it would be more disruptive to ask her, I had quietly gone to the window to adjust the ventilation by opening the window. She smiled and felt reassured in understanding the set of events in a much less hurtful, rejecting way. Airing the *discrepancies in our experiences* further illuminated her particular organization and served as a basis for the establishment of an alternative perspective.

Several months later, my analysand suddenly recalled how at home her mother often stared out the window, oblivious to all around her, providing a very important additional historical piece that closed the loop, if you will, in understanding the particularities of this organized experience in the analytic relationship.

The use of the different listening/experiencing perspectives increased access to and understanding of my patient and, thus, substantially influenced the analytic field. In this instance, my "going to the window" activated in the analytic relationship my patient's pattern of organization that was based on her relationship with her mother.

In my view, not all field theories are the same, for they substantively vary on a range of theoretical and clinical issues. I have chosen only two theoretical issues—the use of different listening/experiencing perspectives and the use of different transference models—to demonstrate the profound impact of these models on our field theories and clinical work, creating considerable diversity.

References

Atwood, G. and Stolorow, R. (1984). *Structures of Subjectivity.* Hillsdale, NJ: The Analytic Press.

Berger, P. and Luckmann, T. (1967). *The Social Construction of Reality.* Garden City, NY: Anchor.

Bromberg, P. (1989). Interpersonal psychoanalysis and self psychology: A clinical comparison. In D. Detrick and S. Detrick, eds., *Self Psychology: Comparisons and Contrasts.* Hillsdale, NJ: The Analytic Press, 275–292.

Coburn, W. (2002). A world of systems: The role of systemic patterns of experience in the therapeutic process. *Psychoanalytic Inquiry,* 22: 655–677.

Coburn, W. (2013). *Psychoanalytic Complexity: Clinical Attitudes for Therapeutic Change.* New York: Routledge.

Fosshage, J. (1992). Self psychology: The self and its vicissitudes within a relational matrix. In N. Skolnick and S. Warshaw, eds., *Relational Perspectives in Psychoanalysis.* Hillsdale, NJ: The Analytic Press, 21–42.

Fosshage, J. (1994). Toward reconceptualizing transference: Theoretical and clinical considerations. *International Journal of Psycho-Analysis,* 75(2): 265–280.

Fosshage, J. (1995). Countertransference as the analyst's experience of the analysand: Influence of listening perspectives. *Psychoanalytic Psychology,* 12(3): 375–391.

Fosshage, J. (1997). Listening/experiencing perspectives and the quest for a facilitative responsiveness. In A. Goldberg, ed., *Conversations in Self Psychology: Progress in Self Psychology,* Vol. 13. Hillsdale, NJ: The Analytic Press, 33–55.

Fosshage, J. (2003). Contextualizing self psychology and relational psychoanalysis: Bi-directional influence and proposed syntheses. *Contemporary Psychoanalysis,* 39(3): 411–448.

Fosshage, J. (2011). The use and impact of the analyst's subjectivity with empathic and other listening/experiencing perspectives. *Psychoanalytic Quarterly,* 80(1): 139–160.

Freud, S. (1895). *Studies on Hysteria.* In *The Standard Edition of the Complete Psychological Works of Sigmund Freud.* London: The Hogarth Press [*S.E.* from hereon], Vol. 2.

Freud, S. (1905). Fragment of an analysis of a case of hysteria. In *S.E.*, Vol. 7: 7–122.

Freud, S. (1912). The dynamics of transference. In *S.E.*, Vol. 12: 97–108.

Freud, S. (1914). Remembering, repeating and working-through. In *S.E.*, Vol. 12: 145–156.

Freud, S. (1915). The unconscious. In *S.E.*, Vol. 12: 166–215.
Gabbard, G. (1997). A reconsideration of objectivity in the analyst. *International Journal of Psycho-Analysis*, 78: 15–26.
Ghent, E. (2002). Wish, need, drive: Motive in the light of dynamic systems theory and Edelman's selectionist theory. *Psychoanalytic Dialogues*, 12(5): 763–808.
Gill, M. (1982). *Analysis of Transference I: Theory and Technique*. New York: International Universities Press.
Gill, M. (1984). Transference: A change in conception or only in emphasis? *Psychoanalytic Inquiry*, 4(3): 489–523.
Goldberg. A. (1999). Between empathy and judgment. *Journal of the American Psychoanalytic Association*, 47: 351–365.
Hoffman, I. (1983). The patient as interpreter of the analyst's experience. *Contemporary Psychoanalysis*, 19: 389–422.
Hoffman, I. (1991). Discussion: Toward a social-constructivist view of the psychoanalytic situation. *Psychoanalytic Dialogues*, 1: 74–105.
Katz, M., ed. (2013). *Metaphor and Field Theory: Common Ground, Common Language, and the Future of Psychoanalysis*. New York: Routledge.
Kohut, H. (1959). Introspection, empathy, and psychoanalysis. *Journal of the American Psychoanalytic Association*, 7: 459–483.
Kohut, H. (1977). *The Restoration of the Self*. New York: International Universities Press.
Kohut, H. (1982). Introspection, empathy, and the semicircle of mental health. *International Journal of Psycho-Analysis*, 63: 395–408.
Kohut, H. (1984). *How Does Analysis Cure?* Hillsdale, NJ: The Analytic Press.
Lewin, K. (1935). *A Dynamic Theory of Personality*. New York: McGraw-Hill.
Lewin, K. (1951). *Field Theory in Social Science: Selected Theoretical Papers*. Ed. D. Cartwright. New York: Harper & Row.
Lichtenberg, J. (1981). The empathic mode of perception and alternative vantage points for psychoanalytic work. *Psychoanalytic Inquiry*, 3: 329–356.
Lichtenberg, J. (2002). Values, consciousness, and language. *Psychoanalytic Inquiry*, 22: 841–856.
Lichtenberg, J., Lachmann, F. and Fosshage J. (1992). *Self and Motivational Systems: Toward a Theory of Technique*. Hillsdale, NJ: The Analytic Press.
Lichtenberg, J., Lachmann, F. and Fosshage, J. (1996). *The Clinical Exchange: Technique from the Standpoint of Self and Motivational Systems*. Hillsdale, NJ: The Analytic Press.
Lichtenberg, J., Lachmann, F. and Fosshage, J. (2010). *Psychoanalysis and Motivation: A New Look*. New York: The Analytic Press.
Mitchell, S. (1988). *Relational Concepts in Psychoanalysis*. Cambridge, MA: Harvard University Press.
Orange, D. (1995). *Emotional Understanding: Studies in Psychoanalytic Epistemology*. New York: Guilford Press.

Ornstein, P. and Ornstein, A. (1985). Clinical understanding and explaining: The empathic vantage point. In A. Goldberg, ed., *Progress in Self Psychology*, Vol. I. New York: Guilford Press, 43–61.

Piaget, J. (1954). *The Construction of Reality in the Child*. New York: Basic Books.

Racker, H. (1968). *Transference and Countertransference*. New York: International Universities Press.

Schwaber, E. (1981). Empathy, a mode of analytic listening. *Psychoanalytic Inquiry*, 7: 261–275.

Schwaber, E. (1997). A reconsideration of objectivity in the analyst. *International Journal of Psycho-Analysis*, 78: 1219–1221.

Schwaber, E. (1998). From whose point of view? The neglected question in analytic listening. *Psychoanalytic Quarterly*, 67: 645–661.

Shane, M., Shane, E. and Gales, M. (1998). *Intimate Attachments: Toward a New Self Psychology*. New York: Guilford Press.

Smith, H.F. (1999). Subjectivity and objectivity in analytic listening. *Journal of the American Psychoanalytic Association*, 47: 465–484.

Smith, H.F. (2003). Analysis of transference: A North American perspective. *International Journal of Psycho-Analysis*, 84: 1017–1041.

Stern, D.B. (1997). *Unformulated Experience: From Dissociation to Imagination in Psychoanalysis*. Hillsdale, NJ: The Analytic Press.

Stern, D.B. (2013). Field theory in psychoanalysis, Part I: Harry Stack Sullivan and Madeleine and Willy Baranger. *Psychoanalytic Dialogues*, 23(5): 487–501.

Stolorow, R. (1997). Dynamic, dyadic, intersubjective systems: An evolving paradigm for psychoanalysis. *Psychoanalytic Psychology*, 14: 337–346.

Stolorow, R., Atwood, G. and Orange, D.M. (2002). *Worlds of Experience*. New York: Basic Books.

Stolorow, R., Brandchaft, B. and Atwood, G. (1987). *Psychoanalytic Treatment: An Intersubjective Approach*. Hillsdale, NJ: The Analytic Press.

Stolorow, R. and Lachmann, F. (1984/1985). Transference: The future of an illusion. *Annual of Psychoanalysis*, 12/13: 19–37.

Sullivan, H. (1940). *Conceptions of Modern Psychiatry*. New York: W.W. Norton & Co.

Thelen, E. and Smith, L. (1994). *A Dynamic Systems Approach to the Development of Cognition and Action*. Cambridge, MA: The MIT Press.

Wachtel, P.L. (1980). Transference, schema and assimilation: The relevance of Piaget to the psychoanalytic theory of transference. *Annual of Psychoanalysis*, 8: 59–76.

Wachtel, P.L. (2008). *Relational Theory and the Practice of Psychotherapy*. New York: Guilford Press.

The field is a situation in which there is more variety and richness of feedbacks and in which we can come in touch with ourselves. A common denominator is helping patients come in touch with parts of themselves in which they are not in touch with. This is a major aim of our work and using the field concept best realizes this than through the classical concept of the analyst interpreting. The field concept is richer than the hierarchical concept of the analyst interpreting something to the patient because he comes in touch with something in himself. He discovers something new, and this is neglected by the classical analyst.

Marco Conci

Chapter 4

Dialectics of transferential interpretation and analytic field

Beatriz de León de Bernardi[1]

I would like to review a central aspect of the field theory: the dialectic character of transferential interpretation. Transferential interpretation undoubtedly emerges in the context of a specific analytic relationship. This implies complex verbal and non-verbal phenomena, which go beyond interventions and explicit interpretations from the analyst. This aspect has been highlighted by accumulated clinical experience, different psychoanalytic theorizations and empirical research. Non-interpretative moments between patient and analyst (Stern et al., 1998) have a central influence in the strengthening of the therapeutic relationship. Another aspect that has been noted is how the analytic encounter supposes an "engagement or closeness between therapist and patient which characterizes the 'positive therapeutic alliance'" (Levenson, 1974, p. 359), generating a global commitment from the patient's and analyst's personalities and contributing to reveal intimate and unconscious aspects from the analysand's subjectivity.

The focus of this paper will be, however, the study of those analytic moments when transference becomes explicit. I will primarily take a closer look at the analysis of metaphoric language used by either the analyst or the patient, or co-constructed by the dyad (de León de Bernardi, 2013; de León and Altmann, 2014). I also revisit contributions by Bleger (1969) about the situational, dramatic and dialectic character of psychoanalysis.

Bleger emphasized the dialectic character of psychoanalysis. Later, Ogden (1992) pointed to the dialectic character of the constitution of the psychoanalytic subject, highlighting the dialectic permeability between the conscious and unconscious systems, as I mentioned in a previous paper (de León de Bernardi, 2000).

Bleger integrated and widened some psychoanalytic notions of thinkers from the Río de la Plata, such as Pichon-Rivière, Racker, and M. and W. Baranger (who developed their thought in Buenos Aires and Montevideo from the start of the 1940s). These notions included, but were not limited to, "analytic bond" and "dialectic spiral" (Pichon-Rivière), "complementary countertransference" (Racker), and "dynamic field" (the Barangers).

Dialectic perspective in the analytic situation and process

Bleger's situational, dramatic and dialectic perspective about psychoanalysis leads him to revisit the notion of "analytic bond" (Bernardi and de León de Bernardi, 2012), understood by Pichon-Rivière as a dialectic structure established between subject and object. This notion of bond, which used to put special emphasis on its unconscious aspects, modified the notion of object relationship which was present in Klein, who had specially considered object relationships and unconscious fantasies belonging to the subject's internal world. Pichon-Rivière, however, conceived bond as a complex structure of two participants who dialectically interrelate with each other. This aspect had an influence in the conception of shared unconscious fantasy in the analytic field by M. and W. Baranger. Pichon-Rivière considered the "internal group" of primary, internalized figures not only in the analytic scene but also in tight interrelation with the analysand's family and social bonds. "All unconscious mental life, for which I mean the domain of unconscious fantasy, has to be considered as the interaction among internal objects (internal group) in permanent dialectic interrelation with the objects from the outside world" (Pichon-Rivière, 1998, p. 42).

Besides, not only the analytic relationship is conceived dialectically, but also the analytic treatment was understood as a dialectical process by different authors. As Etchegoyen (1986/2002) later stated, different authors from the Río de la Plata offered an analysis of the analytic situation, with a synchronic perspective, but also of the analytic process considered in its entirety and diachronically. The dialectical view incorporates a vision of temporality in relation to the interpretation, in the "here and now," but also in relation to the process of analysis. This temporal dimension is especially expressed in the metaphor of the "dialectical spiral" proposed by Pichon-Rivière, which was revisited by M. and W. Baranger.

The "dialectical spiral"

Pichon-Rivière's idea of the "dialectical spiral" appears as a metaphor of the interpretative movement of analysis, which is placed as a hinge between the "here and now" of the analytic scene and the "there and then" of the infantile past. The turns of the spiral suppose a hermeneutic circle of opposed senses, rooted in the emotional experience of the patient, which are amplified in a game of oppositions that gradually integrate in new syntheses and meanings along the analysis. In this sense the transferential interpretation has, for Pichon-Rivière and also for M. and W. Baranger, not only a retrospective value but also a prospective one, integrating the present of the analytic situation to the infantile past and the history of the analysis while, at the same time, taking a step into the future. In this perspective, transference is conceived not only as an update of the past but also as an opening to a new relationship with the analyst, which can transform repetitive circuits.

This game of oppositions, proposed by Pichon-Rivière as a characteristic of the analytic experience—both in the structure of the established bond between patient and analyst (in which phenomena of deposit and symbiosis become manifest) and between the present of the current relationship and the past of primary relationships—also appears in Racker's (1953/1957) vision of complementary countertransference. The analyst is placed in a complementary role, meaning opposed to an object of the internal world of the patient. This role is often silently acted, favoring resistances to the process. The clearest examples provided by Racker are those in which the analyst is put in the place of the patient's superego acting sadistically (with answers of talionic nature to the patient) or in the place of the analysand's self taking a masochist place to face the patient's sadistic demands (de León de Bernardi, 2014). Besides, the game of opposites becomes manifest in both Pichon-Rivière's and Bleger's descriptions of mechanisms of projective identification and splitting processes. The categories proposed by Pichon-Rivière of depositor, depositary and what is deposited are taken up again by Bleger (1978) in the analysis of María Cristina (Bernardi and de León de Bernardi, 2012) to illustrate deposit aspects of one in the other, which is in the basis of underlying symbiosis in the bond of María Cristina with her mother.

It is necessary to take into account the cultural framework that had an influence on these thinkers' reflections. As they themselves noted, they received, among others, the influence of phenomenology through the thought of Merleau-Ponty as well as Marx's and Hegel's ideas about dialectics. The phenomenological approach led to highlighting of the situational and dramatic perspective of the psychoanalytic experience. The dialectic approach highlighted the dynamism of opposites emerging in the heart of the clinical experience and the integration processes by insight lead to a new restructuring of the analysis field. Undoubtedly, these ideas have been confronted by new developments in psychoanalytic theory and new cultural paradigms. The dialectic perspective has been especially opposed due to the change of cultural paradigms in various thinkers. Lacan, in the structuralist framework, opposes the notion of breakup and subjective repositioning to the emotional integration or synthesis. Interpretation and condensation and substitution processes of verbal signifiers provoke breakups in the analysand's conscious known discourse and restructurations in the analysand's psychism (de León de Bernardi, 2013). Bion, in turn, highlighted the negative capacity of suspending thought and making place to what is not known, what is not thought, which enables capturing basic emotions in the analytic experience. This paradigm confrontation between a perspective highlighting the dialectic integration of processes and a view emphasizing the experiences of breaking and lack of awareness is noted by Szpilka (1976) when he refers to the changes that are produced in the epistemological perspective. From his point of view, there is a break between a positivist and empiricist perspective and a negative epistemology, which privileges the experiences of rupture, discontinuity of sense and absence of object. From my perspective, moments of breakup and mobilization of unconscious defenses dialectically alternate with integration moments. I will return to this aspect when considering the clinical examples. Now, though, I will briefly consider the subject of metaphors in psychoanalysis.

Metaphors

In a previous paper (de León de Bernardi, 2013) I referred to different meanings of the word "metaphor" in psychoanalysis. In a wide sense, Borbely (1998) noted how analytic communication can be understood, in general, as a metaphoric process in which connections are established between the literal sense of the analyst's and patient's expressions and their latent sense. In the same way, Wallerstein (2013), in one of his last papers, revisits the notion of Lakoff and Johnson (1980), whose studies showed that metaphor is an essential part of the cognitive process from the beginning of life, just as it is in philosophical and scientific thought, and culture. From this perspective, Wallerstein affirmed that metaphors are not only products of language but mental products that are part of the thought process. He stressed the value of the different psychoanalytic theories considered as metaphors, as far as they are not taken in their literal sense but in their polysemic sense, so as to adjust to the complex characteristics of clinical practice.

In a strict sense, the term "metaphor," as language figure, has suffered modifications through time. Traditionally it has been considered as an abbreviated comparison. Aristotle emphasized the transmission processes and scope of meaning when considering metaphor as a shortened comparison, by which the literal sense of a term is figuratively used when it is transferred to another, then widening its original meaning. Later perspectives added new definitions. Ricoeur (1970) suggests metaphor emerges when it encounters semantic vacuums, generating new senses which become "impertinent" to the literal and usual sense of terms. For Davidson (1978), metaphors propose new meanings, creating conceptual changes in the listener. Metaphor does not substitute the literal sense of a term for a figurative one. In the metaphor the literal sense of terms is retained, but the degree of indetermination among them is relevant, enabling new associations and emotions in the listener. Davidson stresses more the effects that the metaphor produces in the listener than in the transmission and scope of meaning.

Metaphors emerged in the analytic field and it is necessary to investigate their latent sense in the analysis. Occasionally they are integrated in transferential interpretations, in which they have significant figurative and dramatic impact. They generate dialectic dynamisms in communication and new restructuring of the analytic field. These dialectic dynamisms gradually include the movement of opposed perspectives in the mind of analyst and patient according to the analysand's answers, which contribute to reestablish fluidity and permeability among them. This happens among the analysand's bonds and the current bond with the analyst; between the current bond with the analyst and the infantile past; between the infantile history of the analysand and the history of the analysis in its different moments; among the intrapsychic experiences and the analysand's experience in the external world; among his emotional, bodily and verbal experiences; among interpretative moments and non-verbalized moments of encounter with a big emotional load; among moments of rupture and lack of knowledge and moments of integration and insight; among others. When establishing links among the different areas of the analysand's psychic experience, interpretation may promote transformation.

Besides, metaphoric expressions are imbued with implicit preconscious theorizations from the analyst, giving rise to "mini-theories" (Leuzinger-Bohleber and Fischmann, 2006, p. 1360), which include alternative "open" hypotheses about the analysand, the analyst's own participation and the process of analysis. Although we know that interpretative processes are complex and often implicit, the moments in which transference makes itself explicit have a retrospective and prospective value, marking, through their meaning, the history of the analysis (de León, 1993).

Two clinical moments

Juan is a forty-five-year-old man who consulted due to frustration feelings in regards to the achievement of some aims in his life. His tendency to postpone valued goals calls my attention because this does not seem to fit with his potential.

Juan describes himself as someone who suffered from significant shyness for a great part of his infantile life, meaning he found great difficulty in group integration. Others easily occupied their places and he felt left aside. In one session he relived the painful feeling of being left aside. Metaphors condensed the infantile experience of self: "I was considered a 'little bug.' I was a little bug. It was very hard for me to modify that." Besides, he was considered fragile because he was very thin and often fell ill. "It was the allocated place."

Throughout the session, he showed another aspect of himself: "They also called me 'little lion' because occasionally I seemed to be a furious lion, but they mocked me and they didn't take me seriously."

Juan also explained how, in different moments of his life, it had been difficult to realize his potential. At the end of this session he mentioned a dream: "In the dream you told me: 'Now you can let go.'"

I answered: "Let the lion go here?"

We smiled at the end of the session.

I will now refer to a clinical situation with very different characteristics. It comes from a systematic study about clinical materials from candidates during their curricular training (de León, 2010). The candidate's patient had experienced child abuse and aggressive acts from others and himself, he suffered depression and he had made a suicide attempt. In his second year of analysis, prior to his analyst's vacation, he began a session by saying:

> I wanted to apologize because I didn't call you on Thursday when I did not come. I was in bed all day; I couldn't go out. The following day my girlfriend would be arriving. I only went out at night. I drank, I took drugs . . . Since my girlfriend told me that she was with another man I have been feeling a pain in my chest that is growing . . . *I feel stronger but I don't know how I will react. When I went out I span out of control, though I remembered you.*

His analyst replied:

> You could remember me and you trust that we, together, can process this pain without wishing death, as was the case last year (suicide attempt, before my vacation) or when you were a child and you wanted to disappear so as not to suffer.

A memory of the patient's infantile history and the history of the analysis arose in the analyst and formed the basis of the interpretation:

> The patient always remembered how, as a child, when he crossed the hot sand, his father told him as a motto: "Hot sand does not burn or hurt." This phrase was taken by the patient as a maxim that expressed the impossibility of manifesting pain. In the session I sought his expressing pain through words instead of acting.

Summarizations

In both clinical situations metaphoric thought operates in the minds of the analyst and the patient in a dynamic process, which gradually includes different perspectives on the analysand's mind and the relationship between both. These different facets appear as opposite in the first place; but as different moments of the session pass by, the sense of those oppositions is modified at the time that they, even when differentiated, get bonded, as in metaphors, in a dialectic to-and-fro movement. There are not only hermeneutic circuits of meanings and verbal signifiers. These gradually include different circuits of emotional embodied experiences which gradually acquire new density in the present situation of the analysis. So, the "little bug" metaphor evokes feelings of being diminished, abandonment, loneliness, suffering and stillness, due to the analysand's infantile inhibitions, but also bodily representations of himself and ways of bodily contact with others, which hide the impulse to fight for his things and are expressed in the "lion" metaphor, which partly represents the wish to expand his emotions and aggression and bodily movements. In this sense we can talk about "embodied metaphors." My intervention to "let the lion go here"—which specifically indicates the action of the joint movement of analyst and patient—adds other dimensions, and the smile from both shows an emotional moment of encounter. To a certain extent, this was a moment of synthesis of what had previously been worked, but, keeping an interplay, as Davidson (1978) stated, a jungle of significations and emotions among the different poles that are represented by the images in the session. It was a restructuring moment of the analytic field with the more explicit opening of the transferential dimension. I, undoubtedly, bear in mind the dimension of implicit sexuality, but the interpretative work about it will depend on the later development of the analysis.

The second case is different. The analyst's interventions seek to compensate for the patient's difficulties in processing mental pain. In this way, moments of the history of the analysis emerge again in the analyst through the words of the patient's father—"Hot sand does not burn or hurt"—which were lived by the patient as a mandate to deny physical pain, then put in the same level of denial of mental pain by the analyst. We cannot talk about metaphor in a strict sense, as a figure of language, but we can talk about the metaphoric thought of the analyst, which generated a new mental product when reestablishing the relations between the words of the father as a negation of physical suffering and the tendency to act and negation of mental pain by the patient. The intervention "you could remember me" seeks to modify the bond of the infantile scene of demand and ignorance of suffering. The words of the father experienced as an unquestionable truth together with the characteristics of the patient lead the analyst to reflect on the influence of traumatic effects from the primary bonds of the patient. If, in the first case, the patient could metaphorize his different emotional states in conflict and his primary bonds regarding his internal objects, in this case the symbolic levels (of image and word and sub-symbolic—emotional and bodily), the areas of the mind, the body and the world, such as Bleger (1969) stated, appear rigidly separated. The strength of the paternal mandate shows the patient's difficulty to find (symbolize, mentalize) a voice of his own. To Bleger, the mayeutic process of interpretation has an effect of dealienation and dialectization, as far as defenses keep the terms of the psychic conflict separated. In this case we are not dealing in the first place with the Oedipal conflict but with more primary deficits in the ways of mental functioning, which undoubtedly color the ways in which the patient perceives the paternal mandate. Changes occur not only through the verbal interpretative work but also, as the patient states, through the interiorization of a new "presence" and analytic relationship.

In this preliminary analysis I have chosen to pay special attention to a particular aspect of field theory that is related to the dialectic character of transferential interpretation, linking it to the ways of metaphoric thought. Undoubtedly, several aspects remain open for discussion. Similarly, the notion of dialectics that emerged in a specific ideological and philosophical context needs to be revisited in light of current psychoanalytic knowledge and interdisciplinary contributions about complex thought (Morin, 1977). It is also necessary to rethink the characteristics of transferential interpretation. In both of the cases presented here, transference naturally emerges in the words of the patient within the established analytical bond, not answering to the explicit will of the analyst. At the same time, the language is brief and non-saturated, but it has a high dramatic impact.

In which sense do we talk today about interpretation and transference? Undoubtedly, the ways to interpret it have changed through time according to the evolution of theory, psychoanalytic practice and cultural developments. However, certain moments of explicit interpretation of transference call our attention to one permanent, implicit dimension of the analytic encounter which needs to be listened to and worked according to the needs and characteristics of the patient and the moment of analysis.

Finally, in the Freudian vision, a regressive sense was assigned to figurability, according to the idea of formal regression belonging to Freud's conception about dream mechanisms. Taking the notion of bastion of the analytic field as it was formulated by M. and W. Baranger (1961/2008), it was supported, in the framework of Kleinian thought, by Susan Isaacs'

(1948) ideas about unconscious primitive fantasies. In this sense, the bastion as formation of the field is constituted by infantile fantasies of regressive and defensive character shared by analyst and patient. These mutual implications may lead to acts of various types and to paralysis of the analytic process when it is impossible to achieve the decoding in a retrospective look at the participation of the analyst in the session and in periods of the process.

It is important to bear in mind not only the regressive character of figurability and the image in the analysis, but also the progressive and dialectic character of the construction of figurative processes and their contribution to mentalizing the emotional states and bodily experiences of the patient. In these cases, the image contributes to the interpretative process and it does not follow a regressive path. Integrated to metaphoric thoughts co-created by patient and analyst, it follows a progressive path, such as a spiral, in successive levels of mental integration in the session and in later elaborations by patient and analyst. Undoubtedly, this is not the only way of intervention from the analyst, nor the only way of elaboration in the communication established in the analytic field, but I believe it constitutes one of the key elements in the analytic process.

Summary

This paper deals with the subject of transferential interpretation and its characteristics. Bleger's ideas about the situational, dramatic and dialectic character of psychoanalysis and Pichon-Rivière's idea of "dialectical spiral" as a frame to reflect on the explicit and implicit aspects of transferential interpretation are revisited. This supposes paying attention to the analyst's participation in the process, but also consideration of different facets of the analysand's mind, sometimes opposed, which are occasionally articulated dialectically, in a to-and-fro movement in the interpretative task. Developments about metaphor in psychoanalysis and in the interpretative process are integrated, reviewing, synthetically, one aspect of field theory. Finally, on the basis of the presentation of two clinical situations, there is reflection on the variations in the form and content of the explicit interpretation of transference in different patients, situations and analytic processes.

Note

1 Beatriz de León de Bernardi is a full member of the Uruguayan Psychoanalytic Association. Email: deleon.bea@gmail.com.

References

Baranger, W. (1979). "Proceso en espiral" y "campo dinámico". *Revista Uruguaya de Psicoanálisis*, 59(17), 32.
Baranger, W. and Baranger, M. (1961/2008). The analytic situation as a dynamic field. *International Journal of Psycho-Analysis*, 89, 795–826.
Bernardi, R. and de León de Bernardi, B. (2012). The concepts of *vínculo* and dialectical spiral: A bridge between intra- and intersubjectivity. *Psychoanalytic Quarterly*, 81, 531–564.
Bleger, J. (1969). Teoría y práctica en psicoanálisis. La praxis psicoanalítica. *Revista Uruguaya de Psicoanálisis*, 11, 287–303.
Bleger, J. (1978). *Simbiosis y ambigüedad. Estudio psicoanalítico*. Buenos Aires: Paidós.
Borbely, A. F. (1998). A psychoanalytic concept of metaphor. *International Journal of Psycho-Analysis*, 79, 923–936.
Davidson, D. (1978). What metaphors mean. *Critical Inquiry*, 5(1), 31–47.
de León, B. (1993). El sustrato compartido de la interpretación. Imágenes, afectos y palabras en la experiencia analítica. *Revista de Psicoanálisis y Boletin de la API*, 50(4–5), 809–826.
de León, B. (2010). La formación psicoanalítica en un contexto de pluralismo teórico y técnico. *Revista Latinoamericana de Psicoanálisis*, 9, 119–138.
de León, B. and Altmann, M. (2014). The three-level model in psychoanalytic training. In M. Altmann (ed.), *Time for Change: Tracking Transformations in Psychoanalysis: The Three-Level Model* (pp. 281–294). London: Karnac.
de León de Bernardi, B. (2000). The countertransference: A Latin American view. *International Journal of Psychoanalysis*, 81(2), 331–351.
de León de Bernardi, B. (2013). Metaphor, analytic field, and spiral process. In S. M. Katz (ed.), *Metaphor and Fields: Common Ground, Common Language, and the Future of Psychoanalysis* (pp. 182–203). New York: Routledge.
de León de Bernardi, B. (2014). Commentary on: "The Compulsion to Confess and the Compulsion to Judge in the Analytic Situation" by Stefano Fajrajzen. *International Journal of Psychoanalysis*, 95, 995–1006.
Etchegoyen H. (1986/2002). *Los fundamentos de la técnica psicoanalítica*. Buenos Aires: Amorrortu.
Isaacs, S. (1948). The nature and function of phantasy. *International Journal of Psychoanalysis*, 29, 73–97.
Lakoff, G. and Johnson, M. (1980). *Metaphors We Live by*. Chicago, IL: University of Chicago Press.

Leuzinger-Bohleber, M. and Fischmann, T. (2006). What is conceptual research in psychoanalysis? *International Journal of Psychoanalysis*, 87, 1355–1386.

Levenson, E. A. (1974). Changing concepts of intimacy in psychoanalytic practice. *Contemporary Psychoanalysis*, 10, 359–368.

Morin, E. (1977). *Le Méthode* (Vols. 1–5). Paris: Le Seuil.

Ogden, T. H. (1992). The dialectically constituted/decentred subject of psychoanalysis, I: The Freudian subject. *International Journal of Psychoanalysis*, 73, 517–526.

Pichon-Rivière, E. (1998). *El Proceso Grupal. Del Psicoanálisis a la Psicología Social*. Buenos Aires: Nueva visión.

Racker, H. (1953/1957). The meanings and uses of countertransference. *Psychoanalytic Quarterly*, 26(3), 303–357.

Ricoeur, P. (1970). *Freud: una interpretación de la cultura. Siglo XXI*. Mexico: Ed. SA.

Stern, D. N., Sander, L. W., Nahum, J. P., Harrison, A. M., Lyons-Ruth, K., Morgan, A. C. and Tronick, E. Z. (1998). Non-interpretive mechanisms in psychoanalytic therapy: The "something more" than interpretation. *International Journal of Psychoanalysis*, 79, 903–21.

Szpilka, J. I. (1976). Complejo de Edipo y "a posteriori." *Revista de Psicoanálisis*, 33(2), 285–300.

Wallerstein, R. S. (2013). Metaphor in psychoanalysis and clinical data. In S. M. Katz (ed.), *Metaphor and Fields: Common Ground, Common Language, and the Future of Psychoanalysis* (pp. 22–38). New York: Routledge.

Resonance is a central aspect of clinical work. How the patient, the interaction, and our own experience resonate in us is a significant part of our work. During the psychoanalytic session, different theoretical perspectives implicitly resonate in us, remaining, suspended, in our mind. After the session, our different theoretical perspectives contribute to the elaboration and conceptualization of the dialectics of the analytic field.

Beatriz de León de Bernardi

Chapter 5

About the theory of the analytic field

Elsa Rappoport de Aisemberg

Introduction

I am very grateful that Montana Katz, the editor of *Metaphor and Field*, decided to give some of the contributors to that text, plus several others, the opportunity to share new thoughts on this theme and hopefully display both affinities and differences on the subject.

When I think about its origins, and specifically about W. and M. Baranger's (1961–1962) *princeps* statement – the analytic field – I remember the authoress saying that the concept was constructed by both of them in Montevideo, while they were organizing the Uruguayan Psychoanalytic Society, and that it was the product of continuous and endless dialogues between the two of them about their work.

On the same lines, S. and C. Botella (1997, 2001) also worked together to produce some conceptualizations to deal with what happens in sessions between patient and analyst. Thus, they describe figurability, regredience, and the work of the double with borderline patients.

In addition, C. Botella (2014), in his work on metapsychology, which I had the pleasure of discussing recently, suggests that we should start thinking about the metapsychology of the analytic encounter and of the session. I agree, and view the Barangers' concept of field as an answer to his request.

I used to believe that such a statement was an intermediate hypothesis between metapsychology and clinical work, but now I feel that it has to do with the metapsychology of the analytic encounter and of the session. That is to say, it is a high-level theory to account for this encounter.

I would also like to mention here R. Roussillon's (2013) paper, in which, when he refers to the plurality and complexity of contemporary psychoanalysis, he states that we have to accept the differences among cultures and authors that influence the theoretical models and, connected to this, points out that W. and M. Baranger have had significant influence on the way of thinking of the Argentine Psychoanalytic Association and the Uruguayan Psychoanalytic Society. I fully agree.

In Buenos Aires, where I trained as an analyst, most of us were immersed in E. Pichon-Rivière's ideas and those of his followers, who were my teachers: J. Bleger, D. Liberman, and the Barangers. All of them shared the view of the session as an encounter between two people in dialogue in an asymmetric way. Therefore, I think that the intersubjective dimension implied in the theory of the field has been in my implicit theories ever since the beginning of my training.

In this intersubjective dimension of the analytic field, the communication of unconscious to unconscious is an essential point. As I have pointed out in a previous work (Aisemberg, 2013), this kind of perception has been referenced since the Freudian formulation of 1912 up to W. Bion's statements about maternal reverie and/or the analyst's mind in the regressive context of the session, M. de M'Uzan's work on the use of the analyst's mind as the patient's auxiliary when he is still unable to translate his emotions into representations, and the Botellas' previously mentioned statements.

I would also like to mention an interesting idea that J. Rolland (2014) recently presented in a lecture to the APA concerning the importance of the unconscious to unconscious transmission. This is a model that, in my opinion, accounts for the singularities we observe in our clinical work on the analytic field: for example, the construction of an unconscious fantasy common to both participants or the particular relationship established between a determined patient and a determined analyst that constitutes a very special field, which M. de M'Uzan has beautifully conceptualized as "the Chimera." I should also mention T. Ogden's (2014) recent account of a session where he could not remember whether the text was his or the patient's. According to my reading, this is related to the concept of common unconscious fantasy of the field formulated by the Barangers.

At this point, it would be useful to state my differences with American intersubjective colleagues who emphasize the interpersonal relationship, whereas I adhere, for my training and my ideas, to a model of communication of unconscious to unconscious, a movement that goes from the intrapsychic to the intersubjective and then back again.

On contemporary psychoanalysis

I think that as we have extended our work as analysts, especially since the sixties and seventies, we have started to investigate non-neurotic functioning in addition to the classic psychoneurotic functioning. On the whole, this is called "contemporary psychoanalysis."

This has been dealt with by numerous authors, including: W. Bion, W. and M. Baranger, D. Winnicott, A. Green, M. de M'Uzan, R. Roussillon, C. and S. Botella, T. Ogden, S. Bolognini, A. Ferro and G. Civitarese.

1. In 1962 W. Bion wrote about beta elements that work as discharge to the act or to the soma. He also described reverie – the capacity for grasping in the counter-transference, like the mother with her baby, what the patient cannot yet put into words.
2. Around the same time, 1961–1962, the Barangers described the theory of the analytic field between patient and analyst and the unconscious fantasy that is common to both.
3. Shortly after, in 1967, D. Winnicott, the "analyst of the frontiers," according to A. Green, provided, with his transitional phenomena, a creative dimension for the clinical work.
4. In 1975, A. Green described non-neurotic structures and the construction of the analytic object in the session in his excellent book *On Private Madness*.
5. Three years later, M. de M'Uzan highlighted the use of the analyst's mind when the patient is still unable to transform his own emotions into words and representations. Later, in 1994, he described the Chimera—a brilliant metaphor close to the Barangers' field formulation.
6. In 1991, R. Roussillon referred to frontier situations in analysis, stressing the importance of transference–counter-transference dynamics, and set forth the idea of reconstruction hypotheses as moments in the analytic treatment.
7. In 1997 and 2001, the Botellas wrote about figurability, regredience and the work of the double in the session with borderline patients.
8. Likewise, in 1994, T. Ogden advanced the notion of the analytic third as well as the tendency to dream dreams that are never dreamed (2007). In his most recent work (2014) he wrote about a fantasy shared by patient and analyst in the session.
9. In *Psychoanalytic Empathy* (2004) and *Secret Passageways* (2011), S. Bolognini described the peculiarities of the counter-transference

and analytic relationship in some patients who require a creative activity from the analyst, on the assumption that communication in these cases is from preconscious to preconscious.
10. A. Ferro presented his most recent version of his theory about the field in 2012 and 2013 in two excellent papers written with G. Civitarese, in which they refer to those aspects in the patient that have not reached a mental level and demand the development of the capacity for dreaming and thinking.

In my opinion, all these authors aim to give theoretical status to the clinical approach to other functioning beyond neurosis that is now also the object of current psychoanalysis.

In my previous work (Aisemberg 2001, 2007, 2008, 2010, 2012) I have described in the sphere of psychosomatics two coexistent psychic functionings: the psychoneurotic and the non-neurotic; somatosis appears in the latter. The psychoneurotic field originates in the experience of satisfaction (it is Oedipus domain), whereas the non-neurotic field comes from the experience of pain (it is the early trauma sphere). This experience of pain has not had the possibility of guardian masochism binding as described by B. Rosenberg (1991).

All this has led me to state that a trauma or a present mourning can awaken those sensory traces that have not been resolved psychically and that appear in scene as act or as somatic phenomenon or even as hallucination in non-psychotic people.

Bodily counter-transference

In a previous text (Aisemberg, 2013) I referred to the importance of the use of counter-transference in the analytic field and included an account of its evolution and use in our discipline. Although I emphasized then its mental dimension, I think it is important now to stress its bodily dimension.

Thus, I believe that the analyst's body is constantly involved in our work. As I have previously pointed out, to be able to accomplish our work, aware of the asymmetry of the setting, besides verbal listening, we have to let ourselves be partly affectively and sensorially involved by the unconscious messages sent by the patient.

Before the statement of the analytic field, everything concerning the analyst's body had to be excluded, or was considered of no use in analytic work. The big change that was brought about by the concept was that we were able to accept or take into account or think about the importance of the analyst's person or presence in the construction of the analytic situation with the patient. This meaningful, general change has taken place recently, even for those colleagues who do not use the field concept: for example, O. Renik,[1] with his theory of intersubjectivity in the United States, although he is quite far from our theoretical models. Instead we find in Europe ideas (Winnicott, Bion, de M'Uzan, Bollas and the Botellas) closer to those of the Barangers.

In their *princeps* work, the last-mentioned authors (Baranger and Baranger, 2008, p. 802) point out that:

> The participation of the body in the analytic situation is by no means limited to the patient. Every analyst participates in the physical ambiguity and responds with his or her own body to the patient's unconscious communication. The analyst also elaborates a body language with which to respond to certain modifications of the field.

This opens a new road for exploration.

Unconscious to unconscious communication

S. Freud announced this communication as early as 1912, when he pointed out that the physician "must turn his own unconscious like a receptive organ towards the transmitting unconscious of the patient. He must adjust himself to the patient as a telephone receiver is adjusted to the transmitting microphone" (Freud, 1912, pp. 115–116). This implies, to my mind, the use or disposition not only of the analyst's mind but also of his/her body and his/her whole person. Since internal and external perceptions of the relationship with the object become sensory or perceptive traces, previous to the word, I think they would lie between soma and psyche, in the Id of the second topic with their roots in the soma as Freud draws in 1933 (p. 79). This is the proper or genuine unconscious which has not been translated, which was never conscious, as Freud asserts in *Moses* (1939, p. 96).

Thus, I formulated (Aisemberg, 2007, 2008, 2010, 2012) the hypothesis of the two unconscious: the repressed unconscious (Oedipus domain, organized drive, representations, psychoneurosis); and the proper or genuine unconscious (never conscious, field of the archaic, of endosomatic excitation, of disorganized drive, which can find expression in passage to act or to soma or to hallucination in a non-psychotic person).

It is the approach to the latter functioning in the transference–countertransference situation in the analytic field that makes it possible to transform sensory traces into memory traces which will give rise to representations and dreams. Therefore, we help to construct the repressed unconscious. It is the use of the mind that produces the translation of perceptive traces into useful representations, introducing the word.

Bodily perception is the origin of unconscious to unconscious communication that naturally has to be translated by the analyst, who in these cases functions as an "auxiliary" who lends his/her mental capacity, as M. de M'Uzan stated in 1978, because the patient cannot yet transform those traces into words or representations. We are in the figurability field as developed by the Botellas, as well as in the analyst's dreams when the patient cannot dream yet (Aisemberg et al., 2012).

I would now like to illustrate these ideas with two clinical vignettes.

Silvio

Silvio was a patient of one of my colleagues, and she brought the case to me for discussion. He was a thirty-three-year-old entrepreneur, married with two children, who suffered myocardium infarction. A physician called my colleague to interview the patient at the coronary unit. He had characteristics of overadaptation; he was a workaholic and pragmatic. When he was discharged from the clinic, he started treatment on a two-session basis, face-to-face, during which he reported his everyday life in a matter-of-fact manner, using an operative language, in the phrase coined by P. Marty (1990).

After a couple of months, during which the patient never mentioned the heart attack, the analyst felt *angor*, a pain in her chest, at the start of a session. Later, she asked my advice during supervision, and I told her to see a cardiologist, and also to think about how disturbed or worried she was about Silvio, who did not talk about his anxiety in relation to suffering a heart attack at such a young age.

Once my colleague had checked that her coronary arteries were fine, she was in a position to transform her corporeal sensations and include the split affects: the fright; the fear Silvio must have felt when he had his heart attack; the pain; and his concern about the present and the future.

This was a slow reintrojection that gave rise to the emergence of psychic mourning: for his mother's death a few years before; for detachment from his two older sisters, who lived abroad and whom he had not seen for years; and for the lack of communication with his father, who had remarried. Little by little, during a process that took ten years, he began to work through mourning psychically and not with the soma, and there appeared transferences, dreams, sexuality, Oedipus and aggression, all of which were no longer suppressed. All of these belong to psychoneurotic functioning.

Pablo

I think that a paradigmatic use of the analyst's body takes place in the face-to-face setting. Previously (Aisemberg et al., 2000), when referring to the transference narcissistic dimension, I have described this treatment as a way to meet the patient's need to be sustained in the analyst's gaze, to be mirrored in the therapist's face in the manner described by D. Winnicott (1967/1971).

A colleague shared the following clinical material with me.

Pablo was forty, an entrepreneur, married with four children. María, his first child, suffered fetal distress during delivery and had irreversible neurological damage. Now fifteen, she was the cause of much suffering in the family. She screamed at night and could not control her body, so she had to be tied to her wheelchair to avoid serious falls (several of which she had previously suffered). When Pablo started treatment he recounted his lonely and sad childhood and María's illness as if they were someone else's stories, without affect, stating that these events did not disturb him. He described himself as a practical man, always looking ahead, a workaholic who traveled constantly but "not to run away": "I can cope with a lot."

He struck my colleague as false-self or anti-analysand or overadapted. The following fragment from one of their sessions is revealing.

Pablo reported an episode that had happened a couple of days earlier. María had started to scream at night, as she often did, and to move in a compulsive way until she finally fell off the bed, hit her nose badly and broke a tooth. Pablo related the story in his usual matter-of-fact way. In the counter-transference the analyst felt that little by little she was becoming immersed in the sordid and extremely painful atmosphere he was unwittingly transmitting. Suddenly, she noticed his eyes were filling with tears.

"Pablo, your eyes are red and full of tears."

"You know something? This has never happened to me before. When I saw your face, saw the way you look at me, the horror on your face, I realized through you how painful all this is. Only now am I aware of that, because of the way you are looking at me."

These moving words showed how this tough, apparently cold man weakened like a child. I feel that Pablo was able to contact his emotions through the most primary path: by seeing himself reflected in the analyst's face, a face that worked as the mirror that had probably been missing in his early life.

J. Semprún's (1995, pp. 15–16) words come to mind. In *La escritura o la vida* (Writing or life) he describes meeting the soldiers who had just freed him and his fellow inmates from Buchenwald concentration camp:

> They are in front of me, their eyes wide open, and suddenly I see myself mirrored in their terrified gaze: in their shock. I had lived without a face for two years. There are no mirrors in Buchenwald . . . It is the horror in my eyes that their eyes are revealing, a horrified gaze.

In conclusion

The analyst as a person with his/her own desires, transferences and ideologies is brought into play in the transference situation, and although the ethical aspiration of neutrality and abstinence is present and should be preserved as an ideal, there are resonances in action, singular resonances that emerge in each analytic field, which proves that the relation between each patient and each analyst is different. The problem lies in how we understand these resonances and what we do with them; how much belongs only to the analyst and how much to the patient. We have to bear in mind that this is facilitated by the therapist's vulnerability or his/her own vibrations.

Addenda

After our fruitful meeting in Cambridge, organized by Montana Katz, I would like to thank our coordinator and all of the colleagues who participated for the high quality of the work accomplished in an atmosphere of respectful and intelligent dissent. There was an active exchange of the ideas held by the three groups about the theory of the analytical field, as M. Katz pointed out in her work: the Americans, with their singular nuances; the Italians, starting from A. Ferro's statements; and the Latin Americans, with the Barangers' ideas and those of the Río de la Plata.

It was a very interesting interchange in a friendly atmosphere, which I highly appreciate as a model of scientific interchange, and there were moments of useful confrontation leading to further reflection. For example, which points did we most share and which were the greatest areas of differences among us?

It was a true moment of communication.

Note

1 Now, after our meeting in Cambridge, I think that the American colleagues who belong to the third group (as described by M. Katz in her paper) also work with their theory of the analytic field.

References

Aisemberg, E.R. (2001). Revisión crítica de las teorías y los abordajes de los estados psicosomáticos [Critical review of the theories and approaches to psychosomatic conditions], *Revista de Psicoanálisis*, 58, 2: 507–517.

Aisemberg, E.R. (2007). Repetición, transferencia y somatosis [Repetition, transference and somatosis], *Revista de Psicoanálisis*, 64, 2: 309–317.

Aisemberg, E.R. (2008). The shadow of heritage in contemporary psychoanalysis, *EPF Bulletin*, 62: 93–103.

Aisemberg, E.R. (2010). Psychosomatic conditions in contemporary psychoanalysis, in M. Aisenstein and E.R. Aisemberg, eds., *Psychosomatics Today: A Psychoanalytic Perspective*, London, Karnac, pp. 111–130.

Aisemberg, E.R. (2012). Más allá de la representación: los afectos [Beyond representation: the affects], in Aisemberg, E.R et al., eds., *El Cuerpo en Escena*, Buenos Aires, Lumen, pp. 119–140.

Aisemberg, E.R. (2013). The analytic relationship in field theory, in S.M. Katz, ed., *Metaphor and Fields*, New York, Routledge, pp. 209–213.

Aisemberg, E.R. et al. (2000). El autorretrato [Self-portrait], *Revista de Psicoanálisis*, 57, 3/4: 493–508.

Aisemberg, E.R. et al. (2012). *El Cuerpo en Escena* [The Body at the Scene], Buenos Aires, Lumen.

Baranger, M. and Baranger, W. (1961–1962). *Problemas del Campo Psicoanalítico*, Buenos Aires, Kargieman (reprinted 1969).

Baranger, M. and Baranger, W. (2008). The analytic situation as a dynamic field, *International Journal of Psychoanalysis*, 89, 4: 795–826.
Bion, W. (1962). *Learning from Experience*, London, Karnac.
Bolognini, S. (2004). *La Empatía Psicoanalítica*, Buenos Aires, Lumen.
Bolognini, S. (2011). *Pasajes Secretos. Teoría y técnica de la relación interpsíquica*, Buenos Aires, Lumen.
Botella, C. (2014). Rememoración y verdad, in *Metapsicología*, Buenos Aires, APA, Lugar, pp. 193–203.
Botella, C. and Botella, S. (1997). *Más Allá de la Representación* [Beyond Representation], Valencia, Promolibro.
Botella, C. and Botella, S. (2001). *La Figurabilité Psychique*, Paris, Delachaux et Nestlé.
Ferro, A. and Civitarese, G. (2012). Desarrollos actuales del concepto de campo, *Revista de Psicoanálisis*, 69, 2–3: 391–398.
Ferro, A. and Civitarese, G. (2013). Metaphor in analytic field theory, in S.M. Katz, ed., *Metaphor and Fields*, New York, Routledge, pp. 121–142.
Freud, S. (1912). Recommendations to physicians practising psychoanalysis, in *The Standard Edition of the Complete Psychological Works of Sigmund Freud*, London, Hogarth Press [*S.E.* from hereon], 12: 115–116.
Freud, S. (1933). Lecture 31 in *New Introductory Lectures on Psychoanalysis*, in *S.E.*, 22: 57–80.
Freud, S. (1939). *Moses and Monotheism*, in *S.E.*, 23: 6–137.
Green, A. (1990). *De Locuras Privadas* [On Private Madness], Buenos Aires, Amorrortu.
Marty, P. (1990). *La Psychosomatique d'Odulte*, Paris, PUF.
M'Uzan, M. de (1978). *Del Arte a la Muerte*, Barcelona, Icaria.
M'Uzan, M. de (1994). *La Buche de l'Inconscient*, Paris, Gallimard.
Ogden, T. (1994). The analytic third: Working with intersubjective clinical facts, *International Journal of Psychoanalysis*, 75: 3–19.
Ogden, T. (2007). On talking as dreaming, *International Journal of Psychoanalysis*, 88: 575–589.
Ogden, T. (2014). Sobre el hablar como soñando, in A.W. Marucco, ed., *Metapsicología*, Buenos Aires, APA, Lugar, pp. 115–132.
Rolland, J.C. (2014). Lecture to the Argentine Psychoanalytic Association.
Rosenberg, B. (1991). Masochisme mortifére et masochisme gardien de la vie, *Monografies de la Revue Française de Psychanalyse*, 62: 5.
Roussillon, R. (2013). Plurality and complexity in psychoanalysis, *EPF Bulletin*, 1 October: 208–220.
Semprún, J. (1995). *La Escritura o la Vida* [Writing or Life], Barcelona, Tusquets.
Winnicott, D. (1967/1971). *Playing and Reality*, New York, Basic Books.

We emphasize the affective ambience that is co-created in any dyad or group that engages and works together regularly. By ambience we mean an affect state, a way of being together. It can be hostile or argumentative; it can be pleasant; it can be sexual. The emotional state you are in with each other is going to influence the inferences you are going to draw. This idea of the co-created between state that affects how we are in a given moment has a completely different language than reverie; it is another way of looking at things.
Joseph Lichtenberg

Chapter 6

Notes on transformations in hallucinosis

Giuseppe Civitarese

> Receptiveness achieved by denudation of memory and desire (which is essential to the operation of "acts of faith") is essential to the operation of psycho-analysis ... It is essential for experiencing hallucination or the state of hallucinosis ...
>
> Hallucinosis, which can be *observed* by divesting oneself of memory and desire, must have had some corresponding mechanism in the events that led to its inception. If the analyst can take certain steps that enable him to "see" what the patient sees, it is reasonable to suppose that the patient has likewise "taken steps," though not necessarily the same ones, to enable him to "see" what he [the analyst] sees.
>
> (Bion, 1970/1993, pp. 35–36, 40; original emphasis)

In four short vignettes, two from supervision sessions and the others from therapy sessions, I will try to show how the concept of transformation in hallucinosis (TH from hereon) (Civitarese, 2015, 2016) can be used, within the frame of a post-Bionian field theory, instead of the classical notion of parapraxis (which I use here also as an allegory of a certain way of conceptualizing the unconscious). Following Bion, but also developing his ideas, by TH I mean the more or less lasting analyst's "errors" in thinking and perceiving, close to "hallucinations" and "delusion," from which eventually he/she may wake up and so see them as a field phenomenon or dream.

Instead of experiencing surprise as a separate individual at the moment when one of his/her repressed formations breaks out from the prison of the unconscious – what we call parapraxis when we realize it almost immediately – the analyst considers the error as a co-created dream, or, in other words, as a kind of poetry of the mind that serves to make personal sense of an experience – something that is generated by the field set up by the communication between the unconscious minds of both parties. This dream gives virtual information about the emotional quality of the relationship and is thus invaluable as proof that the analyst is in unison with the patient.

It is to be noted that the key step is when the analyst "wakes up" from the hallucinosis, or perhaps it would be better to say from the "hallucination" – both terms could be used here, depending on which metaphorical aspect one wishes to emphasize. At this point, the analyst can interpret the hallucinatory images as coming from a real dream dreamed in a waking state and thus also "deeper" than a reverie.

To make best use of this new conceptual tool, the analyst should as far as possible put aside everything he/she already knows and every reference to external reality and the past. In this way he/she actively sets himself/herself up to be visited by the productions of the unconscious, having "faith" – another conceptual tool – in the fact that, if he/she has enough patience and is able to put up with anxiety and the sense of guilt entailed in not understanding, sooner or later some fact or other will come along and deliver meaning.

"How do you think I am now?"

What follows is a small fragment of dialogue presented in a supervision. It is important to observe the way in which my colleague – N – visually organized the text, with new sentences placed on new lines, because this led me into an error; or, rather, into hallucinosis.

P. You changed your hair. Change is good.
    How do you think I am now?
A. [Smiling] How do you feel?
P. As you see. Moderately fluctuating.
    I often come here drunk. Alcohol affects me in a bad way. It makes me depressed, sad. But marijuana, pure marijuana, is different. I often get aggressive with alcohol. I drink a little bit before coming here, it is OK. But after going out, I drink more, and it is something different.

As soon as my colleague has read the first two lines, I make a comment and tell her that maybe the patient is telling her that he finds her changed for the better since the last time, or even *in* the last time. She might have shown herself to be different then; or, compared to then, she might have given the patient the impression of being different because of the way she welcomed him when he arrived. I add that obviously it is not a question of hair, but of the head and of ideas. The patient – all the more so if there is a seductive aspect to the comment, or rather a recognition of the fascination that the object exercises on him, implicit in the compliment ("Change is good") – nevertheless wonders what N really has in her head, what she really thinks of him. I add, partly as a joke, that she does well to be a little coquettish with him when asking him, "How do you think I am now?" because that is a way, while being in the patient's text, of expanding the narrative that he is proposing to her; in general, that of knowing more about her anxieties and how she is feeling.

N quickly points out that it was not she who asked the question "How do you think I am now?" but the patient! I immediately acknowledge my mistake, and on a superficial level attribute it to the positioning of the new sentence on a new line in the transcript that she has presented to me. However, as can be seen in the extract above, there is no letter at the beginning of that sentence to indicate a change of speaker from patient to analyst. N explains to me that she wrote it in that way because there was a short silence after the patient said, "good." The actual question which N asks ("How do you feel?") distances her from his good-natured comment, because it merely asks him how he is in general. It is true that by smiling she indicates that she has accepted the compliment. The patient responds by bringing the discourse back to the level of the visual ("As you see"), to the reciprocal mirroring which is perhaps the essence of analytic dialogue beyond its contents, and answers, "Moderately fluctuating." Immediately afterwards, with his story, he indicates two modes of functioning in the analytic field, two forms of dependency: one more toxic and dangerous (that of alcohol); the other more innocuous, which brings him calm (oscillation alcohol↔marijuana). It is as if he is indicating the two ever-alternating qualities of the object, arousing and calming, and at the same time his desperation at not being able to integrate a single sufficiently reliable way of relating to the other. The patient is speaking of his dependence on the analyst. But he says more: that he has to drink in order to manage his emotions before/during the meeting, and even more so afterwards. At this moment the field does not seem to be functioning well enough to help him transform his emotions.

It is as if he left the session more weighed down than when he entered. But then, at this point, we wonder what meaning (I wrote "breast"[1]) my "hallucination" may have had (there is a precise visual component in my misreading of the text). The fact that the patient asks how the analyst finds him makes us see that, under the guise of a compliment, the first comment was hiding an enquiry about what was *in* her head. But a confirmation of this kind would not have needed my mistake. I think that the unconscious emotional truth expressed by my/our hallucinosis is, perhaps banally, that the analyst is seriously preoccupied by what the patient thinks of her. It is worth saying that a judgemental dimension is very much present, that it is intense, a field in which the patient worries about how he will perform, to the point where he needs to "drink to talk." Alcohol (a certain eroticization of the relationship?) eases this persecutory waiting a little, but it is a type of defence that intoxicates him.

The rest of the session seems to confirm this reading. The analyst, who in turn is worried about the supervision, confines herself to asking many questions, and does not sufficiently pick up the emotion expressed by the patient. This is how the central theme of the session passes into the supervision and can be "dreamed." My hallucinosis is in fact a dream (nightmare) from which I wake and which I can thus use as a fragment of waking dream. The question that I attribute erroneously to the analyst – "How do you think I am now?" – reflects the patient's distress about herself, her concerns about the patient and about me, but also, conversely, my anxiety about being judged by her, all the more so in a week when another colleague with whom I was working on a case had lost it and made me feel her disappointment and anger to some extent.

In conclusion, the functioning of the analytic field seems to be characterized by a climate of menace and danger. The aim of the therapy becomes how to pass from alcohol to marijuana, from a pathological dependency to a less immature dependency. The hallucinosis also allows me to flirt with my colleague (when I describe her as coquettish). This means that perhaps I emphasize a mutually seductive feature of her (us) – which perhaps should be kept more under control (although it is not said: it could have its purpose, like marijuana or alcohol) – but also of the patient and myself.

Parapraxis

In a record of a session I read the sentence, "She is learning to be a mother to her mother." This concerns a patient with a compulsive obsession about killing her little boy with kitchen knives. In the group discussion a salient fact emerges – that the father is missing from the case history. But this is interpreted as an important deficiency in a function of thirdness, paternal but symbolic, in the mother's mind. It is as if, not being able to regulate her distance from the object and fearing difference more than anything else, she could imagine either keeping the child in her womb for ever (she often says how she misses her pregnant belly) in an eternal pregnancy, or eliminating it by killing it. We can see how the lack of a symbolic paternal function brings into play what we might call a "Medea" function. I say "function" because it is nevertheless appropriate to see it as a desperate defence, as the way of coming back to life, even if only in a desperate act of fury. The shame of not-being, of carrying stamped on one's skin the brand of a maternal verdict of non-existence, lives again in the profound shame of thinking oneself capable of killing one's child. Yet we understand that the shame comes first and that the compulsive obsession arrives only as a justification, a "delusional production," *a posteriori*, to give it a painful form. In a sense the child is like the monster in the film *Alien*.

Now let's return to my *lapsus*: as soon as I read the sentence as I quoted it earlier, I notice almost instantly that what it actually says is: "She is learning to be a mother *with* her mother"! The sentence recounts the fact that she used to take the child to her mother so as to see how she did things with him, taking her as a positive model with which to identify. But my *lapsus* tells a different story and, to my surprise, directs my attention to the fact that a double identification may be in play: if she is learning to be a mother *to* her mother, it means that she identifies her mother with the child (she wants to kill in the child the "dead" mother she has inside her, and thus placate her furious narcissistic rage), but that in the past she herself has been the child of her mother. Thus, there has been a reversal of roles: this time the mother is her son.

But if this is how things stand, it is also true that unconsciously she identifies herself *with* the mother (her mother) who "killed" her, or rather did not "recognize" her at birth. My lapsus can now be seen as a lightning flash of hallucinosis, which becomes a dream as soon as I realize my error and shows me an intricate narrative in which the victims are executioners and vice versa, as in the stories of Greek tragedy. In the dreaming perspective of the session I intuit that at the same time a crucial game is being played in which the patient is the therapist of the therapist.

You and Giulia

"A, seeing us together once, said to us, 'You and Giulia are very different.'" Giulia is speaking to me about her relationship with her boyfriend (S), with whom she shares a workplace, and repeating a comment made by a mutual acquaintance (A). Her boyfriend had answered with annoyance because he refused to accept the idea that he had no affinities with Giulia. The moment I hear Giulia express herself in these terms, I seem not to understand and ask her, "Who is this Giulia?" Giulia replies, "*I'm* Giulia!" I realize that I had immediately identified Giulia with the person to whom A was referring – saying "You" – and by whom she meant, instead, the boyfriend. So I was superimposing Giulia onto S, the boyfriend.

What my hallucinosis brings us to ask ourselves is if I might be disclosing a "Zelig" feature, an imitative attitude in Giulia in relation to S; the need not to be authentically herself, for fear that if she were, she would run the risk of losing him. Moreover, by asking her "Who is this Giulia?" it is almost as if I had identified *two* Giulias – one who can show herself and one who must stay hidden – and a certain difficulty in communicating between them.

From a viewpoint more linked to the actuality of the meeting, the point becomes how much difference in views, opinions, emotions I (we) can bear.

Permission

Stefania's phone sounds in her handbag, which she has left on the floor near the couch. In a tone of (affectionate) tolerance she says to me, "Well? You have my permission to read the message!" A little disconcerted and also amused, I answer, "Actually . . . it's yours." At which point, surprised, Stefania takes the phone out of her bag. Here the hallucinosis seems to be in the service of a role reversal in which it is the patient who is treating me like a child, putting herself in the place of a parent. At the same time, perhaps she wants to tell me she has forgiven me for the fact that when we first resumed our sessions on the usual day after the summer break, I had absent-mindedly not expected her, even though I was in my consulting room. In other words, her anger having largely cooled, she was giving me permission to be distracted for a moment. Was this a bit like a *fort-da* game? At the end, she invites me to "read" or interpret the message.

From parapraxis to transformation in hallucinosis

The concept of *parapraxis* – in Italian, the term for this notion (for example, a slip of the tongue) is *lapsus*, which has the primary meaning "fall" or "tumble" – returns in the framework of classical psychoanalysis. A representation escapes from the unconscious in which it was isolated and returns to consciousness as a symptom, as a compromise formation. A banal *lapsus* in reading might be investigated in the same way. But if we see the poetry of the mind at work there – i.e., the narrative derivatives of what Bion calls the waking dream thought – we can think of the repression itself as being in the service of expression. For Freud the only purpose of the dream work is to conceal the meaning of the dream thought, to make it latent. Hence the censorship. The censorship does not create effects which have meaning, except accidentally. We, however, have realized that all thinking is dreaming. That the form of meaning-creation that expresses itself in dreaming is the only one we have in language, even though it obviously extends along a range that runs from an extreme emotional and sensory richness to the extreme simplification of the concept.

Visiting the Chris Ofili exhibition entitled *Night and Day* at the New Museum in New York, at a certain point one enters a large room cloaked in semi-darkness. One can barely make out the large panels on the walls. Even when one's eyes have adjusted to the darkness, it is still difficult to see the painted figures on the panels. It is only by moving around slowly that the play of weak light coming from small spotlights reveals the outlines of some large, disturbing, though incomplete, figures. The device Ofili has used reveals the invisible and arouses feelings of awe and reverence, not only towards the figures but because the interaction itself becomes a figure in an irremediably solitary vision.

Similarly, if one is to capture the visions of the unconscious, there needs to be a delicate and alternate encounter between a game of darkness and a cautious movement of exploration. The light of memories must be set aside to make way for the experience of remembering (Bion, 1970/1993), which means putting "faith" in the fact that what is initially disturbing – the semi-darkness – and what is almost irritating to the point that one feels like running out of the room is actually the necessary premise for evocative visions. Avoiding casting a bright light on the facts of the analysis (which can also mean not reducing ambiguity) and using instead an updated version of the Freudian concept of a "beam of darkness" can in some cases cause literal hallucinations (a concept which for me encompasses not only the phenomenon of TH itself, but also the way in which we use an interpretation of the dream of the session; Civitarese, 2006). It is then that, starting from the invisible of the unconscious, we cast a glance on holograms present in the analytic field (which we regard as created by both the patient and the analyst) at any given moment, and on the figures, no less sublime than those created by Ofili, of the unconscious.

Note

1 Translator's note: the author wrote "*seno*" (breast) instead of "*senso*" (meaning).

References

Bion, W.R. (1970/1993). *Attention and Interpretation.* London: Karnac.
Civitarese, G. (2006). Dreams that mirror the session. *International Journal of Psychoanalysis*, 87: 703–723.
Civitarese, G. (2015). Transformations in hallucinosis and the receptivity of the analyst. *International Journal of Psychoanalysis*, 96: 1091–1116. Available online at: http://onlinelibrary.wiley.com/doi/10.1111/1745-8315.12242/epdf, accessed May 18, 2016.
Civitarese, G. (2016). *Truth and the Unconscious.* London: Routledge.

Is the theory of the unconscious necessary to the theory of the field or not? There are two theories—the theory of the unconscious and the theory of observation. Field theory is a theory of observation. We can observe and theorize about what we observe. When we observe we have theories but they are implicit theories. All of us worked with field theories before we knew that they were field theories.

Roosevelt Cassorla

Chapter 7

Psychoanalytic field theory
Good for all analysts

Martin A. Silverman

I should like to begin with a story, which I heard from my traditional, Freudian analyst.

A man was in analysis. For a while, everything seemed to be going well, but then it bogged down. The patient was frustrated. The analyst was frustrated. Neither could find a way to get things going again. It remained like this for quite a while. One day, the analyst said:

> You know, we're stuck. Things have plateaued, and we haven't been able to get back on track. I don't seem to be able to do anything for you right now. Nothing's being served by my being here. I tell you what. Why don't you come in each day, lie down on the couch, and speak out loud. I'll be downstairs in the coffee shop, but I'll leave a tape-recorder here. At the end of the day, I'll listen to the tape and hear what you've said. When I think I can be useful to you again, *I'll* be here instead of the tape-recorder.

At first the patient wasn't very happy with the idea, but then he figured he'd give it a try. For a while, he followed his analyst's suggestion.

Then, one day, when the analyst was sitting at the counter drinking coffee and reading a book, he heard a familiar voice.

"Hi, Doc," his patient said.

The analyst was surprised. "Why aren't you upstairs talking to my tape-recorder?" he asked.

"Oh, it's okay," the patient replied. "My tape-recorder is talking to your tape-recorder."

My analyst said to me, "Analysis can only be done by two human beings."

I've thought about that story periodically over the years. And one of the thoughts I've had is that, in a certain way, the analyst's tape-recorder stands for psychoanalytic theory. Theory can be very useful—but it can also muck things up. To quote Liran Razinsky (2013, p. 6):

> Theory creates blindness. Even useful, fruitful theories bring about a certain blindness. In illuminating reality, they *ipso facto* relegate other parts of it to darkness. Concepts we use sharpen our perception of certain aspects of reality, but necessarily blind us to others.

We shall return to this later.

Transference–countertransference interaction

It is quite true that it takes two people to make an analysis work. And the interaction between those two people is complex indeed. Sigmund Freud learned this the hard way, when the young lady whom he called Dora taught him very painfully that an analyst brings as much into what develops within the analytic process that unfolds between them as does his or her patient. Both participants in the analytic process bring their internal worlds into the interaction between them, and all the people past and present who populate those worlds come into the room with them. They bring with them all the human struggles, conflicts, attitudes, beliefs, and personal strivings that reside within them. Dora taught Freud about *the analyst*'s transference. And psychoanalysts have been wrestling with and trying to understand what is involved in so-called transference–countertransference interaction ever since.

Now, what does this have to do with psychoanalytic field theory? *Everything!*

What is psychoanalytic field theory? Where did it come from? How are we to define it? And what does "theory" actually mean? *Webster's Third New International Dictionary* offers several definitions of the word:

> (1) "imaginative contemplation of reality"; (2) "a belief, policy or procedure proposed or followed as the basis of action"; (3) "the body of generalizations and principles developed in association with practice in a field of activity"; (4) " a judgment, conception, proposition, or

formula ... formed by speculation or deduction or by abstraction or generalization from facts"; and (5) "an unproved assumption."

(Gove, 1971, p. 2371)

If we were to put these definitions together into one composite statement, we might come out with something like: "A theory is a body of general principles, derived from speculative and partly imaginative ideas that emanate from repeated observations, which forms the basis for practice in a field of activity—although the assumptions upon which it is based have not necessarily been proven to be correct."

Theory can be very powerful, for good and/or for ill. And words are also very powerful—and we tend, in general, to use language both to reveal and to conceal. More often than not, we do both at the same time. As Bonnie Litowitz has felicitously put it (2014), we speak with one another for three reasons—to establish contact, to convey information, and to lie. The terms we use can clarify, obfuscate, or do both at the same time. Language, to a large extent, shapes our perception of the world around us. What we *say* about things powerfully influences what we think those things are. How we define things very much influences what we believe to be true. As psychoanalysts, *we* have to be careful with the words (and the theories) we use, and about the ways in which we use them. A Canadian psychoanalyst, Sheldon Heath (2008), told me that he noticed, as a supervisory session he was about to have with Wilfred Bion was about to begin, that Bion was scowling and shaking his head.

"What's the matter?" Heath asked him.

"People talk about my ideas," Bion replied, "as though they are facts. They are *not* facts! They are *ideas*!"

It *is* a fact, furthermore, that Bion was a strong proponent of tolerating uncertainty and of being willing *not to know* while doing psychoanalytic work.

We can extend what Bion said about his ideas to the realm of theory. Theories are not truths. They are theories. As such, they can be very useful to us in organizing our ideas, but they can also misguide us if we impart more power to them than they should be given or if we apply them without *thoroughly* researching and understanding them. Psychoanalytic field theory is not a prescription but a *concept*.

As human beings, we are not omniscient, and our nature tends us toward reductionism. When we focus upon something that is important to us, something about which we have strong feelings, and especially something which *we ourselves* have created, we tend to revert back to pre-operational thinking, in which, while we focus upon one part of a whole, we lose sight of other parts of it and become blurred in our perception of the whole of which it is a part. Our baby *clearly* is the most beautiful, most wonderful baby of all. *Everyone* should recognize that. Something must be wrong with them if they don't.

When we construct a theory, we tend to valorize it above all else, and shunt aside that which does not fit neatly into our conceptualizations. We do this by minimizing the significance of anything that might disturb our thesis or even by denying its existence altogether. A good number of years ago, I was teaching a course on child development. I could not find anyone where I was teaching who could explain Piaget's ideas in a way that was clear and understandable, so I studied them myself. I read books written by and about Jean Piaget, Barbel Inhelder, and their work. I also repeated some of the ingenious experiments they designed. My older daughter served eagerly as one of my subjects. One day, when she was not quite four years old, she was happily sorting a number of cards of various shapes and colors into overlapping "families." She accomplished the task rather quickly and easily. Incapable, at that age, of more than pre-operational thinking, however, she was not yet able to appreciate a group that consisted of a single member. Among the cards I had given her was one that had a unique shape and a unique color. She furrowed her brow, frowned, and showed increasing consternation at finding herself unable to fit it with any of the other cards.

All of a sudden, she pointed over my left shoulder, toward the window behind me, and asked, "Daddy, what's that?" I turned to look out the window but failed to see anything remarkable. "I don't see anything," I said. "What were you asking about?"

"Oh, nothing," she said. "I thought I saw something." Then she sat there, beaming.

"You look happy," I said. "Why's that?"

"I've finished!" she declared.

And, indeed, she appeared to have sorted all the cards neatly into overlapping families. Something, however, did not seem quite right. Then it dawned on me. "Where's the purple rectangle?" I asked.

"I hid it!" she declared gaily.

We tend to do something very similar when we elaborate psychoanalytic theories.

(Incidentally, my daughter delighted her teachers by bringing the game into her nursery school class for her friends to play.)

Theoretical constructs, by their very nature, are limited, incomplete, and subject to revision as fresh observations or inputs point in new directions. They never give the all-important, final say which we might like them to give. Richard Feynman, together with two of his colleagues, did groundbreaking research that led to elaboration of the concept of quantum electrodynamics, for which they received a Nobel Prize. He wrote a little book, to which he attached the ironic title *QED: The Strange Theory of Light and Matter* (1985/2006). He emphasized in the book that we can never know anything with absolute certainty, because everything involves an order of probability. He and his colleagues discovered what appeared to be very strange things going on inside atoms and involving the properties and actions of subatomic particles in general. He stated, whimsically, at the beginning of the book, that if someone wants to understand quantum electrodynamics, he or she could either go to school for six years or read his book. I read the book (although I had to do a crash course in integral calculus to get through it and form some idea of what the theory of quantum electrodynamics can tell us). I was reassured that Feynman said at the outset that readers need not be dismayed after reading the book to find that they still do not understand what the theory is all about, because he didn't understand it himself! He also indicated that he and his colleagues could not be certain that their conclusions were correct, no matter how impressed the Nobel Committee might have been. It is quite possible, he said, that one of the graduate students they taught would one day demonstrate that they were totally wrong.

Reading *QED* strengthened my belief that it is necessary for us to be ever open to new ideas, as the educators I have most admired tend to emphasize, and to think about and question those ideas with open-minded skepticism, rather than idealize them and leap into glib and superficial application of them to what we do.

Alexander Pope (1711), three hundred years ago, similarly advised those who would be poets or critics of poetic work to study Homer and the ancient Greek poets, and to do so in depth so as to learn the basic principles of poetry from them before (carefully) devising new principles. Then he penned these oft-quoted words:

> A little knowledge is a dang'rous Thing.
> Drink deeply from the Pierian Spring or taste not at all.
> There shallow draughts intoxicate the Brain.
> And drinking deeply sobers us again.

The term "psychoanalytic field theory" refers to a valuable contribution to existing psychoanalytic theory and practice rather than a new school of thought. Its emphasis is upon the importance of focusing in detail on the total field within which psychoanalytic treatment takes place and, in particular, upon the collaborative and creative interaction that takes place between the two participants. The aim is to assist the patient in overcoming or ameliorating emotional difficulties that arose in the course of past interaction with key figures in his/her life. Psychoanalysis involves reliving the past so as to create a better future. As the patient and the analyst throw themselves into the work, something new emerges that derives from what each of them brings into their interaction but is more than merely the sum of the parts. Analyzing this new configuration is the most powerful and most mutative component of what is done in a successful analysis.

This sounds simple, but it is not. And one of the reasons why it is not simple is that, as Madeleine and Willy Baranger (2008) indicated when they introduced the concept, while the relationship between the two participants in the analytic enterprise is symmetrical in some ways, in another, important way, it is *asymmetrical*. One of the participants, the patient, is suffering and has come for help. The other possesses training and experience which he or she is expected to use to assist the participant who has come for assistance. Analytic treatment is designed to benefit the patient rather than the analyst, who is paid for providing that assistance. The analyst, of course, inevitably grows from the experience, just as a good parent grows from the experience of raising his or her children. And analysts have expectations of their patients, just as parents have expectations of their children. The therapeutic aim of psychoanalytic treatment is an important and unavoidable aspect of the Barangers' observations about the field within which analytic work takes place. People *pay us* for helping them. We work for them. But there are limits to what we allow them to do to us and what we allow them to expect from us.

I am reminded, for example, of a very angry, intermittently deeply depressed woman who was one of the nastiest people I have ever met. One day, she said to me, "The way I treat you probably isn't worth what I pay you."

I replied, in a firm voice, "That's right!"

She looked startled and asked what I meant. I explained that being subjected to abuse and torture was *not* part of my job. This exchange marked an important turning point in the treatment. I might add that this was a psychotherapy case, not psychoanalysis. Many years earlier, in a fit of rage at the psychiatrist with whom she was in treatment at the time, she had stepped out of a window in his waiting room—on the twelfth floor! It was only because a series of well-constructed awnings broke her fall that she came out of it alive, although with multiple fractures. She is still alive and well, and now in her nineties. She did not become seriously depressed again after our work together.

Madeleine and Willy Baranger's concept of the psychoanalytic field

Madeleine and Willy Baranger, working in Argentina during the 1950s and 1960s, introduced the concept of psychoanalytic field theory. They were influenced by the work of a number of people. Foremost among these was Wilfred Bion, especially his ideas about the way in which mothers and babies appear to project and introject mental and emotional contents into and from one another as the mother receives the baby's communications about its distressingly overwhelming, chaotic and inchoate, negative and as yet indefinable sensations ("beta elements"). The mother willingly contains them within herself while she empathically detoxifies and organizes them, via "reverie," and she returns them to the child in a clearer and more manageable form ("alpha elements") through her container-contained "alpha function." Bion also observed that we think in dream-like fashion as much when we are awake (including within the dreamscape of an analytic session) as when we are asleep. He also embraced the poet John Keats's emphasis on the importance of "negative capability"—that is, of willingness to tolerate not knowing—even at times to a large degree and for relatively long periods, and to be open to encountering things that might be foreign to us and may even conflict with what we have previously believed.

They were similarly impressed by Heinrich Racker's ideas about concordant and complementary identification by an analyst with his or her patient's internal objects and with elements in the patient's self-representations as important determinants of the way in which the analyst perceives and responds to the patient, and by Kurt Lewin's ideas about the complex, dynamically changing and evolving field of interaction that takes place between us and our physical, interpersonal, and social environment, within which whatever affects one element also affects other elements in the field. Merleau-Ponty's "phenomenological–existential" philosophy, which stresses personal experience over perceptual experience, also impressed them.

The Barangers' (2008) ideas center on the analytic setting as a bi-personal field of operation within which the analyst, consciously and unconsciously, contributes actively to the perceptions, ideas, fantasies, and emotional configurations that emerge within the analytic field of operation. The two participants in the analytic process jointly create a new, functionally basic fantasy about the patient, which the analyst eventually needs to recognize, analyze, and understand. *Their creative interaction with one another* gives major access to the analysand's internal struggles and conflicts. Important components of the transference–countertransference interaction between the participants *arise out of* the basic, unconscious fantasy which they jointly create within the field. The analyst's interventions aim to promote clarity about what is taking place—for the patient and, perhaps even more so, for the analyst. Interventions need to be timed and constructed in such a way that they can be understood, accepted, and processed by *both* participants. The analyst's ability to offer an effective, useful intervention derives from the ability to recognize where, in the field of interactional expression by and between the patient and the analyst, as transference objects to one another, there is a point of entry into an area in the field on which both participants can safely focus as they *look together* at what is taking place between them. The Barangers term this the *point of urgency*. It requires training, skill, and expertise.

Impasses and stagnation in the analytic process can often be understood, the Barangers indicate, as resulting from blockages in the field that stem from unconscious collusion by the analysand and the analyst to remain blind to elements in the analytic field that are undermining it. To overcome them, the analyst needs to *take a second look* at what is taking place within the analytic field—as a whole and with regard to its various components—in order to identify what is causing the blockage. The blockage, they maintain, is most often created by the intersection between a heavily defended area of emotional conflict (a bastion) within the analyst and a corresponding bastion within the patient. Recognition by the analyst of his or her own contribution to the stalemate does not necessarily always require self-disclosure on the part of the analyst. The Barangers emphasize that the mutative effect of the treatment derives largely from working with and within the analytic field, especially within the basic fantasy that is created by the two people who are collaborating in the analysis. It is from this that real change can occur.

The Barangers did not intend to create a new body of psychoanalytic theory to replace or supplant the existing Freudian and Kleinian contributions to theory and practice that informed their work. Their intention, it seems to me, was to focus upon just one, albeit extremely important, aspect of psychoanalytic theory and practice—namely, the transference–countertransference *interaction* that takes place as analysand and analyst work together.

The post-Bionian field theory of Ferro and Civitarese

Three decades after Willy and Madeleine Baranger first introduced their ideas about the bi-personal, psychoanalytic field, a group of Italian analysts was inspired to expound and expand upon them. They also derived their ideas to a great extent (probably to an even greater extent) from those of Wilfred Bion—as well as from the contributions of the Barangers, Herbert Meltzer, Harold Searles, Umberto Eco, Rene Descartes, Jacques Derrida, and a number of other philosophers. The group includes Roberto Basile, Michele Bezoari, Francesco Corrao, Giovanni Foresti, and, most influentially, two extremely articulate and prolific Italian psychoanalytic writers: Antonino Ferro and Giuseppe Civitarese. In their works on "post-Bionian psychoanalysis," which they continue to produce, Ferro (1992/1999, 1996/2013, 1999/2006, 2006/2009) and Civitarese (2006, 2008/2010, 2013, 2014) present impressive and at times dazzling ideas about:

- the central importance of focusing on the bi-personal interaction taking place in a dream-like framework;
- the importance of viewing what is expressed as waking dream thoughts;

- the importance of the analyst's recognition of and joining in with the narrative or story created by the analysand, in which a host of past and present figures holographically occupy the stage;
- the need for analysts to be free to be spontaneous and to resist being controlled by whatever theory they have learned as they "metaphorize" what is appearing on the analytic dreamscape or stage;
- the need of the analyst to balance immersion in the patient's psychic reality with joining into it in a spontaneous and creative fashion;
- the task imposed upon the analyst of increasingly supplying alpha function to the alpha and beta elements that emerge from the analysand—at first largely interpersonally and interactively but increasingly verbally—so that "knowing" can be created, as Bion emphasized; and
- the centrality of baseline projective identification and baseline reverie.

They also join with the Barangers in stressing the importance of following Bion in appreciating the value of Keats's "negative capability"—that is, of tolerating not knowing, and being willing to be taken by surprise, en route to acquiring knowledge.

Their emphasis upon the necessity of viewing analytic sessions as encounters between the patient's dream and the analyst's dream and upon entering into the patient's emotional world by entering into the patient's dreaming process is epitomized in Civitarese's assertion (2014, p. 12) that:

> Today we no longer regard the dream as the royal road that helps to reveal the disguises dream-work imposes on latent thoughts; rather we valorize its function of transformation and symbolic creation. The ambiguity of the manifest text of the dream no longer arouses suspicion. We consider it instead the expression of its poetic function . . . Understood as a communication between one unconscious and another, it is something we listen to as an intersubjective production. We read every session as if it were a long shared dream and conceive the whole of analysis as an exchange of reveries. In principle, it would be difficult to tell what belongs to one and what belongs to the other. In interpretation, also the associations and reveries of the analyst rightfully come into play, and they too help us understand the patient's dream.

They do not eschew solid theoretical grounding, however, nor are they proponents of wild analysis or of the "anything goes" approach about which David Tuckett (2009), Fred Busch (2008), and others have urged caution. They are careful to distinguish between the "virtual reality" that prevails in the analytic consulting room and the actual reality in which the analysand lives, outside of the psychoanalytic field, and they stress the need for psychoanalytic humility—for example, with regard to the realities of the patient's life and to physical aspects of psychosomatic illness and of the somatic expression of emotional contents, which, to paraphrase Blaise Pascal, exist despite theory.

They provide plentiful clinical illustrations of the ideas they share and the principles they value as central to the analytic process, although they do not always do so at length. The clinical material they provide amply attests to the usefulness of their approach in the treatment of seriously disturbed patients—psychotic, borderline, and developmentally stunted. Its application to this patient group is not surprising, especially since they derive so many of their ideas from Bion. Its suitability for analytic work with more neurotic patients is less clearly evident.

They are strong proponents, furthermore, of open exchange of observations and ideas among psychoanalysts who are adherents of different schools of thought within what, in a larger frame of reference, we might characterize as another kind of "analytic field." I quote Ferro (1996/2013, p. 54):

> Two analysts of one and the same school adhesively reinforce each other's positions without any development, whereas two analysts belonging to different schools will clash, each convinced of the correctness of his own school and the falseness of the other's. Conversely, two analysts who are "recipe-less cooks" not only understand each other but succeed in mutually enriching each other.

Ferro (1996/2013, pp. 90–91) has indicated that post-Bionian field theory differs in some ways from that of the psychoanalytic field theory of the Barangers:

> I understand the field differently from Willy and Madeleine Baranger. They talk about the analytic couple's unconscious fantasy, which can only be revealed with the aid of the analyst's second interpretative gaze. I see the field as the place where all possible stories can be told, stories that have their origin when the patient's undigested facts

encounter the transformative ability of the analyst. It does not matter which direction the story will take later. The important thing is that it transforms the material the patient has been unable to digest, and I think that analysts with different models can perform this type of transformation equally well.

This is because if the undigested facts are transformed it matters little in which dialect this is done: in the dialect of the reconstruction of the child's story of events, or in the dialect of the events of the inner world, and of the vicissitudes of his internal objects; or else via a relational explanation of the here and now; or simply—which I prefer—by means of constant co-narrative transformations involving analyst and patient.

Similarly, I might be permitted to question or even respectfully disagree with Ferro and Civitarese with regard to how they work with their patients. I appreciate the care they take to respect their patients' sensitivity about being shamed, humiliated, demeaned, or otherwise abused, because of painful past experience, and to respect their patients' need for containment (Bion) or even holding (Winnicott). Nevertheless, I wonder if they may go too far at times in avoiding engagement with the rage, hatred, and aggressiveness their patients are feeling and (indirectly) directing toward them. An example—involving a session that Montana Katz (2015) presented as illustrative of their clinical approach in a paper upon which I had the honor to comment as a prepared discussant—is the following:

> I tell Lucio that I shall be away for a couple of weeks (for professional reasons). He begins the next session by saying that he has not had any dreams. He then tells me that he took the cat to be neutered and that he feels quite calm. He adds that he has met with one of the leaders of a pacifist association, who has been abandoned by his wife and weeps inconsolably. His wife cheated on him, taking up again with a female fellow student with whom she already had a relationship.
>
> I tell him that, if we were to look at these two communications as if they were two dreams (that is always one of my listening vertices when a patient speaks to me), we might think that he was worried that, if the cat had not been neutered, it might perhaps scratch me. What is more, who knows what might happen if the member of the pacifist organization who cried because of my cheating on him, even if the

cheating was in a way "justified" (for a congress, as he tells me he has discovered on the internet), was actually the Mexican revolutionary Pancho Villa or simply the national hero Garibaldi.

I cannot help but be puzzled by this exchange between patient and analyst. As it comes across to me, the patient, in a thinly veiled fashion, tells his analyst, who has announced that he will be away for professional reasons, that he is hurt and angry at being abandoned, is sobbing inside in anguish, and is so angry that he wants to cut off his balls! The analyst understandably indicates to the patient that he appreciates his anger at him for leaving him and that he appreciates even more his wish to protect the analyst from it. But he goes on to tell him, in essence, that he ought nobly to accept the abandonment rather than complain about it, because the analyst is a very important person, doing very important things, like Pancho Villa (my guess is that he was leaving to attend the IPA meetings in Mexico City in 2011) and Giuseppe Garibaldi, a revered Italian hero.

Of course, I was not present in the analytic session or in the analysis as a whole, so I have to consider the possibility that there were good reasons for the analyst to tread carefully while he was responding to his patient's rage, but I do wonder whether we might at times overdo the care we take to provide containment for a patient's intensely negative feelings.

An eighteen-year-old girl consulted me in connection with her chronic unhappiness and anger. She informed me that she believed that "now [she was] ready for therapy." She had gone to a therapist in the past, she said, but she had not liked the overly gentle way the therapist treated her. "I'm not fragile!" she declared, in a very irritated voice. Overprotection is not protection, she maintained. Her complaint about the therapist's underestimation of her ability to deal with troubling issues was mirrored recently in an opinion piece by Judith Shulevitz (2015), in which she lamented the current tendency in US universities to overprotect their students from exposure to ideas and discussions that might be offensive or disturbing to them. She asserted that doing so weakens rather than strengthens the students.

The concept of the analytic third

Before (and perhaps en route to) giving further consideration to the matter of how we might deal with aggression, hate, and rage in the analytic situation, I should like to address the relationship between analytic field theory and the related concept of the analytic third, which also derives in large measure from the ideas of Wilfred Bion. Andre Green, Thomas Ogden, and Donald Meltzer are some of the other prominent contributors to the development of this concept.

In 1975, Green (pp. 1–2) wrote:

> Psychoanalysis has always changed and developed from its very beginnings ... I shall take as a working hypothesis the proposition that the perception of the change which is beginning today is that of *a change within the analyst* [original emphasis] ... I will confine myself to the theory and practice which emerges from the analytic situation; that is, to the view of psychic reality as seen in the analytic situation to the way that *the patient enacts it and makes the analyst experience it* [emphasis added] ... This does not necessarily mean that we must deny changes in the patient [over the years], but they are subordinated to changes and perceptivity in the analyst himself ... Analysts are becoming more and more aware of the part they play in it.

Green spent the next thirty years studying this. By 2004, he was able to describe the analytic situation in terms of the individual subjectivities of the analysand and the analyst joined by the intersubjectivity of the two of them into something new. Interestingly, he did not abandon the concept of drives, and he connected his ideas about the central importance of the interpersonal relationship between patient and analyst with Freud's ideas about primary and secondary thought processes within the mind. He spoke about a *tertiary process* in analysis that links primary process with secondary process as it re-binds disconnected, unbound forces of sexuality and aggression and constructively reintegrates love and hate. He emphasized that a key to understanding "thirdness" in analytic work is appreciation of the central place of ambivalence within human nature.

Before going on to Ogden's observations, I would like to return to the very beginnings of the concept of the analytic third. Wilfred Bion constructed an important set of ideas about a mother's accepting her infant's unformed and inchoate emotions, feelings, and impressions, which are beyond its capacity to apprehend or comprehend, containing and detoxifying them within her mind (via "reverie"), and returning them to the child in a tamed, transformed, and therefore more tolerable, manageable, and useful form. He perceived a similarity between this and what takes place during psychoanalytic treatment, most dramatically with borderline and psychotic patients. The analysand's and the analyst's conjoined mental activity, which takes place largely outside of consciousness, constitutes a *third* entity that contains elements of both the child's mind and the mother's mind at the same time that it is something new—more than merely the sum of their two contributions. Bion also emphasized (as did Winnicott) the vital importance in the interaction between infant and mother, as well as between patient and analyst, of the expression, acceptance, and taming of murderous rage. A crying baby, he averred, is a dying baby—a terrified, frantic, enraged infant that is fighting for its life. Bion derived his ideas from those of Melanie Klein, especially with regard to the centrality of ambivalence and of projective and introjective identification in the developmental process and in psychoanalytic work.

Ogden, in 2004 (pp. 168–169), described the concept of the analytic third as comprising

> the vicissitudes of the experience of being simultaneously within and outside of the intersubjectivity of the analyst and analysand. This subjectivity, the intersubjective analytic third, is the product of a unique dialectic generated by/between the separate objectivities of analyst and analysand within the analytic setting. It is a subjectivity that seems to take on a life of its own in the interpersonal field that is generated between analyst and analysand ... A successful analytic experience [he says] involves [eventual] superseding of the third by means of mutual recognition by analyst and analysand [of themselves] as separate objects and a re-appropriation of the (transferred) individual subjectivities of the participants.

There are two aspects of Green's and Ogden's views that I believe warrant emphasis. One involves the need to be aware of and respect the unique, individual subjectivity of the two participants in the analytic endeavor while engaging in what Ogden terms the "subjugating intersubjectivity" that temporarily blurs awareness of their independence, as two very different individuals, playing very different roles, participating in the analytic encounter. If an analyst, succumbing to the mythical caricature of Sigmund Freud as a dispassionate, distant, silent analyst, which in reality he never was, assumes an authoritarian and/or cold and distant stance, he is seriously losing perspective. When an analyst gives a paper she is writing to her patients to read and asks them to assist her by offering editorial assistance, she is losing perspective. When an analyst *permanently* sidesteps disturbing issues to avoid embarrassing or shaming the patient, he or she is losing perspective. An analyst who does not allow the patient to claim and reclaim his or her separateness and individuality, via eventual dissolution of their intersubjective merging, has done only part of the job. If an analyst allows a patient to self-destruct masochistically, rationalized as respecting the patient's right to self-determination, something is *very* wrong. When analysts organize their theory and practice around the Oedipus complex and scant the importance of pre-Oedipal and post-Oedipal experience and development, they are just as wrong as those who look away from the role of competitive, triangular conflicts within human psychology. When you shine a spotlight on just one part of an elephant, as Razinsky observed, you don't see the rest of it. Theoretical formulations can help us organize and understand data, but they muddle things when they get in the way of clinical observation.

Love and hate in the brain stem and within the psychoanalytic field

This brings me to the centrality of ambivalence in human nature and in interpersonal interaction. It applies to analysand and analyst alike, as Winnicott (1947/1975, 1969) points out. Children hate as well as love their parents, just as parents hate as well as love their children. Our brain stem does not allow it to be otherwise. And, *pari passu*, so it is in psychoanalysis. When I began analytic training, one of my instructors recalled Sandor Lorand saying to his class, when *he* began his training: "People talk about patients falling in love with their analyst. Patients don't fall in love with their analyst. They fall in *hate* with their analyst!" Laplanche (1970) observed that an analysis begins when the patient hates his analyst.

It is comprehensible that some analysts are inclined to make psychoanalysis more palatable to potential analytic patients by speaking of abstruse motivational systems rather than thinking in terms of animalistic, instinctual drive pressures, but I am not sure that we benefit from throwing out the concept of drives altogether. Antonio Damasio (2010) concludes from neuro-scientific research that brain generates mind by assessing strategies for interacting with the environment in such a way as to gratify imperative needs and desires more or less safely. This seems, to me, to correlate well with Freud's ideas about peremptory drives and an executive apparatus that seeks to satisfy them while struggling to contain and regulate the power those drives exert over people. Damasio theorizes the existence of a purely somatic *protoself* operating within the most phylogenetically primitive part of our brain, which functions within us, semi-independently, throughout our lives. Around this, a somatopsychic *core self* develops out of repeated interaction with the environment that mediates between bodily needs and the environment. Around that, there develops, via ongoing patterning and mapping within the brain, a completely psychological *autobiographical self* that continually appraises our reaction to and our interaction with our internal and external environments, over time, so as to assure effective functioning. The psychological grows out of the biological, and it never loses its connection with it.

Jaak Panksepp concludes that there are seven powerful, neurologically-based, emotional systems that operate within the brain stem of mammals (and to a greater or lesser extent in other animals) (Panksepp and Biven, 2012). Some of them sound very much like the source of what Freud referred to as drives (which are not biological but psychological). They are the Fear, Rage, and Lust systems. The Fear and Rage centers are very close to each other and tend to operate in unison when danger threatens. Other brain stem centers appear to be biological sources of the interpersonal, relational inclinations that make us social creatures. They are: Care (notably for one's young but extending into social interaction and attachment behavior); Panic/Grief (the reaction to traumatic separation and loss); and Play (which contributes to both affectionate and competitive social interaction). The seventh Panksepp calls the Seeking system, which generates curiosity about our animate and inanimate environment. It operates in unison with other systems. With Care and Play (and perhaps with Panic/Grief), it mediates social interest and interaction. With Lust, and with Play and Rage, it mediates the search for a mate and willingness to engage in competition with a rival to obtain and maintain possession of it. Even on a purely biological level, of course, this is far from the whole story. Hormones, including estrogen and testosterone, vasopressin, oxytocin, progesterone, thyroxin, and ACTH also play powerful roles. And we have a limbic system and a frontal cortex, which maintain continuous, bi-directional communication with our primitive brain stem centers. But our reptilian past continues to exert power over us, as Paul

Maclean (1990) and his co-investigators have observed. We do not have a single brain organization but a triune brain—a reptilian brain, a feline-like brain, and a primate brain—each of which can assume dominance over the others, depending on circumstances.

Even in our primitive brain stem we are quite complex in our makeup—and are any of the fundamental systems that Panksepp suggests are driving us any more important than the others? I am reminded again of the wonderful fable from India about the seven blind men, each of whom examined one part of an elephant and then was so convinced that what he had examined was the whole elephant that they began to argue heatedly and then descended into fighting with one another, much as psychoanalysts can when their favorite theories are challenged.

Stephen Porges (2011), drawing upon decades of research, informs us that we have two distinct components within our vagus nerve that mediate parasympathetic control of our visceral organs and thereby our emotional experience and expression. One, which originates from the dorsal motor nucleus of the brain stem and is unmyelinated, derives from our phylogenetic evolution from distant reptilian ancestors. It impels us to react to danger by freezing (playing dead) or diving under water (figuratively, rather than literally, as reptiles do). The other, which is myelinated, originates from the nucleus ambiguus (which contains nerve cells that migrated away from the dorsal motor nucleus in the course of our evolution into warm-blooded mammals). It serves the vital function of exercising a "vagal break" upon the mammalian, sympathetic nervous system that mediates mammalian fight-or-flight reactions to danger and the intense bursts of energy necessary for pursuing prey or scrambling for food or for a mate—which, paradoxically, would endanger us were they not dampened down sufficiently to keep them under control. The vagal break dampens the vigorous cardiovascular activity that takes place during hunger-driven, infantile suckling, and during states of intense excitement later in life; this is necessary for interpersonal bonding and social interaction to take place. Together with oxytocin, it also dampens the effect upon us of bursts of unmyelinated, reptilian vagal nerve activity, in response to danger—which, if unchecked, can lead not only to fainting but to heart attacks, voodoo death, and, quite possibly, sudden infant death syndrome. In his whimsical and wise poem "For an Amorous Lady," Theodore Roethke (1941/1975) employed ironic understatement when he told the woman in question that she was one in a million, because she not only enjoyed receiving caresses the way mammals do but also enjoyed giving them the way reptiles do, according to a natural history book he had read. In fact, *we are all* both mammalian and reptilian!

Ferro has not abandoned the concept of instinctual drives within human psychology. For example, he states (1996/2013, p. 91):

> In today's psychoanalysis, can we still speak of drives or unconscious fantasies that belong exclusively to the patient or, conversely, are they connected to the mental qualities of the analyst? Must the unconscious fantasies and drives that enter the field be thought of as belonging to the patient, or to the analytic couple, and therefore include the analyst? Can there be a neutral analyst or does the analyst come along with their history, with their private life, with their drives, with their unconscious fantasies?

I began this essay with a story. Two other stories about love and hate (as well as about cooperation and competition) in human interaction come to mind. In one of them, two lawyers are walking down the broad steps that descend from a courthouse. A beautiful woman walks by on the sidewalk. One of the men turns to the other and says, "Oh, I'd like to screw her!" The other asks, "Out of what?"

The other story involves a man who is in intensive psychotherapy, which seems to go well for a while, but then bogs down—from the intersection of bastions perhaps. After months of frustration, one Friday afternoon the therapist tells the patient that they are no longer getting anywhere and perhaps should take a break. The patient is upset but agrees to think about it. The following Monday, he comes in looking haggard, disheveled, and wild-eyed.

"What's wrong?" asks the therapist.

"I was so upset by what you said to me on Friday," the patient replies, "that I was on edge and irritable all weekend. My wife began bugging me about something. She was giving me a really hard time. After a while, I just couldn't take it any longer. We got into a big fight and I lost it. I grabbed her around the neck and I squeezed hard to shut her up. Suddenly I realized that she was dead. I'd killed her. I didn't know what to do. I dragged her into the next room and stuffed her body in a closet. What do I do now?"

"Ah," says the therapist, "now we have something to work on. What do you have about closets?"

Let me say just one more thing about the concept of the analytic third. I heard of a wonderful quip that was made by a senior faculty member at the Institute for Psychoanalytic Education, affiliated with NYU School of Medicine in New York (Stein, 2014). He had been present when a proponent of an interpersonal approach presented an example of his work to a group of students. Afterward, a candidate said, "It seems to me that the work you did reflected a one-person psychology, not a two-person psychology."

The faculty member said, "Maybe it was a one-and-a-third psychology."

The presenter thought for a moment and said: "You might be right."

If I too may be permitted to play poetically with words, it seems to me that meaningful analytic work involves both a one-person *and* a two-person psychology—raised to the third power. Psychoanalysis in general and psychoanalytic field theory in particular are not simple. They are complex and challenging. We need to study and think about them carefully, eschew oversimplification, and take care not to lose sight of the whole elephant while we focus upon a part of it.

"Is you is or is you ain't my baby?"

I should like to make one last comment about the subject of definition and domain. As Piaget (Silverman, 1971) emphasized, logical thinking involves the coordination of inclusion and exclusion. Psychoanalytic field theory, it seems to me, needs to be defined not only as to what it is but also as to what it is not. It is not a substitute for any established school of thought but rather a concept that can enhance and sharpen any of them. It is what it is—no more, no less. The emphasis within it upon appreciating the contributions of both parties to what arises in the course of and is dealt with during psychoanalytic treatment is invaluable, and it applies to work that is carried out in accordance with any school of thought. The way in which awareness of the intersubjective interaction between analysand and analyst develops and unfolds within the field and is applied to the work can vary considerably, however.

Bacal and Herzog (2003) are among the many who stress the importance of fitting the treatment to the specific needs of each patient rather than requiring everyone to conform to the demands of a particular psychoanalytic school of thought. The analytic couch should not be a Procrustean bed. The observation about variation among patients, furthermore, also applies to analysts, each of whom is an individual and cannot be expected to work exactly like everyone else—although we can learn from one another.

It is natural, moreover, not only to over-idealize something that impresses us and to which we hope to make a further contribution (hence, the line from an old song that was popular while I was growing up, which I chose as the heading of this final section), but also to be inclined to extend it so as to make it widely inclusive. It can be counterproductive, however, to broaden a concept so far that one dilutes its significance and blunts its impact. Self psychology emphasizes the centrality in clinical work of interaction between two people. So does the Kleinian emphasis upon projective and introjective identification. It was my dyed-in-the-wool Freudian analyst who told me the joke about analytic work requiring two human beings to carry it out if it is to be successful. As a child analyst, I have long been aware that when I am working with children and their families I am playing on a very large ball field indeed, but child analysis is not synonymous with psychoanalytic field theory and it is not conducted in identical fashion by all child analysts. There are ball fields and there are ball fields, furthermore. A number of sports can be played on the same ball field, but baseball, football, soccer, field hockey, and lacrosse are all quite different from one another.

Relational theory puts great emphasis upon the intersubjective interaction between analysand and analyst (some say too great an emphasis), but it is hardly uniform or monolithic. There is an understandable inclination to view relational theory as a form of psychoanalytic field theory, but I am not at all sure that it is appropriate to do so. For one thing, there are enough conflicting points of view within relational theory that we might think of it in the plural, as consisting of a number of "relational theories." It remains to be seen whether greater synthesis and condensation will take place over time. Analytic field theory is also a specific—relatively limited—*concept*. I have qualms about making it into a large, roomy container for many and often quite diverse points of view. Broadening the definition of psychoanalytic field theory so as to make it widely inclusive can blur its distinctiveness and dilute its significance. At times, less is more. There undoubtedly is conceptual correspondence between psychoanalytic field theory and relational theory, but it probably would serve each of them well to view them as separate, discrete entities rather than conflating them together under a single, broad tent. Each is important in its own right, and it probably would be good to allow each to stand alone, with a unique existence of its own.

References

Bacal, H. A. and Herzog, B. (2003). Specificity theory and optimal responsiveness: an outline. *Psychoanalytic Psychology*, 20: 635–648.

Baranger, M. and Baranger, W. (1961–1962/2008). The analytic situation as a dynamic field. *International Journal of Psycho-Analysis*, 89: 795–826.

Busch, F. (2008). Distinguishing psychoanalysis from psychotherapy. *International Journal of Psycho-Analysis*, 91: 23–34.

Civitarese, G. (2006). Dreams that mirror the session. *International Journal of Psycho-Analysis*, 87: 703–23.

Civitarese, G. (2008/2010). *The Intimate Room: Theory and Technique of the Analytic Field*. London: Routledge.

Civitarese, G. (2013). *The Violence of Emotions: Bion and Post-Bionian Psychoanalysis*. London: Routledge.

Civitarese, G. (2014). *The Necessary Dream: New Theories and Techniques in Psychoanalysis*. Trans. Ian Harvey. London: Karnac.

Damasio, A. (2010). *Self Comes to Mind: Constructing the Conscious Brain*. New York: Pantheon.

Ferro, A. (1992/1999). *The Bi-personal Field: Experiences in Child Analysis*. London: Routledge.

Ferro, A. (1996/2013). *Supervision in Psychoanalysis: The São Paolo Seminars*. Trans. Ian Harvey. London: Routledge.

Ferro, A. (1999/2006). *Psychoanalysis as Therapy and Storytelling*. Trans. P. Slotkin. Hove: Brunner-Routledge.

Ferro, A. (2006/2009). *Mind Works: Technique and Creativity in Psychoanalysis*. Trans. P. Slotkin. Hove: Routledge.

Feynman, R. P. (1985/2006). *QED: The Strange Theory of Light and Matter*. Princeton, NJ: Princeton University Press.

Gove, P. B. (ed.) (1971). *Webster's Third New International Dictionary, Unabridged*. Springfield, MA: G. & C. Merriam.

Green, A. (1975). The analyst, symbolization, and absence in psychoanalytic theory (on changes in analytic practice and analytic experience)—in memory of D. W. Winnicott. *International Journal of Psycho-Analysis*, 56: 1–22.

Green, A. (2004). Thirdness and psychoanalytic concepts. *Psychoanalytic Quarterly*, 73: 99–136.

Heath, S. (2008). Personal communication.

Katz, S. M. (2015). Contemporary psychoanalytic field theory: comparative perspectives. Paper presented to the National Psychological Association of Psychoanalysis, March 8.

Laplanche, J. (1970). *Vie et mort en psychoanalysis* [Life and Death in Psychoanalysis]. Paris: Flammarien.

Litowitz, B. E. (2014). Coming to terms with intersubjectivity: keeping language in mind. Plenary address to the American Psychoanalytic Association Annual Meeting, January 17.

Maclean, P. D. (1990). *The Triune Brain in Evolution: Role in Paleocerebral Functions*. New York: Plenum.

Ogden, T. H. (2004). The analytic third: implications for psychoanalytic theory and technique. *Psychoanalytic Quarterly*, 73: 167–196.

Panksepp, J. and Biven, L. (2012). *The Archaeology of Mind: Neuroevolutionary Origin of Human Emotions*. New York and London: Norton.

Pope, A. (1711). *An Essay on Criticism, with Introductory and Explanatory Notes*. Available online at: http://poetry.eserver.org/essay-on-criticism.html, accessed May 19, 2016.

Porges, S. W. (2011). *The Polyvagal Theory: Neurophysiological Foundations of Emotions, Attachment, Communication, and Self-Regulation*. New York: Norton.

Razinsky, L. (2013). *Freud, Psychoanalysis and Death*. New York: Cambridge University Press.

Roethke, T. (1941/1975). For an amorous lady. In *The Collected Poems of Theodore Roethke* (p. 22). Garden City, NY: Anchor/Doubleday.

Shulevitz, J. (2015). Hiding from scary ideas. *New York Times Sunday Review*, March 22: 1, 6–7.

Silverman, M. A. (1971). The growth of logical thinking: Piaget's contribution to ego psychology. *Psychoanalytic Quarterly*, 40: 317–341.

Stein, H. (2014). Personal communication.

Tuckett, D. (2009). Does anything go? *International Journal of Psycho-Analysis*, 92: 2–9.

Winnicott, D. W. (1947/1975). Hate in the transference. In *Through Pediatrics to Psychoanalysis* (pp. 194–203). London: Karnac

Winnicott, D. W. (1969). The use of an object and relating through identifications. In *Playing and Reality* (pp. 86–94). New York: Basic Books.

In a session with a patient we and the patient are using dream language that is a mixture of beta elements and alpha elements. We are also using a much more slow and reflective syntax, grammar, and word-organized derivative. The only way that we can function together is to both dream together and have separate dreams and conjoint dreams and join in each other's dreams. That's the way we do it. We all have had the experience of struggling with a patient, struggling through a session when it's very unclear what's happening and all of a sudden something begins to gel. We have to be able to not know what's going on, be able to tolerate it, use our reflective ability, and trust ourselves and our patient to use alpha function.

Martin A. Silverman

Chapter 8

Dreams and non-dreams
A study on the field of dreaming

Roosevelt Cassorla

Faced with the complexity of reality the human mind tries to discriminate, separate and isolate aspects such as facts and phenomena that, when named, are brought into the symbolic network of thought. However, although discrimination facilitates thought, it also causes difficulties related to contact with complexity. Apparently "simple" phenomena are linked together in complex ways and the relationships among them indicate that knowledge of reality cannot be approached without taking into account the complicated dynamics of the connections among supposedly "simple" objects.

Reality can be "simple" or "complex" depending on how the observer views it. Ideas about the concept of *field* lead observers to pay less attention to facts than to the relationships and influences that exist among them. These relationships are in constant movement and it is this perception that makes a field dynamic.

The field is the product of the observer's capacity to observe and it must be remembered that any observer influences the facts he or she observes. In other words, the observer is part of the field. Any concept of "objective observation" loses its meaning and, for this reason, observers, as participants in the field, must learn to objectify their own subjectivity.

Certain rules determine the functioning of fields. The principles of uncertainty and incompleteness show that observation is always provisional, uncertain, partial and transitory. As something is observed, it changes, not only because it is in constant movement but also because the very process of observation has affected it. But there is no way to determine the degree of influence of the observer over what is observed, or vice versa. A supposed paralysis of the field is often nothing more than paralysis in the observer's capacity to move from one vertex of observation to another.

There are many different models and metaphors (Katz, 2013) referring to fields, some of which are specific to certain areas of knowledge. The military model, for example, describes battlefields. There, a strategist can study, as "simple objects," the geographical accidents of a location where a battle is to occur in order to gain the best advantage over the enemy. A psychoanalyst might be interested in the structure of the ego. A good military strategist will broaden his observations beyond the geographical field and become interested in the complexities of war, such as the relationships among types of weapons, relations among soldiers, and between soldiers and their leaders, the objectives of the battle, economic, political and ideological factors relating to war, the emotional states of the persons involved, the motivation of the enemy and so on. In the model proposed the strategist himself participates in the battle as he influences and is influenced by the rapid and constant changes that are occurring in the field. The strategist's ability to observe depends on his ability to keep his stand despite the terror and the threat of death.

Developments

In psychoanalysis, the difficulty involved in describing what happens in an analytic process led to the creation of metaphors that gradually became ever closer to ideas about the analytic field.

Freud (1912) compared the analytic process to a battlefield. From this point of view an analysis should conquer "fixation points"—in other words, fortresses occupied by defending "troops." The analyst attracts the libidinal troops to himself with the objective of dominating them. The battlefield can be seen in the transference. The analyst must deal with suffering, seduction and other threats of destruction to his analytic capacity.

Using a historical and archaeological model, Freud (1930) describes a field where mental layers are excavated and where, based on the elements that are found, hypothetical reconstructions can be made (Freud, 1937). The situation becomes more complicated when residues belonging to different "geological strata" (Bion, 1965) are uncovered.

In the chess-game model (Freud, 1913) we know the possible opening moves but we do not know anything about how the game will continue. Analyst and analysand play a game that has infinite variables, and if we include the emotions involved in the game, everything becomes a much more complex phenomenon.

The knowledge of what goes on between analysand and analyst was broadened through gradual new discoveries that contributed to different intersubjective approaches (Brown, 2011). Among these discoveries are projective identification (Klein, 1946), its importance in the perception of reality (Bion, 1962b), the productive uses of countertransference (Heimann, 1950; Racker, 1953; Grinberg, 1962), transference as a total situation (Klein, 1952; Joseph, 1989), the recruitment of the analyst by the analysand's projections (Joseph, 1989), the transitional space (Winnicott, 1951), factors, functions, links and transformations (Bion, 1962b, 1965, 1970) that are all part of the analytic process, and many other approaches. These facts influence the perception and creation of analytic fields.

The field of dreaming

In this paper I shall discuss *functions* of the analytic field that may be of interest to psychoanalysts. We can investigate what functions a given analyst imagines for the field and the factors that led that psychoanalyst to choose the points of view that determine these functions. This approach allows each analyst to use and identify the explicit and implicit theories that have led him or her to belong to a given field.

I propose the capacity to transform and broaden the symbolic network of thought as the vertex observing the functions of the field. The transformation of this network can be seen in the growing capacity of analysands to attribute meaning to their experiences—that is, to think about the conscious and unconscious facts of their lives. In this way, mental resources develop that allow them to deal with reality and transform it to benefit themselves and, hopefully, mankind as a whole.

Among the factors of the field proposed, some phenomena can be identified that are articulated in very complex ways, such as the quality of the links between analysand and analyst, the quality of the emotional experiences resulting from these links, the analyst's capacity for containing, and the reverie that allows him or her to transform emotional experiences into waking and nocturnal *dreams*. Also important is the ability of the analytic dyad to broaden the meanings of the dreams that are dreamed, the analyst's capacity to identify and deal with elements that cannot be dreamed, the ability of the dyad to deal with attacks on the processes described, and many other aspects.

Factors that led me to choose the points of view described included personal characteristics of my own and my encounter with the theory of thought (Bion, 1962a, 1962b, 1992) and its outcomes and transformations.[1] The work of the Barangers (1961–1962/2008, 1982/1983) and the Italian psychoanalytic literature as presented by Ferro are also among these influences.

In the model proposed the field has been taken over by emotional turbulence and catastrophes (Bion, 1976). Analyst and analysand are linked together by emotions, and the field is in constant transformation, thus indicating the quality of the links and the forms of attacks on the links. Everything that happens to one of the members of the dyad has emotional repercussions for the other.

Investigation into the qualities of emotions puts us in contact with the limitations of verbal symbols in describing them. In this sense, poetry and music might be better containers. The adventure of the analysis is stimulated in both members of the analytic dyad by the connections among *love, desire to know* and *hate of suffering*. These initial emotions give rise to further complex sets of emotional links named by the letters L (love), H (hate) and K (knowledge), which influence one another and join together in many different ways. Inversely, their negativity (–L, –H, –K) attacks the positive links (Bion, 1962b). Link K was hinted at by both Freud (1905) (Instinct for Knowledge) and Klein (1932) (Epistemological Instinct). But it was Bion who eventually included this instinct among the emotions, and this inclusion broadened the perception of the field.

As observation of the field develops, more complex, subtle and sophisticated combinations of the emotions are identified, such as arrogant curiosity, possessive love, hatred for the truth, envious seduction, fearful hypocrisy and other forms of generosity, ill-will, despair, terror, solidarity, fanaticism and sacrifice, among others.

One of the characteristics of the analytic field is its capacity to connect L and H to K, or to transform them into K so that knowledge can develop. To know oneself through analysis is an emotional process, and each K attained is an ephemeral step in the search for ultimate reality (O). But O is never really attained, meaning that, from this vertex of observation, the analytic field is infinite.

Transformation into K and the search for transformation into O are determined by the capacity to symbolize proto-mental facts. Symbols are metaphors that attribute meaning to that which has no emotional meaning by transforming raw elements into mental facts. Symbols are characterized by their capacity for emotional attraction and linking, which results in a network—the symbolic network of thought. The first symbolic formations (alpha elements) are in the form of images or, we might say, of affective pictograms (Barros, 2000), which, connected to one another, produce predominantly visual scenes. The scenes seek verbal symbols in order to be narrated.

One important factor in the field of dreaming is the capacity to *imagine* experiences that have no meaning. The transformation of such experiences into predominantly visual *images* is analogous to a mother's capacity to *dream* her baby. This *dreaming* begins before the baby is born and seems to attain its high point soon after birth. Maternal containing allows the mother's capacity for reverie to give meaning to the raw elements projected by the baby. Reverie is related to imagination, visual images, fantasies, perceptions, feelings, daydreams (Ogden, 1999; Civitarese, 2013a; Barros and Barros, 2015). The mother's *dreams* are returned to the baby through emotions, actions and words. This process allows the baby gradually to introject the mother's alpha function and make it its own.

Reverie, a factor of the alpha function, is a complex intersubjective phenomenon between mother and baby. The alpha function was first called dream-work-alpha (Bion, 1992) because the attribution of meaning is analogous with the dream-work described by Freud. In Bion's model, emotional experiences (including perceptions and affects) that initially have no meaning are transformed by the dream-work-alpha. "Bionian" dreams give rise to the repressed unconscious, the area from which "Freudian" dreams arise.

Dreaming goes on twenty-four hours a day, just as other biological functions, such as breathing and digestion, do. Dreaming is a "theater for the generating of meaning" (Meltzer, 1983, p. 93), permanent unconscious dreaming, the content of which is manifest through daydreams and nocturnal dreams. These dreams, in turn, are constantly re-dreamed, and the symbolic network and the capacity to think more abstract thoughts is expanded.

Just as mothers do with their babies, analysts apply their capacity for reverie during sessions. The analyst must let himself go adrift as he waits for reverie to make sense naturally. Untrained analysts often ignore their own reverie or imagine that it is a product of their own conflicts, without bothering to investigate them.

When dreaming is possible the analysand unconsciously dreams what is happening here and now in the analytic field. Through free association, the analysand then tells the analyst these dreams—which are deformed through defenses—by describing images, fantasies, feelings and ideas that come to mind as he or she freely associates. The narratives involve emotions and actions, and since the analysand is awake, secondary working through makes the narrative more or less organized, thus challenging the analyst's skill, as the analyst himself is also transferentially included in these dreams.

The analyst also dreams about what is happening in the analytic field. The asymmetry of the relationship turns the analyst into "the other" of the intersubjective relationship, and he or she re-dreams the analysand's dreams, and dreams the emotional experiences that could not be dreamed. Bion's (1992) proposal that "the analyst dreams the analytic session" (Sandler, 2005, p. 220) can be expanded to "the analyst and analysand dream the analytic session" or "the analytic dyad dreams both dreams and non-dreams that are part of the analytic field." It can also be said that "the analytic field dreams the dreams and non-dreams that make it up." The term *dreams-for-two* can be used to describe dreams that are the product of the field involving dreams of patient and analyst, but that are beyond the set of dreams of both participants of the dyad. As we can see, the expansion of the ideas depends on the vertex used to observe the *dreaming field*.[2]

Non-dreams

When the analytic field is occupied by non-symbolic elements they are discharged in the form of actions, in the body (somatization) or transformed into hallucinosis (Bion, 1965). These transformations take the form of hallucinations in the senses or disorders in thinking, such as beliefs, fanaticism, omniscience or delirious ideas. Non-represented areas can be manifest also as voids.

I proposed the term *non-dreams* for the set of phenomena described above. This nomenclature calls attention to a disorder in the capacity to dream. Since non-dreams are not adequately connected to the symbolic network of thinking, they are experienced as foreign bodies and seek to be eliminated through projective identifications. These projective identifications enter the field and stimulate the analyst's dream-work-alpha. The analyst, using his or her reverie, transforms non-dreams into dreams, thus giving them meaning. If the meaning cannot be borne by the patient, the analyst's dream is reverted into a non-dream. The analyst tries to dream the non-dream in other ways, and so forth.

Sometimes the analyst may encounter difficulties in imagining—that is, in visualizing the images in his or her mind. Outlines of images are static and do not connect with the symbolic network. The patient can describe scenes and plots that are repeated over and over without the meaning becoming any clearer or expanding. At other times scenes appear that are apparently symbolic but the symbols have lost their function of expression. The analyst senses that the patient thinks in a concrete manner and finds it impossible to create or understand metaphors (Barros, 2011).

During an attempt to dream a non-dream an analyst may discover that no creative image comes to mind. In this case, he or she must remain in a receptive state of mind until imagetic symbols come up that can be verbalized, and this process can take quite a long time. The verbal symbols attract new, sensory, imagetic and, especially, further verbal symbols, thus broadening meanings and opening up to new symbolic connections and new meanings in a continuous development of the capacity to think.

Eventually the analyst imagines that he is dreaming a non-dream of the patient but, in reality, he or she was recruited to non-dreaming and does not perceive this fact. The analytical field is taken by *non-dreams-for-two*, a situation that will be discussed below, from clinical material.

The field of dreams and the setting

The *setting* encompasses some aspects of the analytic field but not its complexity. I consider the *mental setting* as more important than the setting defined by spatial and temporal rules. The mental setting shows the analyst's ability to maintain a state of mind whereby he becomes involved in the analysis. But the analyst's mental state must also allow him to be aware of when the dyad is distancing itself from what the analyst considers to be psychoanalysis. With this awareness, the analyst will return to his task of psychoanalysing, anywhere and at any time, even outside the consulting room. Strictly speaking, the field of dreaming includes not only the temporal and spatial setting, but also the mental setting. But the field goes beyond them since it includes all situations where symbolization can occur as a reflection of the analytic process.

The emotional involvement between analyst and analysand begins even before the first interview and then continues after each session, outside the consulting room. The analyst has the advantage of being able to perceive how his mental universe broadens when he writes about a session, when he talks about his analysand with colleagues, supervisors and analysts, when a nighttime dream of his throws light on one or another analytic process, or when he has insights about an analysis while reading a book, watching a film or participating in a scientific meeting. The same thing happens with analysands, but analysts have access to these facts later, during the sessions.

The analytic field also implies taking into account situations when psychoanalysis is not happening. For example, interruptions in the spatial, temporal or mental setting are parts of the analytic field and constitute a privileged aspect of analysis. When the setting is destroyed the analytic field continues to be present and this makes it possible to observe and understand breaks in the setting.

The complex of transference and countertransference is part of the field but should not be confused with it. In the field all emotional links are transitory, even if, at first impression, certain patterns are followed. It should also be recalled that any changes in the vertex of observation can alter these patterns.

The real person of the analyst, the real person of the analysand, and aspects of external reality are also parts of the analytic field. Gender, age, religion, ideology, beliefs and life experiences of both analyst and analysand are aspects of the field. Financial difficulties may be articulated in fantasies but they can also be real facts. Likewise, an act of terrorism can serve as material for a dyad's dreams, but its consequences are nonetheless real.

The analyst is trained to deal with dreaming and difficulties in dreaming, but he must expand his perception of the field to encompass factual reality and be aware of the consequences of this reality in the dyad's work. The analyst works to discern the area in which the dyad is working at any particular moment, even though he knows that moments are transitory and that areas overlap.

Sonia

Sonia, age forty-five, tells me she suffers from nightmares. They are always the same and she has had them since she was a child. She dreams she is walking through certain places until she comes to a dark place where she has the feeling that she is about to be crushed by something very heavy that is falling on her. She wakes up feeling desperate and as she awakens she becomes petrified that something might come from the hallway toward her bedroom to do her some evil. This is why she sleeps with the light on. Sometimes she has to get up and check the rooms in the house to make her feel more at ease. There are no associations and I cannot persuade her to go further into the facts.

Sonia tries to dream emotional experiences without meaning but the outlines of meanings generated are felt as traumatic. Her dreaming apparatus is attacked and the original meanings are inverted. Since she cannot dream, she seems to wake up. In fact she is neither dreaming nor awake. The bizarre and threatening objects continue to be present, even with the light on, like internal phantasms that will come from the lighted hallway.

Despite this horrifying narrative, the analytic field does not seem to be overcome by terror. On the contrary, it is the patient's indifference that catches my attention. I cannot relate the affects described, or the affects felt, to images or words. At one point I have an isolated reverie: I see the body of a person falling on Sonia. This image disappears instantly and I cannot give it any meaning.

Over a period of months, Sonia told me the details of a dispute with her sisters about their inheritance from their father. She showed no sign of anger or hatred against her siblings and believed that each sister was struggling for what she thought was right. My impression was that she was trying to observe the facts impartially in order to avoid coming into contact with her feelings.

Little by little her capacity to dream and think seemed to be developing but I continued to feel dissatisfied with our analytic work. I felt something was escaping me. At certain moments Sonia's ready acquiescence to my interventions bothered me and she did not seem to broaden her capacity to think. When she began insisting that she was "much better" I could not see in what way, and I knew I had to continue observing the analytic field.

One day I end the session with a patient, and Sonia will be the next. I am sure she has not arrived yet because the light connected to the waiting room has not gone on. Even so, I go out to the waiting room to check, and I see that she has not arrived yet. So I go back into the consulting room but leave the door open as usual. Ten minutes go by and I start feeling uncomfortable about her being late. This is an emotional experience searching to be dreamed. What is not there is inside me seeking meaning. Fifteen minutes go by and I go to check out the waiting room again. There is Sonia, standing and nervous. (Later I realized that the previous analysand had left the outside door open, which was why the light hadn't gone on.) Without reflecting, I say: "Are you here?" But, inwardly, I think of saying: "What is she doing here? Why didn't she come into the consulting room?"

I ask her to come in and she lies down on the couch and remains silent. I feel uncomfortable and ask if she has just arrived. She says she has been there for ten minutes. Yes, she saw the door to the consulting room open but she didn't know if she should come in or not. I tell her that the door is always open for her. She answers that she did not come in because she thought she would be intruding, that she would be a bother to me. I want to know more. Sonia says that when she saw me she was certain that that was not her place, that I was not waiting for her and that it was not her scheduled time. I am surprised because she is expressing feelings she had never given even an inkling about.

After this episode, I realized that there were a number of facts that had taken over the analytic field and to which I had not paid enough attention until then. Sonia appeared to be an elegant and discreet person with careful gestures, and her clothes and makeup reflected these characteristics. She had a warm smile and a pleasant voice, and she was very polite—someone whom other people would consider civilized. In short, she was a lady. Correspondingly, in her presence, my gentleman side was stimulated. When I opened the door she was there waiting and, as always, she looked at me. I invited her in with a gesture of welcome. She thanked me with a smile and came in discreetly. I waited until she took the five or so steps to the couch. Then she stopped and turned toward me. I, the gentleman, invited her to lie down. She smiled and delicately lay down as I went to my chair behind the couch.

It was only after the episode described above that I noticed that Lady Sonia and her gentleman analyst were involved in a dual collusion of mutual idealization. Sonia's characteristics had induced me to behave correspondingly to her. We were relating to one another in a gentle, delicate and polite way, and the lack of energy in the analytic process was a reflection of this collusion. I had a certain notion of these phenomena but they were not clear. In other words, emotional experiences of the dyad, which appeared as repetitive behavior of politeness, were not being sufficiently dreamed, and this was keeping them from connecting to the symbolic network of thought. Thus, the analytic process was blocked in this area.

The hesitations in the waiting room, when we expressed dissatisfaction with each other, undid the collusion of mutual idealization. This event was, at one and the same time, both cause and consequence of the behaviors taking place in the field. Sonia was late, I was worried about her being late, I looked for her twice in the waiting room, she was anxious, I invited her in but I was irritated, and so forth. The lady turned into Cinderella, someone who was unwelcome and felt like a bother, someone who inspired neither admiration nor love. The gentleman analyst, on the other hand, became insensitive, left the patient waiting, received her with irritation and asked a silly question ("Are you here?"). My intuition was that I should investigate what had happened between us and that I would have to deal with my own embarrassment and discomfort.

This investigation made me realize that Sonia hid very deep suffering without meaning, strongly masked by defenses that were expressed as delicateness, politeness and niceness. I had been insufficiently aware of these mechanisms that had even recruited me to behave in the same way as she did.

Later, the broadening of her capacity to dream allowed me to review these facts. The collusion of mutual idealization led both of us to live in symbiosis in certain areas of the field. Collusion, consisting of non-dreams that could not be dreamed, showed up the defenses against the trauma of contact with triangular reality. The traumatic threat and the evident distinction between self and object became clear when analyst and analysand came together that day.

Sonia felt crushed by the perception that the analyst is not an extension of herself, that he does not wait for her in the waiting room and that he criticizes her because she did not come into the consulting room. The analyst was also crushed in his analytic capacity. When he realized what was happening—in other words, what was going on thanks to the uncomfortable encounter between them—the situation could be understood and the capacity to dream could be restored.

The collusion might easily have returned. It would be enough for Sonia and the analyst to apologize politely and their idyllic paradise could continue. Situations of this type often happen without the dyad noticing them. There was also the danger that the collusion of mutual idealization would be transformed into collusion of mutual resentment, with demands and responsibility for the misunderstandings. The analyst is unhappy with Sonia, and she is resentful of the analyst. She feels like she is a bother, the analyst feels attacked, and so forth. In other papers (Cassorla 2008, 2009, 2012) I show that in situations of this type there is oscillation between "thin-skin" aspects (mutual idealization) and "thick-skin" aspects (mutual demands).

It is important to remember that the perception of the dual collusions described above occurs only *a posteriori* (*Nachträglichkeit*)—after the dual collusion is undone.

Returning to the mutual behavior between Lady Sonia and her gentleman analyst, we see that all our sessions began in the same way. The theater model is clear for the situation: this is mimicking, mere static and repetitive theater or an exchange of niceties that remind one of meeting rituals among members of the nobility. These rituals also have to do with traumatic dreams that return repeatedly, with the difference that there is no manifest anxiety here. The analyst is insufficiently aware of the ritual, even though he participates in it. We are dealing here with what are known as *non-dreams-for-two* or *chronic enactments* (Cassorla 2001, 2005, 2008, 2009, 2012). Obviously, they continued over many sessions.

While these non-dreams-for-two continued to occur the analyst believed he was dreaming, even though he also felt that the analytic process was paralyzed. But his perception was not enough. Recruited by the massive projective identifications, the analyst became stupid (Cassorla, 2013b, 2014) and therefore failed to perceive that he was dreaming *false dreams* (Cassorla, 2009).

Chronic enactments are related to Freud's concept of *Agieren* (Freud, 1914), where the analysand behaves in ways he cannot symbolize into words because they were recorded in the mind before verbal symbolization was possible. They also have a similarity with Klein's (1957) concepts about *memory in feelings*. They are very primal ways of experiencing others, influenced by the traumatic projection of the unconscious from previous generations (Sapisochin, 2013). In chronic enactment both members of the dyad are involved without being aware of it. In *Agieren* (acting out) by the analysand, the analyst observes without participating.

Chronic enactments indicate discharges and attempts at symbolization through behavior. These symbolic forms have low capacity for connecting with the rest of the symbolic network and, for this reason, they are repeated. They are looking for triangular reality in order to be symbolized by words.

The entire set of facts that undoes chronic enactment is known as *acute enactment*, a term that describes configurations which include both simultaneous discharges and non-dreams being dreamed.

After acute enactments are perceived and interpreted, analytic capacity is restored and the field's dreaming functions are also reestablished. The broadening of the symbolic network puts the dyad in contact with other traumatic facts that are being dreamed or in search of dreamers. Deformed memories eventually emerge, and reveries lead to constructions (Freud, 1937) that restore areas where there are no memories.

Sonia: two years later

Sonia's nightmare of being crushed had disappeared from the field even though she continued to be frightened of it. Now it returns and is in the process of being transformed into dreams. The nightmare produces the same scene: it is dark and something falls on Sonia; something that is going to crush her. Gradually the outline of an image emerges that she describes in one session: "It looked like a . . . a guitar . . . or a piano, maybe a violoncello."

Associations remind Sonia of her childhood when she took piano lessons. She does not remember much about this phase but she knew how to read musical scores and play classical works, although today she does not remember anything. She cannot read a note. She is certain that she was an excellent student and that her teacher, Miss Violet, was stern but liked her because she was dedicated and serious. Bit by bit we realize that the image of the piano, condensed together with the violoncello (related to "Violet") symbolizes responsibility, efficiency and sternness. There were facts that fell on her dramatically and crushed her. These perceptions (dreams-for-two) reminded Sonia of when she was four years old and would tell the adults about her ability to read, while actually repeating childhood stories they had read to her. In her view, this was a motive for admiration until, one dark evening, her father came home from work with a children's book in his hand. He sat down with her and asked her to read it. Sonia was petrified. She cried desperately and ran to her mother. Very touched, in the session, she tells me: "The moment meant death. It meant losing my father's love for me."

After that session Sonia told the memory to her mother, and the mother told her that the episode had really happened, but not in the way Sonia had remembered. Her parents knew that she did not yet know how to read and took her demonstrations as playfulness. It was true that her father brought a book home, but it was not a story-book; it was a coloring book. No one could understand why she was so upset, but her mother supposed that she was afraid her father would demand something from her, and her mother said, "Your father likes you very much."

We can see here that Sonia brought into the analytic field (and into her life) collusion of persecution and mutual seduction with the imago of the internalized father. The analyst had let himself be attracted by the seduction, which covered over the threats of being crushed under demands that fell on her. The situation was broadened during analyses to fantasies about the primal scene, also idealized and crushing. She felt she was a bother to her highly sexualized mother, who crushed her relationship with her father. These facts that were remembered were covering over other, previous facts, consisting of very early inscriptions of transgenerational facts that were impossible to remember. Facts related to her maternal grandparents, who were musicians, also came up, and there were memories of a relative—a well-known writer and family idol—who was an inspiration for her father. Hypothetical constructions broadened the symbolic network. I realized, however, that I should be careful to identify any compulsion to acquiesce on Sonia's part, which is a seductive maneuver of hers to reestablish the collusion.

During later periods in the analysis Sonia talked of other traumas that had continued. Her mother had had an abortion before she was born and felt guilty and afraid of losing Sonia during her second pregnancy. The newborn child faced a mother with postpartum depression. Sonia's younger brother was always sick and we gradually speculated that Sonia had had to develop resources to care for her mother, an experience that reinforced her already-present characteristics of niceness and efficiency.

Some time later, Sonia told me that between the ages of four and six she was sometimes aroused by a neighbor who caressed her. She felt beautiful and lively when she was with this neighbor, which led her to seek him compulsively. During her adolescence she became aware of the sexual content involved but she was unable to summon the courage to tell anyone. The traumatic dream about someone falling on her included all these aspects. The violoncello represented male violence (and the violence of her mother/Violet) and one could note that the chronic enactment also had an erotic component. When, in the waiting room, I asked her, "Are you here?" the question reminded her of what her neighbour would say when she went to his home and excitedly waited for him to be free for her. Only then did the analyst's reverie (about a man falling on her) make sense and the large number of non-dreams being dreamed during acute enactment become clearer.

Functions of the analyst

I suggest using here the theater model to study some of the functions of the analyst as an observer–participant in the analytic field, where she is both the object of fantasies and a real person (Cassorla, 2003).[3] When facing scenes placed in the analytic theater, an analyst, with her analytic function intact, will carry out the following functions *simultaneously*:

1. *Character*, by interacting with the other characters that come into the field.
2. *Spectator*, by observing and trying to understand what is happening. (The power to participate and observe at the same time allows her to exercise the functions described below.)
3. *Co-author*, to the extent that, when interacting with the characters in the field, the analyst does not necessarily do so simply according to the pressure she feels. Much of her analytic activity will consist of pointing out this pressure in order to make it understandable for the analysand (for whom it is not conscious).
4. *Director*, by analytically acting together with the characters in the field as she seeks the best way for the original plot to be understood and changed.
5. *Theater critic*, by standing back from the scene and using her knowledge to evaluate critically how the drama was carried out, how the characters behaved or whether the scene could have occurred in some other way. (Here, she will emphasize the analyst's critical function.) She may also evaluate what explicit and implicit psychoanalytic theories were used for both observing and understanding the phenomena and how they could be understood on the basis of other theories, or even if new concepts or models are required. The role of critic becomes more powerful after the dramatization has occurred. In short, *the analyst's critical capacity* is an important factor for defining her vertices of observation.
6. *Light and sound technician*, by aiding the director in seeing and hearing what is happening. Theatrical presentations are impossible without sound or lighting and, for this reason, technicians should seek

to light up dark aspects or aspects that are trying to disappear into the wings. A good lighting technician throws light on the characters with appropriate nuances of brightness and color.

The analyst's lighting function depends on her capacity to enter into the context of the scenes and live them "at-one-ment" (Bion, 1970). Adequate lighting is equivalent to psychoanalytically trained intuition (Sapienza, 2001). Since the analyst is simultaneously co-author, character and/or director, these functions will complement her capacity for psychoanalytic observation. Focusing on direction and lighting by the director–analyst (who is also co-author and actor) is the spontaneous product of dreams that are being dreamed. The capacity to make the adequate splits becomes an important factor for these functions to be carried out as well.

The analyst's critical capacity determines which functions of the field she should become involved in as participating observer. In this text we have emphasized the capacity of the dyad to become involved in the analytic field of dreaming, which generates meanings and expands the symbolic network of thought. This capacity is determined by factors in the analyst's intuition that allow her to work "without memory, without desire, without the intention to understand," thus allowing herself to be led by what happens and without blocking meanings. It should be remembered, in fact, that one of the objectives of analysis is exactly to broaden meaning capacity. As we have seen, the field of dreaming may include sub-fields. For example, the models of movies (Cassorla, 2003), theater, circus, storytelling and playground are different ways for the field to function, and the models are interwoven and swirl and mix together.

If necessary, the analyst may change his vertex of observation and transform the field (of dreaming, for example) into other fields. Such transitions among different aspects of the field or among different fields depends on the cohesion of his analytic identity, which allows the analyst to be himself, regardless of the field in which he participates.

As was seen, the field of dreaming includes facts of the dream↔non-dream gradient, with different degrees of symbolic representation and non-representation. In this respect, the palimpsest model may help. Any dream covers over other dreams which, in turn, cover over areas of non-dreams that represent traumas, which cover up undreamed childhood traumas, which cover over other traumas transmitted transgenerationally, which cover over other dreams and non-dreams, and so forth. We should broaden the model to a multidimensional palimpsest model in constant movement, like the holograms suggested by Ferro. Communication between areas leads us to suppose that, when an analyst re-dreams a symbolic dream through a dream-for-two, he may also, implicitly, be dreaming areas of non-dreams and vice versa.

The hypotheses and ideas presented in this paper should be understood as provisional and in constant transformation. It is therefore important that they be dreamed by other dreamers who may be interested in them. The author also hopes that non-dreams which he has not yet realized may be identified.

Notes

1 Carried out by Meltzer (1983, 1986), Grotstein (2000, 2007), Ferro (1992/1999, 2002/2005, 2006, 2009), Ogden (1999, 2005), Civitarese (2013b), Sandler (2005, 2009), for example.
2 Numerous authors have taken viewpoints close to the one I am describing here: see Bezoari and Ferro (1999), Ogden (2005), Ferro (2009), Civitarese (2008/2010), and the books edited by Ferro and Basile (2009) and Katz (2013).
3 I have always dreamed a good deal, and when I was a child I had a feeling that my dreams would enrich my life and make things clearer, although I did not know how. I think this was one of my first steps toward my future choices.

References

Baranger, M. and Baranger, W. (1961–1962/2008). The analytic situation as a dynamic field. *International Journal of Psychoanalysis* 89: 795–826 (reprint of the 1968 version).
Baranger, M., Baranger, W. and Mom, J. (1982/1983). Process and non-process in analytical work. *International Journal of Psychoanalysis* 64: 1–15.
Barros, E.M.R. (2000). Affect and pictographic image: the constitution of meaning in mental life. *International Journal of Psychoanalysis* 81: 1087–1099.
Barros, E.M.R. (2011). Reflections on the clinical implication of symbolism. *International Journal of Psychoanalysis* 92: 879–901.
Barros, E.M.R. and Barros, E.L.R. (2015). The function of evocation in the working-through of the countertransference: projective identification, reverie and the expressive function of the mind. In Levine, H.B. and Civitarese, G. (eds.), *The Bion Tradition: Lines of Development – Evolution of Theory and Practice over the Decades*. London: Karnac, pp. 141–154.
Bezoari, M. and Ferro, A. (1999). The dream within a field theory: functional aggregates and narrations. *Journal of Melanie Klein and Objects Relations* 17: 333–348.
Bion, W.R. (1962a). A theory of thinking. In *Second Thoughts: Selected Papers on Psycho-Analysis*. London: Heinemann, 1967, pp. 110–119.

Bion, W.R. (1962b). *Learning from Experience*. London: Heinemann.
Bion, W.R. (1965). *Transformations*. London: Heinemann.
Bion, W.R. (1970). *Attention and Interpretation*. London: Tavistock.
Bion, W.R. (1976). Emotional turbulence. In Bion, F. (ed.), *Clinical Seminars Brasilia, São Paulo and Four Papers*. Abingdon: Fletwood Press, pp. 223–233.
Bion, W.R. (1992). *Cogitations*. London: Karnac.
Brown, L.J. (2011). *Intersubjective Processes and the Unconscious: An Integration of Freudian, Kleinian and Bionian Perspectives*. New York: Routledge.
Cassorla, R.M.S. (2001). Acute enactment as resource in disclosing a collusion between the analytical dyad. *International Journal of Psychoanalysis* 82: 1155–1170.
Cassorla, R.M.S. (2003). Estudo sobre a cena analítica e o conceito colocação em cena da dupla [A study on the analytical scene and the "enactment" concept]. *Revista Brasileira de Psicanálise* 37: 365–392.
Cassorla, R.M.S. (2005). From bastion to enactment: the "non-dream" in the theatre of analysis. *International Journal of Psychoanalysis* 86: 699–719.
Cassorla, R.M.S. (2008). The analyst's implicit alpha-function, trauma and enactment in the analysis of borderline patients. *International Journal of Psychoanalysis* 89: 161–180.
Cassorla, R.M.S. (2009). Reflections on non-dream-for-two, enactment and the analyst's implicit alpha-function. In Levine, H.B. and Brown, L.J. (eds.), *Growth and Turbulence in the Container–Contained: Bion's Continuing Legacy*. London and New York: Routledge, 2013, pp. 151–176.
Cassorla, R.M.S. (2012). What happens before and after acute *enactment*? An exercise in clinical validation and broadening of hypothesis. *International Journal of Psychoanalysis* 93: 53–89.
Cassorla, R.M.S. (2013a). In search of symbolization: the analyst task of dreaming. In Levine, H., Reed, G.S. and Scarfone, D. (eds.), *Unrepresented States and the Construction of Meaning: Clinical and Theoretical Contributions*. London: Karnac, pp. 202–219.
Cassorla, R.M.S. (2013b). When the analyst becomes stupid: an attempt to understand enactment using Bion's theory of thinking. *Psychoanalytic Quarterly* 82: 323–360.
Cassorla, R.M.S. (2014). Commentary to case Ellen: the silent movies. *International Journal of Psychoanalysis* 95: 93–102.
Civitarese, G. (2008/2010). *The Intimate Room: Theory and Technique of the Analytic Field*. London: Routledge.
Civitarese, G. (2013a). The inaccessible unconscious and reverie as path of figurability. In Levine, H.B., Reed, G.S. and Scarfone, D. (eds.), *Unrepresented States and the Construction of Meaning: Clinical and Theoretical Contributions*. London: Karnac, pp. 220–239.
Civitarese, G. (2013b). *The Violence of Emotions: Bion and Post-Bionian Psychoanalysis*. New York: Routledge.

Ferro, A. (1992/1999). *The Bi-personal Field: Experiences in Child Analysis*. London: Routledge.
Ferro, A. (1996/2002). *In the Analyst's Consulting Room*. London: Routledge.
Ferro, A. (2002/2005). *Seeds of Illness, Seeds of Recovery: The Genesis of Suffering and the Role of Psychoanalysis*. Hove: Brunner-Routledge.
Ferro, A. (2006). Clinical implications of Bion thought. *International Journal of Psychoanalysis* 87: 989–1003.
Ferro, A. (2009). Transformations in dreaming and characters in the psychoanalytic field. *International Journal of Psychoanalysis* 90: 209–230.
Ferro, A. and Basile, B. (eds.) (2009). *The Analytical Field: A Clinical Concept*. London: Karnac.
Freud, S. (1905). Three essays on the theory of sexuality. In *The Standard Edition of the Complete Psychological Works of Sigmund Freud* [*S.E.* from hereon]. London: Hogarth Press, 1953–1974, 7, pp. 124–248.
Freud, S. (1912). Recommendations to physicians practising psycho-analysis. In *S.E.*, 12, pp. 111–120.
Freud, S. (1913). On beginning the treatment. In *S.E.*, 12, pp. 123–144.
Freud, S. (1914). Remembering, repeating and working-through. In *S.E.*, 12, pp. 145–156.
Freud, S. (1930). Civilization and its discontents. In *S.E.*, 21, pp. 59–145.
Freud, S. (1937). Constructions in analysis. In *S.E.*, 23, pp. 257–269.
Grinberg, L. (1962). On a specific aspect of countertransference due to patient's projective identification. *International Journal of Psychoanalysis* 43: 436–440.
Grotstein, J. (2000). *Who is the Dreamer who Dreams the Dream? A Study of Psychic Presences*. Hillsdale, NJ: The Analytic Press.
Grotstein, J. (2007). *A Beam of Intense Darkness*. London: Karnac.
Heimann, P. (1950). On countertransference. *International Journal of Psychoanalysis* 31: 81–84.
Joseph, B. (1989). *Psychic Equilibrium and Psychic Change: Selected Papers of Betty Joseph*. Ed. Feldman, M. and Spillius, E.B. London: Routledge.
Katz, S. M. (ed.) (2013). *Metaphor and Fields: Common Grounds, Common Language and the Future of Psychoanalysis*. New York: Routledge.
Klein, M. (1932). *Psychoanalysis of Children*. London: Hogarth Press.
Klein, M. (1946). Notes on some schizoid mechanismos. In *Envy and Gratitude and Other Works: 1946–1963*. London: Hogarth Press, 1975, pp. 1–24.
Klein, M. (1952). The origins of transference. In *Envy and Gratitude and Other Works: 1946–1963*. London: Hogarth Press, 1975, pp. 48–56.
Klein, M. (1957). Envy and gratitude. In *Envy and Gratitude and Other Works: 1946–1963*. London: Hogarth Press, 1975, pp. 176–235.
Meltzer, D. (1983). *Dream-life: Re-examination of the Psycho-analytical Theory and Techniques*. Strath Tay: Clunie.
Meltzer, D. (1986). *Studies in Extended Metapsychology: Clinical Applications of Bion's Ideas*. Reading: Clunie Press.

Ogden, T.H. (1999). *Reverie and Interpretation: Sensing Something Human.* London: Karnac.

Ogden, T.H. (2005). *This Art of Psychoanalysis: Dreaming Undreamt Dreams and Interrupted Cries.* Hove: Routledge.

Racker, H. (1953). A contribution to the problem of counter-transference. *International Journal of Psychoanalysis* 34: 313–324.

Sandler, P.C. (2005). *The Language of Bion.* London: Karnac.

Sandler, P.C. (2009). *A Clinical Application of Bion's Concepts*, Vol. 1: *Dreaming, Transformation, Containment and Change.* London: Karnac.

Sapienza, A. (2001). O trabalho de sonho-alfa do psicanalista na sessão: intuição-atenção-interpretação. In França, M.A. de A., Thomé, M. da C.I. and Ani, M.P. (eds.), *Transformações e Invariâncias: Bion–SBPSP: Seminários Paulistas.* São Paulo: Casa do Psicólogo, pp. 17–25.

Sapisochin, S. (2013). Second thoughts on Agieren: listening the enacted. *International Journal of Psychoanalysis* 94(5): 967–991.

Winnicott, D.W. (1951). Transitional objects and transitional phenomena. *International Journal of Psychoanalysis* 34: 89–97 (also available in his *Collected Papers.* London: Tavistock, 1958).

It seems to me that at different points in a treatment the work is quite different. When things are going along smoothly then we can ride the flow. When Bion refers to alpha-function, I always translate that as reflective function, to become reflectively aware, to reflect on and metabolize unformulated experience. When ruptures occur, however, we must delve into trying to understand as best we can who contributed what to the rupture—what were the analyst's and patient's respective contributions to each other's experience and to their own in order to understand how the rupture occurred. Of course, neither participant is objective, but we do the best we can to explore and ferret out what happened. Mutual understanding substantively contributes to repair.

James L. Fosshage

Chapter 9

Analytic field theory
A dialogical approach, a pluralistic perspective, and the attempt at a new definition

Marco Conci

Introduction

My familiarity with the field concept goes back to the time of my adolescence and it still plays a crucial role in my life. Going to the USA as an exchange student in the summer of 1972 – and living with a Jewish family in a suburb of New York City – allowed me eventually to understand the social, cultural, and psychological field from which I came originally. I am making reference to a famous and old – but provincial – Italian town of Austrian-Hungarian heritage, in which psychoanalysis was very little known, and in which I was later supposed to enter into my father's firm. Experiencing such a different field, including the attendance of an alternative high school program centered on independent study projects, gave me the courage to understand and later to pursue my own personal and professional goals – and eventually to become a psychiatrist and a psychoanalyst.

From this point of view, the field concept can in the first place allow us to reformulate the way in which Freud connected the knowledge we can gain of ourselves to the dialogue with the Other, the "significant other" represented – at the time of his self-analysis – by Wilhelm Fliess. Here is my reformulation of it: we know ourselves, only if we become aware of the field from which we come and/or has shaped us, as such an awareness becomes possible through the dialogue with a significant other – that is, with a "significant field" with which we come in touch.

From such a lucky experience I also learned how important it is for me to look for social fields in which I can function well and be productive. This is what lies behind a whole series of choices I made in my professional and personal life, which culminated in my moving to Munich in 1997, after training as a psychoanalyst at the Milan Associazione di Studi Psicoanalitici (ASP) – the institute founded by Gaetano Benedetti (1920–2013) and Johannes Cremerius (1918–2002) in the early 1970s – and after working as an assistant professor of psychiatry at an Italian medical school. In 2002 I became a member of the German Psychoanalytic Society (DPG), in 2010 a member of the International Psychoanalytic Association (IPA) – i.e., a year after the DPG had been readmitted into it at the 2009 Chicago IPA Congress – and in 2012 a member of the Italian Psychoanalytic Society (SPI). In 2007 I had been elected to the position of co-editor-in-chief of the *International Forum of Psychoanalysis* – the journal of the International Federation of Psychoanalytic Societies (IFPS), to which both the Milan ASP and the DPG belonged.

By giving you all this information, I do not merely mean to introduce myself, but also to show how my interest in the topic of the analytic field has not only personal but specific professional sources. My training and my scientific evolution have allowed me to come in touch not only with a variety of professional and scientific fields, but also with a series of analytic field concepts, which is what my chapter for this book is centered on. In fact, I will try to show how only by considering the variety of analytic field concepts at our disposal (as Donnel Stern started to do in 2013 in *Psychoanalytic Dialogues*) can we come to a new and more adequate definition of it.

I also believe that the position of the participant observer I just described not only represents the kind of pendular movement which we learn from any field we inhabit, but also characterizes the analytic field which Freud himself created and practiced, without wanting to define it as such – at the risk of abandoning his positivistic outlook.

As we will see, the concept of the analytic field was originally formulated by H.S. Sullivan (1892–1949), representing the red thread of his whole work (see Conci, 2012); it was integrated into their Kleinian, Bionian and interdisciplinary viewpoint by Willy (1922–1994) and Madeleine Baranger (born 1920); and it was later taken by Antonino Ferro as the basis of his revisitation of Bion's legacy – to name just the major articulations of the concept, to which I will add a couple of others. By trying to deal with all of them, we can probably come to a new and more general definition of the concept, and thus take it out of the category of our so-called "regional concepts," where it presently seems to belong.

But let me now turn to Sullivan's theory.

H.S. Sullivan's field theory

In her fascinating biography of Sullivan – the first native North American psychiatrist and psychoanalyst to make an original and lasting contribution to our field – Helen Swick Perry (1982) clearly showed how the dissociative crisis he underwent at age seventeen, in the spring of 1909 at Cornell University, represented a crucial ingredient of the brilliant professional and scientific career which he began in the 1920s in the Washington, DC area – first as a collaborator of William Alanson White (1870–1937) at St. Elisabeth's Hospital and then, between 1922 and 1930, as a chief psychiatrist at the Sheppard Hospital in Towson, Maryland. This crisis kept him two and a half years out of school – which he resumed in the fall of 1911 at the Chicago College of Medicine and Surgery – but it allowed him personally to experience (and confirm) the crucial difference established by Eugen Bleuler (1857–1939) in 1911 between what he called "schizophrenia" and Emil Kraepelin's concept of "dementia praecox."

As Jay Greenberg and Stephen Mitchell showed in 1983, Sullivan originally made reference to Freud in his struggle against Kraepelin's very pessimistic view; Freud had in fact created around his neurotic patients a field and an approach of human understanding, contact and communication that allowed them to experience their illness not as a "brain disorder," but as a disturbance arising directly out of their way of conducting their life and/or of reacting to a series of traumatic existential situations. From this point of view, Sullivan was one of the first psychiatrists or psychoanalysts to try to do the same with borderline and schizophrenic patients, combining Freud's dynamic approach with what I would call a "double field theory": the field as the positive environment in which these patients have the right to be treated; and the field as the communicative and constructive qualities of the human relationship which we can develop with them.

In fact, this is the read thread on which centers *Schizophrenia as a Human Process*, the book edited in 1962 by Helen Swick Perry as an anthology of the papers on the features, nature, and treatment of schizophrenia published by Sullivan between 1924 and 1935. As I wrote in my preface to its Italian edition (Conci, 1993a), this should be the first book by Sullivan that everyone should read – or at least everyone who really wants to understand what his *Interpersonal Theory of Psychiatry* (1953) and *Psychiatric Interview* (1954) are all about. In fact, the word itself – "interpersonal" – which later became the connotative adjective of his own psychiatry and psychoanalysis, was originally formulated by Sullivan in one of these papers, "The onset of schizophrenia," in 1927. Here is the context out of which it emerged:

> We have found all sorts of maladjustments in the history of patients who suffered the great psychosis, but regardless of vicious influences subsequently encountered, the sufferer has acquired the tendency to such an illness while in the home situation. *Interpersonal factors seem the effective elements in the psychiatry of schizophrenia.*
> (Sullivan, 1962, 104; emphasis added)

As I showed in the careful examination of *Schizophrenia as a Human Process* which I articulated in *Sullivan Revisited: Life and Work* (2012), Sullivan already knew the concepts of "countertransference" (introduced by Freud in 1910) and "projective identification" (introduced by Melanie Klein in 1946), although he did not use such terms – as this was the case for Freud's knowledge of the phenomenon of "participant observation." As far as the first phenomenon is concerned, he was aware of the fact that the major obstacle to an adequate treatment of the sickest patients is represented by the anxiety they produce in us. As far as the second phenomenon is concerned, he was a good enough therapist to be receptive to and experience the sense of loneliness and mental pain which a silent and regressed schizophrenic patient was able to communicate to him.

But even more important than his pioneering role in the application of Freud's concepts to a group of patients with whom Freud had not directly dealt was what I call Sullivan's "epistemological revolution" – that is, his convincing answer to the question "Where does schizophrenia come from and what can we do about it?" His answer: schizophrenia originates within the interpersonal field which the patient experienced before and during his illness and its therapy centers on creating around him a new and healthy interpersonal field! From my point of view, the dimension of the interpersonal field discovered by Sullivan still represents the foundation of our work, as much as Freud's discovery of the unconscious dimension of our life.

Stephen Mitchell's relational turn

I find it isomorphic to the topic of field theory, to resume the personal thread I hinted at in the introductory section, by telling you that I was lucky enough to meet Stephen Mitchell (1946–2000) in Florence in April 1988, as he and Jay Greenberg were invited to present their 1983 book *Object Relations in Psychoanalytic Theory* – which was translated into Italian in 1986. When I met him, I was already fascinated by Sullivan's work, and it was from sharing this fascination with Mitchell that I received the encouragement I needed to write my book on Sullivan. From Mitchell I not only learned how post-Sullivanian interpersonal psychoanalysis had revisited and modified Sullivan's concept of "participant observation," but also how he had just been working on articulating a new psychoanalytic paradigm – the so-called "relational turn" – in his new book *Relational Concepts in Psychoanalysis: An Integration* (1988a). I not only had the honor of introducing him and his work in the Italian edition of 1993 (Conci, 1993b), but also of organizing two further trips to Italy for him (1991 and 1996, with papers presented in Rome, Milan, Bologna, and Florence).

Since I believe that his work and legacy are crucial for the articulation and new definition of the concept of analytic field which I am developing in this chapter, I will share the concepts he formulated in an important paper of 1988, and in Chapter 10 of the above-mentioned book of 1988.

Before doing so, however, let me explain what Mitchell's "relational turn" was all about: it was the way in which he tried to integrate the points of view of Sullivan, Fairbairn, Bowlby, and Kohut, in terms of their complementary character and their common denominator as alternative perspectives to Freud's original concept of psychoanalysis, which he considered unilaterally dominated by the concepts of drive and intra-psychic fantasy, with the consequence of neglecting external reality and the role of interpersonal relationships. To cut a long story short, the "relational turn" represented Mitchell's way of correcting Sullivan's insufficient emphasis on the internal world by integrating it with compatible ideas, such as the ones mentioned above, and this allowed him to bring Sullivan back into mainstream psychoanalysis without losing touch with Freud. This turned out to be a very successful scientific and political operation.

That Freud kept representing an important point of reference for him clearly emerges also in the paper "The intra-psychic and the interpersonal: different theories, different domains or theoretical artifacts?" (1988b), which I will now try to summarize through the following words, found by Mitchell to clarify and overcome the sterile opposition which these two terms so often gave rise to, and attempt to put them in a dialectical continuity with each other:

> I have suggested that the terms *intra-psychic* and *interpersonal* have been used loosely in the literature as banners representing clusters of different kinds of concepts and emphases, and I have broken the dichotomy down into four contrasts: fantasy vs. perception, psychic reality vs. actuality, inner world vs. outer world, and drive theory vs. a theory of environmental interaction. We noted that Sullivan gave great prominence to both fantasy and psychic reality in general, and that, although tentative, he used concepts referring to the patient's inner world. Only on Freud's concept of drive per se do we find Sullivan uncompromisingly opposed, since drives are, by definition, understood to be sheltered from the interpersonal field, arising independently in the id and encountering the actual world only through the mediating activities of the ego.
>
> (Mitchell, 1988b, 486).

And here are Mitchell's final thoughts on the subject from that paper:

> The distinction between the intra-psychic (taken more broadly than drive theory) and the interpersonal ... represents complementary views of a common analytic experience whose richness and complexity always eludes the efforts we make to grasp it through the inevitable limitations of our language and our ideas.
>
> (Mitchell, 1988b, 494–495)

In other words, all contemporary analytic theories – including post-Sullivanian psychoanalysis – are in Mitchell's view post-Kantian theories: that is, theories in which both reality and fantasy, fantasy and reality, play crucial roles, but in each one of them to a different extent.

Stephen Mitchell's unique capacity to shuffle anew the cards of our analytic work also represents a central ingredient of the revision of the therapeutic action of psychoanalysis which he developed in the last chapter of *Relational Concepts in Psychoanalysis* – "Penelope's loom: psychopathology and the analytic process" – with particular regard for his proposal on how to overcome the sterile opposition between the role of the interpretation and the role of the new relationship that we establish with the patient – a sterile opposition that played a central role in our debates for many years. After examining the theories of technique of the drive-conflict and of the developmental-arrest models, and showing how they differ from the relational-conflict model which he articulates in the book, in terms of the role which human interactions play in shaping our psychic life, here is how he formulates the corresponding model of therapeutic action:

> The third perspective portrays the analyst as discovering himself *within* the structures and strictures of the repetitive configurations of the analysand's relational matrix. The struggle to find his way out, the collaborative effort of analyst and analysand to observe and understand these configurations and to discover other channels through which to engage each other, is the crucible of analytic change.
> (Mitchell, 1988a, 292; original emphasis)

And here is how Mitchell reconceptualized the concept of interpretation as a "complex relational event":

> In the relational-conflict model, both the informational content and the affective tone are regarded as crucial, but their effects are understood somewhat differently – in terms of their role in *positioning* the analyst relative to the analysand. An interpretation is a *complex relational event*, not primarily because it alters something inside the analysand, not because it releases a stalled developmental process, but because it says something very important about where the analyst stands vis-à-vis the analysand, about what sort of relatedness is possible between the two of them.
> (Mitchell, 1988a, 294–295; original emphasis)

This is how analyst and patient do their work according to Mitchell's field concept of psychoanalysis, based as it is on the re-visitation of Sullivan's concept of "interpersonal situation" in terms of a "relational matrix" through which our psychic life gets its basic configuration and through which – through therapy conceived as a new relational matrix – it can also be changed.

Freud's implicit field theory

As much as Sullivan did not use the terms "countertransference" and "projective identification," although he was familiar with the clinical phenomena which these terms aim to describe, I believe the same to be true for Freud, as far as the field concept is concerned. I arrived at this conclusion many years ago, when editing the Italian edition of his letters (1871–1881) to Eduard Silberstein – the friend with whom he shared his self-taught study of Spanish. Although still a candidate in training, due to my Austrian-Hungarian heritage I was familiar enough with Freud's language and cultural world, and also with the main collections of his letters, which Johannes Cremerius had encouraged me to explore.

But here is what the eighteen-year-old Freud proposed to his *"querido amigo"* (who had left Vienna to pursue his university studies in Leipzig) on September 4, 1874, in order to keep in better touch with each other:

> The members of the Spanish Academy are among those modern men whose days number more than twelve working hours and whose nights are robbed of dreams by fatigue ... Hence my proposal amounts to stipulating that every Sunday each of us, the two sole luminaries of the A.E., send the other a letter that is nothing short of an entire encyclopedia of the past week and that with total veracity reports all our doings, commissions and omissions, and those of all strangers we encounter, in addition to all outstanding thoughts and observations and at least an adumbration, as it were, of the unavoidable emotions. In that way, each one of us may come to know the surroundings and condition of his friend most precisely, perhaps more precisely than was possible even at the time when we could meet in the same city ... In our letters we shall transmute the six prosaic and unrelenting working days of the week into the pure gold of poetry and may perhaps find that there is enough of interest within us, and in what remains and changes around us, if only we learn to pay attention.
>
> (Boehlich, 1990, 57–58)

Exactly! If we want to learn to pay attention to a series of things that we would otherwise repress and/or forget, we must create a communication field around us through which it becomes possible.

Apart from this personal reconstruction of mine, what is generally referred to as "Freud's implicit field theory" is, of course, what he wrote in 1912 in "Recommendations to physicians practicing psycho-analysis" to explain the concept of "free floating attention":

> To put it into a formula: he must turn his own unconscious like a receptive organ towards the transmitting unconscious of the patient. He must adjust himself to the patient as a telephone receiver is adjusted to the transmitting microphone. Just as the receiver converts back into sound-waves the electric oscillations in the telephone line which were set up by sound waves, so the doctor's unconscious is able, from the derivatives of the unconscious which are communicated to him, to reconstruct the unconscious, which has determined the patient's free associations.
>
> (Freud, 1912, 115–116)

From this point of view, I am also ready to state that we can easily find an implicit field concept in Freud's work every time he leaves the prescriptive level and embraces the descriptive one (see Greenberg, 1981), as he does, for example, in his book on lay-analysis. When we try to describe what happens in our sessions, the field concept suddenly becomes essential. It represents the best way to try to keep track of all the variables of our work, which go well beyond the simple phenomenology of the patient doing the speaking and the analyst doing the interpreting – as Freud himself well knew.

The bipersonal field of Willy and Madeleine Baranger

After having heard her speak at the Amsterdam (1993) and Berlin (2007) IPA Congresses, I eventually had the chance to meet Madeleine Baranger at the Athens IFPS Forum in October 2010, at which she presented the paper "The intrapsychic and the intersubjective in contemporary psychoanalysis." Meeting her allowed me to develop the following fantasy concerning the forty-six-year delay (see Churcher, 2008) before a groundbreaking paper like "The analytic situation as a dynamic field" was translated into English: she gave me the feeling of such a good "narcissistic balance" as not to need to become too active in promoting her own work, with the exception of its Italian publication in 1990, due to the initiative of Stefania Manfredi and Antonino Ferro.

But here is the central part of the paper:

> We ourselves proposed the "field theory" ... as a new attempt to account for the clinical experience of the interchange. The notion of

field is not foreign to the thoughts found in Freud . . . Our starting point was observation of the analytic situation and its evolution . . . A growing recognition of countertransference aimed to see analysts not only as observers and investigators of patients, but also as full participants in the process. Following a suggestion by Bion (1961) that the analytic couple constitutes a small group . . . we identified "basic assumptions" in this couple as described for large groups. We understood that they referred to a Kleinian conception described by Susan Isaacs (1952): a basic unconscious fantasy subjacent to the psychoanalytic relation that constantly contributes to structure it. It is not a sum or combination of individual fantasies, but an original set of fantasies created by the field situation itself. Rooted in the unconscious of each member, it includes important areas of their individual histories and personalities.

(Baranger, 2012, 133)

Meeting Madeleine Baranger encouraged me to increase my understanding of the context out of which such an original perspective had developed and to read the anthology *The Work of Confluence* (Baranger and Baranger, 2009) carefully. Not only did I find, among the other things, confirmation of the fact that Willy Baranger's training analyst, Enrique Pichon Rivière (1907–1977), knew and appreciated the socio-psychological orientation of H.S. Sullivan (see Tubert-Oklander, 2013, chapter 6), a fact I had originally learned from Salomon Resnik (see Conci, 2009); I also learned what a crucial role Heinrich Racker (1910–1961) played in the series of developments leading to the Barangers' "field turn" (see de León de Bernardi, 2008). Speaking with Robert Oelsner, who recently translated Racker's preliminary communication of 1951 into English, and reading the chapter about Racker I asked him to write for a German anthology on post-Freudian psychoanalysis, I understood how Racker was really the one who had the courage to say, "The king is naked!": that is, "the analytic situation is, essentially, a bipersonal situation" (Baranger and Baranger, 2009, 2). As a consequence, "countertransference reactions can provide evidence to the analyst of what is going on in the analysand" (Racker, 2013, 18).

And here is how, in one of Racker's papers, I was able to find a "preconception" of the Barangers' concept of the analytic field and its way of functioning, with particular regard for the dynamics of the so-called "unconscious fantasy of the couple":

> At the start of a session an analysand wishes to pay his fees. He gives the analyst a thousand peso note and asks for change. The analyst happens to have his money in another room and goes out to fetch it, leaving the thousand pesos upon his desk. During the time between leaving and returning, the fantasy occurs to him that the analysand will take back the money and say that the analyst took it away from him. On his return he finds the thousand pesos where he had left it. When the account has been settled, the analysand lies down and tells the analyst that when he was left alone, he had fantasies of keeping the money, of kissing the note good-bye, and so on. The analyst's fantasy was based upon what he already knew of the patient, who in previous sessions has shown a strong disinclination to pay his fees. The identity of the analyst's fantasy and the patient's fantasy of keeping the money may be explained as springing from a connection between the two unconsciouses, a connection that might be regarded as a "psychological symbiosis" between the two personalities.
>
> (Racker, 1957, 321)

What I find particularly interesting in this example concerns the structure of the unconscious fantasy, with particular regard for its connection with the past interactions between patient and analyst, a connection which the Barangers articulated in 2008 in such a way as clearly to distinguish their concept from the one developed by Susan Isaacs in 1948: that is, more clearly than Madeleine Baranger did in Athens in 2010. In their words, the structure of the unconscious fantasy

> cannot in any way be considered to be determined by the patient's (or the analyst's) instinctual impulses, although the impulses of both are involved in its structuring. More importantly, neither can it be considered to be the sum of the two internal situations. It is something created *between* the two, within the unit that they form in the moment of the session, something very different from what each of them is separately.
>
> (Baranger and Baranger, 2008, 806; original emphasis)

In other words, I find this point of view of the Barangers in line and/or compatible with the perspectives developed by both Sullivan and

Mitchell – also inasmuch as the expression "created between the two" does not mean to restrict our attention to the present, and to the level of the reciprocal projective identifications, but also includes the whole relational history of the couple.

Not surprisingly, in line with Mitchell's concept of interpretation is also the Barangers' critique of what they – in the same article – call "the natural course of treatment," inasmuch as the treatment "must follow the dynamic laws of the bi-personal situation" (Baranger and Baranger, 2008, 813). The same is true for the way in which they conceptualize the therapeutic action of psychoanalysis:

> The field of the analytic situation is the opportunity, through repetition in a new context, of the original situations that motivated the splitting, to break up this defensive process and to re-integrate the split of sectors of experience into the whole of the patient's life.
>
> (Baranger and Baranger, 2008, 816)

Very meaningful in this regard is also a less frequently mentioned paper by Willy Baranger, "Contradictions between theory and technique in psychoanalysis" (1969; included within Baranger and Baranger, 2009), in which he expresses his full agreement with Michael Balint's object-relational orientation, and further distances himself from both Klein and Isaacs: "If we were to think of an analysand's unconscious fantasy as causing the events that occur in the analytic situation," he wrote, "we would be reversing the whole order of how things actually occur" (Baranger and Baranger, 2009, 158). He concluded this important paper with the words:

> Everything that occurs in the analytic situation takes place between two people and is put into words by two people. Any abstraction that tends to make one or the other of these two protagonists disappear will also tend to turn their words into silence.
>
> (Baranger and Baranger, 2009, 176–177)

Gaetano Benedetti's concept of "transitional subject"

Born in Catania on June 26, 1920, Gaetano Benedetti died in Basel on December 2, 2013, as you can read in the obituary I wrote with Brian

Koehler and Maurizio Peciccia (Conci, Koehler and Peciccia, 2014). After graduating from medical school in Catania, he chose to specialize in psychiatry because of his deep sympathy for and empathy with psychiatric patients. Psychiatry was subordinated to neurology at the time in Italy, so Benedetti moved to Zurich, where he had the good fortune of becoming one of the closest collaborators of Eugen Bleuler's son Manfred (1903–1994), who greatly encouraged his pioneering work in the analytic psychotherapy of schizophrenia – work for which he had also been well equipped through his training analysis with Gustav Bally (1893–1966), a Swiss analyst who had trained at the Berlin Institute before the war. Through Bleuler, Benedetti also had the opportunity to spend a year in the USA (1950/1951), where he came into contact with Frieda Fromm-Reichmann (1889–1958) and Harold Searles. In 1956 he organized – together with Christian Müller (1921–2013) – the first conference of the International Society for the Psychotherapy of Schizophrenia (ISPS) in Lausanne. The following year he moved to the University of Basel, where he spent the rest of his career, and from where he traveled regularly to Italy to teach and supervise. Around this time he also promoted Sullivan's work (see Benedetti, 1961), founded the above-mentioned Milan ASP (see Conci, 2014) and began his collaboration with Maurizio Peciccia, a partnership whose chief achievement was the redefinition of schizophrenia in terms of the lack of integration between separate and symbiotic states of the self (Benedetti and Peciccia, 1996).

"Ogden speaks of a 'third' which comes to life between patient and therapist in the course of the analytic process. I believe that Ogden's 'analytic third' corresponds to what I call 'transitional subject,'" declared Benedetti (2006, 83) in an interview with Patrick Faugeras that centered on his life and work, with particular regard for his concept of schizophrenia as a condition of radical loss of self-integration and self-identity. In a co-authored paper of 1998 in which he also summarized more than fifty years of work and research, Benedetti mentioned the following steps in the development of his own "therapeutic field":

- from his personal interest in and sympathy with psychotic patients to H.S. Sullivan's concept of "participant observation";
- from the familiarity with his own countertransference and the creation of a stable therapeutic frame to the gradual substitution of the patient's pathological symbiosis with a "therapeutic symbiosis" (Searles);

- from the role of the patient's "self-object" to the creation of the kind of symmetrical situation and/or unconscious communication, measured by the vicissitudes of the "transitional subject", through which the patient can acquire the symbolic function he lacks; and, last but not least,
- the development of a new identity through what he called the phase of "progressive psychopathology."

(Benedetti and Peciccia, 1998)

As the reader may well imagine, I have chosen to present Benedetti's field model because it allows us – more easily than the Barangers do – to connect Sullivan's participatory stance directly with the crucial level at which the therapeutic action takes place: the dimension of the symmetric unconscious communication, which allows the analyst to transfer (Benedetti would say "donate") to the patient his symbolic function, and/or (using the Bionian language of Lawrence Brown, 2011) his alfa-function.

The field concept in Italy

The publication of Antonino Ferro's book *The Bipersonal Field: Experiences in Child Analysis* (1999) represented a crucial turning point in the history of Italian psychoanalysis, which eventually started to leave the peripheral position it had occupied until then in the international analytic scene and acquired the higher profile it has progressively enjoyed – culminating in the 2013 election of Stefano Bolognini to the IPA presidency. As I showed in the reconstruction I offered in 2008 in the monographic issue *Italian Themes in Psychoanalysis*, behind Ferro's achievement a whole society had worked for many years in the direction of becoming sufficiently familiar with a "foreign discipline" such as psychoanalysis, around which Edoardo Weiss (1889–1970) had been able to create only a very small group of clinicians before the war, and which was not practiced by more than a hundred colleagues by the end of the 1960s.

The first operation consisted of translating, over many years, as many analytic authors as possible. The second, promoted by the publisher Paolo Boringhieri in the early 1960s in conjunction with Cesare Musatti (1897–1989), consisted of the production (between 1966 and 1981) of the Italian edition of Freud's *Standard Edition*. Even more important was the third operation: to invite important foreign analysts to Italy, to organize regular supervisions with them, and eventually to start speaking with them, with the possibility of realizing that they could also come to respect us and our work. Here I am thinking not only of Bion's 1977 Italian seminars (Bion, 1983) but also – for example – of the supervisory groups held in Italy by Herbert Rosenfeld (1910–1986) between 1978 and 1985 (edited by Franco de Masi in 1997).

By all this I mean to say that, on the one hand, the scientific field out of which Ferro's work emerged also represents a topic which deserves to be discussed; on the other hand, around him other colleagues also worked on the concept of the analytic field and from them we can also get some useful inputs concerning our topic – and the new definition of the concept I aim to establish.

Of the four training analysts working in Italy in the immediate postwar period, only Alessandra Tomasi di Lampedusa (1894–1982) had received an adequate training abroad – at the Berlin Institute. A Baltic baroness, she had married the author of the famous novel *Il gattopardo* (Giuseppe Tomasi di Lampedusa, 1896–1957), with whom she lived in Palermo. Her most important training analysand was Francesco Corrao (1922–1994), who had the good fortune of meeting Bion at the IPA Congress in Geneva in 1955, "giving space in his own internal world to the ideas of Bion, from the outset, when they were little known," as Bion's daughter Parthenope (1944–1998) declared in 1993 (Bion Talamo, 2015, 103). He not only actively promoted the reception of Bion's work in Italy but was also a pioneer of analytic group psychotherapy – and, like his training analyst, was himself a president of the SPI between 1969 and 1974. Bion's 1962 *Learning from Experience* was translated into Italian as early as 1972 (it would be another eighteen years before it was translated into German!) and in 1975 Corrao founded the Centro di Ricerche Psicoanalitiche di Gruppo "Il Pollaiolo" in Rome, where he trained a series of colleagues, among them Claudio Neri, whose 1998 book *Gruppo* has been translated into several languages.

Another eloquent example of Corrao's important role in familiarizing the Italian analytic community with the topic of this chapter is represented by *Studi sulla tecnica psicoanalitica*, the Italian edition of Racker's groundbreaking book, which he promoted in 1970. He also wrote a preface to it and persuaded Giuseppe di Chiara, a future president of the SPI (1993–1997), to translate it into Italian. It is no wonder that Antonino Ferro (himself one of di Chiara's trainees in Milan) not only became one of the most creative contemporary interpreters of Bion's legacy, but also valued its group and field aspects highly – to the point of co-celebrating "the marriage of Bion and the field concept" at the end of the Bion Conference held in Boston in July 2009 (see Ferro and Sabbadini, 2010, 424).

In the meantime, several other colleagues from Ferro's generation had worked very hard in the same direction, as exemplified by the important International Bion Conference organized in Turin in July 1997 by Parthenope Bion Talamo and Franco Borgogno (whose proceedings were published in 2002).

The early and positive reception of Bion's work in Italy was also facilitated by the specific attention to the relational aspect which characterized Italian psychoanalysis from the beginning, as shown in the early interest for a topic like countertransference and/or in the choice of the topic *La relazione analitica* (The analytic relationship) for its fourth National Congress, held in Taormina in 1980 under the presidency of Eugenio Gaddini (1916–1985). An important contribution to the creation of such a climate had also been made by Franco Fornari (1921–1985), the pioneer – together with Gaddini – of the reception of Klein's work in Italy (see Fornari, 1963). Luciana Nissim Momigliano (1919–1998) moved in the same direction, and her publication of the anthology *Shared Experience: The Psychoanalytic Dialogue* in 1992 (including chapters by di Chiara, Ferro and de Masi) represented one of the first signs of the establishment of a specific Italian analytic tradition and/or of its visibility abroad.

I had the chance to experience Nissim Momigliano's eagerness to start new conversations when – having just promoted the Italian edition of Mitchell's *Relational Concepts in Psychoanalysis* – she contacted me, curious to learn who Mitchell really was, given the affinity that she felt with his work. At our subsequent meeting in her office in Milan I not only developed an immediate interest in her work, which allowed me to review her second book in English (Conci, 1995), but set the stage for my work on Sullivan and Bion, which I published many years later (Conci, 2009).

It is no wonder that the 1994 SPI National Congress – whose proceedings were edited in 1997 by Eugenio Gaburri – was specifically dedicated to the theme of the analytic field. Rereading that book when preparing this chapter, I was very impressed by the richness of its ideas. In terms of the new definition of the concept that I aim at, I find particularly useful the following perspective developed by Fernando Riolo (one of Corrao's analysands and collaborators, and himself a former president of the SPI between 2005 and 2009) in terms of the relations between the concepts of field and relationship:

> The field is neither the patient nor the analyst, nor the relationship. On the contrary, it is that which does not belong to the relationship ... either because the field comes after all that which does not yet participate of the symbolic nature of the relationship – like drive, feeling, emotion; or because the field comes before all that which has been expelled from it – like projection, hallucination, action.
>
> (Riolo, 1997, 67)

This seems to me another way to say what the Barangers express unclearly when they say that the field stops expanding once a bastion (an unconscious collusion between patient and analyst) has taken place. Riolo says that it ceases to exist!

Another useful point of view in terms of my line of thought was developed by di Chiara at the same conference:

> The problem is therefore not only how to best follow the evolution of the "bipersonal unconscious phantasy," although this represents an interesting point of reference which may go through a variety of configurations. Even more important is to closely follow the evolution of an even more complex relationship between two people, which takes place at different levels, and which we as analysts have on the one hand to understand as best as we can, but which, on the other, implies for us the necessity of nourishing through the most adequate form of participation.
>
> (di Chiara, 1997, 106)

If I understand di Chiara correctly, he agrees with Benedetti that the unconscious symmetry at which therapeutic action takes place can be established only through the hard-won attainment of the best possible form of participation – in the sense intended by Sullivan.

A little-known German field concept

In 2013 Werner Bohleber published in the *International Journal of Psychoanalysis* an important paper by Hermann Argelander (1920–2004),

"The scenic function of the ego and its role in symptom and character formation," which had originally appeared in German in 1970. The New York analyst Leon Balter was able to identify many similarities between the work of Argelander and the work of Jacob Arlow (1912–2004) once he was able to overcome the impression of having to deal with a similar phenomenon to what Darwin had called "the origin of new species promoted by geographical isolation" (Balter, 2013, 355). The concept of "unconscious fantasy" was the principal common denominator that he found in their work, while the other major ingredients of what I define as Argelander's "field concept" are as follows: psychoanalysis is a dialogue which requires the analyst's participation in the emotional life of the patient, and the relationship resulting from such an interaction will allow the patient to express the unconscious conflicts which brought him to ask the analyst for help in terms of concrete unconscious behaviors and/or more or less structured scenes. The motor of such a performance on the side of the patient is what Argelander calls "*die szenische Funktion des Ichs,*" which the analyst can best understand by making use of his "*szenisches Verstehen,*" two crucial German phrases that we may translate as "scenic function of the ego" and "scenic understanding."

Bohleber himself tried to connect Argelander's model with similar past and present developments in psychoanalysis as follows:

> The scene is a dynamic construction shared by analyst and patient, a creation of both parties and not something from the past that is simply found. Scenic understanding is ultimately a modern constructivist concept that was ahead of its time. However, Argelander's thinking always preserved its links to ego psychology. An approach analogous in some respects to this can be discerned in Madeleine and Willy Baranger's view of the analytic situation as a "dynamic field" – these authors too had taken up some ideas of Gestalt psychology – as well as in modern intersubjectivist conceptions of the analytic situation as always being a co-creation of the analyst and the patient. Similarities are also evident between Argelander and, for example, Donnel Stern's hermeneutic conception of the unconscious as "unformulated experience," Stern being another author substantially inspired by the hermeneutics of Gadamer.
>
> (Bohleber, 2013, 335)

Leaving aside why it took our German colleagues such a long time to inform the international analytic community about such an interesting development in their country (see Conci, 2013), I feel it is more worthwhile to ask why they failed to appreciate that Argelander had made such an important contribution to analytic field concepts. Of course, I do not have sufficient room to discuss such an intriguing problem in depth in this chapter, so I will limit myself to presenting the evidence behind my attempt to analyze the variety of field concepts. Who introduced Racker's work in Germany? I learned that it was Argelander, who reviewed the German edition of his groundbreaking book *Übertragung und Gegenübertragung. Studien zur psychoanalyischen Technik* (1978) in the prestigious journal *Psyche*.

An attempt at a new definition

If we now look back at the various ways in which the analytic field concept has been dealt with by the authors I have considered in this chapter, we may characterize it by provisionally establishing the following levels or models:

- Level 1: What I have defined as Freud's "implicit field concept."
- Level 2: Sullivan's concept of "interpersonal situation."
- Level 3: Argelander's concept of "scenic understanding."
- Level 4: Mitchell's concept of "relational matrix."
- Level 5: The example of "bipersonal field" I attributed to Racker; di Chiara's revisitation of the Barangers' concept; Benedetti's concept of "transitional subject."
- Level 6: The Barangers' concept of "bipersonal field."
- Level 7: Riolo's definition of the field in terms of a relationship tending to a condition of symmetry whose complete realization brings the field itself to cease to exist.
- Level 8: Once the symmetrical situation of the so-called "bastion" has been resolved, we can think of the possibility of the field coming into existence again.

If I now were to abstract from these different levels or models a new model of the analytic field concept, I would see it as a model which gives an equal role to the two poles of what Sullivan called the analyst's "participant observation," on the one hand, and what the Barangers called the "bipersonal unconscious fantasy," on the other hand – not as originally formulated by Susan Isaacs, but as the product of a specific interaction with a specific history and/or development. In other words, I also consider Sullivan's concept of "participant observation" and Racker's concept of "countertransference" as two different metaphors: that is, ways of expressing the same clinical phenomenon (see Wallerstein, 1988). Both authors think that, in order to understand the patient, the analyst must participate in his problems and, at the same time, be aware of such participation; this is how, for both of them, such a behavior (Sullivan) and/or such an attitude (Racker) allows us to know the patient better. Both ways of working with our patients have, as a result, the emergence of unconscious fantasies – which also for Sullivan, and even more so for Mitchell, represent an important part of our analytic work.

It is therefore no wonder that Werner Bohleber and his colleagues in the IPA Committee on Conceptual Integration, when describing the second step of their work (i.e., unconscious fantasy as a clinical phenomenon), recently stated:

> Implicit in the phenomenology ... is a close theoretical relation between the concept of enactment and that of unconscious fantasy. It would be erroneous to think that enactment acts out a fantasy existing prior to the act itself. What the analyst calls unconscious fantasy is rather the verbal articulation of an unsymbolized affective experience. Consequently, the illusion that the fantasy exists prior to the affective shared experience, or prior to the act itself, would belong to the phenomenology of unconscious fantasy. The concept of unconscious fantasy can thus be understood as a metaphor that assists in understanding the patient's psychic material and behavior.
> (Bohleber et al., 2015, 711)

In other words, if I understand them correctly, these colleagues see – as I do – the external behavioral level and the internal unconscious level in terms of a mutual correlation.

Concluding remarks

A review of the various definitions which the analytic field concept has received in the course of the evolution of our analytic discourse apparently allows us to shuffle the cards produced by the latter in an even more significant way than the concept of metaphor, as it was dealt with in the volume edited by Montana Katz in 2013.

In fact, if we want to make of the analytic field concept a general analytic concept, as opposed to a so-called "regional concept," we have to take into consideration the theoretical and historical contexts out of which it has been developed in the various regions of the world.

As I have tried to show, by comparing the different field concepts and extracting from them what I consider to be their essential ingredients, we can, for example, eventually close the gap between external reality and/or the way in which the patient and we behave, our analytic attitude and our internal worlds, and/or better see their dialectical and mutual correlation.

Another important implication of the dialogical approach and the pluralistic perspective which I have developed in this chapter is represented by the necessity for us, as analysts, to get to know better the fields in which we ourselves operate – that is, in which our theoretical positions are embedded – and also to bring about a more effective communication among the different analytic communities. It makes little sense to use the field concept in our work with our patients and not to use it when talking with one another – in terms of the fields from which each of us speaks.

Stephen Mitchell (1991) centered the "editorial philosophy" he formulated for *Psychoanalytic Dialogues* on the necessity for us, as analysts, to talk more effectively with one another – as effectively as we talk with our patients. Paul Stepansky (2009) argued that we can survive as a discipline only if we move in the direction of a consensually validated working field, as opposed to a disarticulated group of professionals, each minding only his or her own ideas.

In fact, Freud himself founded psychoanalysis on the basis of his own experience of and familiarity with the Austrian medical tradition, the French psychological tradition and the British empirical tradition, which makes psychoanalysis itself the result of a unique kind of "international synthesis" (see Ackerknecht, 1999) – the very kind of synthesis that I have tried to formulate in this chapter.

References

Ackerknecht, E.H. (1999). *Breve storia della psichiatria*. Ed. M. Conci. Bolsena: Massari (original German edition, 1957).

Argelander, H. (1978). Besprechung des Buches von H. Racker "Übertragung und Gegenübertragung. Studien zur psychoanalyischen Technik." *Psyche – Zeitschrift für Psychoanalyse und ihre Anwendungen*, 32, 871–875.

Argelander, H. (2013). The scenic function of the ego and its role in symptom and character formation. *International Journal of Psychoanalysis*, 94, 337–454 (original German edition, 1970).

Balter, L. (2013). Discussion of H. Argelander's paper "The scenic function of the ego and its role in symptom and character formation." *International Journal of Psychoanalysis*, 94, 355–371.

Baranger, M. (2012). The intrapsychic and the intersubjective in comtemporary psychoanalysis. *International Forum of Psychoanalysis*, 21, 130–135.

Baranger, M., Baranger, W. (2008). The analytic situation as a dynamic field. *International Journal of Psychoanalysis*, 89, 795–826.

Baranger, M., Baranger, W. (2009). *The work of confluence: listening and interpreting in the psychoanalytic field*. Ed. L. Glocer Fiorni. London: Karnac.

Baranger, W., Baranger, M. (1990). *La situazione psicoanalitica come campo bipersonale*. Milan: Cortina.

Benedetti, G. (1961). Prefazione. In H.S. Sullivan, *La moderna concezione della psichiatria*, vii–xxvii. Milano: Feltrinelli.

Benedetti, G., Faugeras, P. (2006). L'esperienza delle psicosi. Colloqui di Riehen. In ASP, ed., *La parola come cura. La psicoterapia delle psicosi nell'incontro con Gaetano Benedetti*, 73–99. Milan: Angeli.

Benedetti, G., Peciccia, M. (1996). The splitting between separate and symbiotic states of the self in the psychodynamic of schizophrenia. *International Forum of Psychoanalysis*, 5, 23–37.

Benedetti, G., Peciccia, M. (1998). The ego structure and the self-identity of the schizophrenic human and the task of psychoanalysis. *International Forum of Psychoanalysis*, 7, 169–174.

Bion, W.R. (1961). *Experiences in groups and other papers*. London: Tavistock.

Bion, W.R. (1983). *Bion in Rome*. London: The Estate of W.R. Bion.

Bion Talamo, P. (2015). *Maps for psychoanalytic exploration*. London: Karnac.

Bion Talamo, P., Borgogno, F., Merciai, S., eds. (2002). *W.R. Bion: between past and future*. London: Karnac.

Boehlich, W., ed. (1990). *The letters of Sigmund Freud to Eduard Silberstein 1871–1881*. Cambridge, Mass.: Belknap and Harvard University Press (original German edition, 1989).

Bohleber, W. (2013). Introduction to Hermann Argelander's paper "The scenic function of the ego and its role in symptom and character formation." *International Journal of Psychoanalysis*, 94, 333–336.

Bohleber, W., Jimènez, J.P., Scarfone, D., Varvin, S., Zysman, S. (2015). Unconscious phantasy and its conceptualization: an attempt at conceptual integration. *International Journal of Psychoanalysis*, 96, 705–730.

Brown, L.J. (2011). *Intersubjective processes and the unconscious*. London: Karnac.

Churcher, J. (2008). Some notes on the English translation of "The analytic situation as a dynamic field" by W. and M. Baranger. *International Journal of Psychoanalysis*, 89, 785–793.

Conci, M. (1991). Presentazione all'edizione italiana. In S. Freud, *"Querido amigo." Lettere della giovinezza ad Eduard Silberstein 1871–1881*, vii–xxvi. Turin: Bollati Boringhieri.

Conci, M. (1993a). Prefazione. In H.S. Sullivan, *Scritti sulla schizophrenia*, v–ix. Milan: Feltrinelli.

Conci, M. (1993b). Presentazione. In S.A. Mitchell, *Gli orientamenti relazionali in psicoanalisi. Per un modello integrato*, ix–xv. Turin: Bollati Boringhieri.

Conci, M. (1995). Review of the book by L. Nissim Momigliano "Continuity and change in psychoanalysis. Letters from Milan," 1992. *Psychoanalytic Books*, 6, 199–204.

Conci, M. (2008). Editorial – Italian themes in psychoanalysis: international dialogue and psychoanalytic identity. *International Forum of Psychoanalysis*, 17, 65–70.

Conci, M. (2009). Bion and Sullivan: an enlightening comparison. *International Forum of Psychoanalysis*, 18, 90–99.

Conci, M. (2012). *Sullivan revisited: life and work*. Second, revised edition. Trento: Tangram (original Italian edition, 2000; German edition, 2005; Spanish edition, 2012).

Conci, M. (2013). Editorial – Psychoanalysis in Germany, part one. *International Forum of Psychoanalysis*, 22, 195–198.

Conci, M. (2014). Gaetano Benedetti, Johannes Cremerius, the Milan ASP, and the future of IFPS. *International Forum of Psychoanalysis*, 23, 85–95.

Conci, M., Koehler, B., Peciccia, M. (2014). Prof. Dr. Med. Gaetano Benedetti (1920–2013), co-founder ISPS. *Psychosis*, 6, 1–3.

de León de Bernardi, B. (2008). Introduction to the paper by M. and W. Baranger "The analytic situation as a dynamic field." *International Journal of Psychoanalysis*, 89, 773–784.

de Masi, F. (1997). *Herbert Rosenfeld at work: the Italian seminars*. London: Karnac.

di Chiara, G. (1997). La formazione e le evoluzioni del campo analitico. In E. Gaburri, ed., *Emozione e interpretazione. Psicoanalisi del campo emotivo*, 103–112. Turin: Bollati Boringhieri.

Ferro, A. (1999). *The bipersonal field: experiences in child analysis*. London: Routledge.

Ferro, A., Sabbadini, A. (2010). Review of the book by W. and M. Baranger "The work of confluence." *International Journal of Psychoanalysis*, 91, 415–429.

Fornari, F. (1963). *La vita affettiva originaria de bambino*. Milan: Feltrinelli.

Freud, S. (1910). The future prospects of psycho-analytic therapy. In *The Standard Edition of the Complete Psychological Works of Sigmund Freud* [*S.E.* from hereon], XI, 139–152. London: The Hogarth Press, 1957–1958.

Freud, S. (1912). Recommendations to physicians practicing psycho-analysis. *S.E.*, XII, 109–120.

Gaburri, E., ed. (1997). *Emozione e interpretazione. Psicoanalisi del campo emotivo.* Turin: Bollati Boringhieri.
Greenberg, J.R. (1981). Prescription or description: the therapeutic action of psychoanalysis. *Contemporary Psychoanalysis*, 17, 239–257.
Greenberg, J.R., Mitchell, S.A. (1983). *Object relations in psychoanalytic theory.* Cambridge, Mass.: Harvard University Press.
Isaacs, S. (1952). *Developments in psycho-analysis.* London: Hogarth Press.
Katz, M., ed. (2013). *Metaphors and fields: common ground, common language, and the future of psychoanalysis.* London and New York: Routledge.
Klein, M. (1946). Notes on some schizoid mechanisms. *International Journal of Psychoanalysis*, 27, 99–110.
Mitchell, S.A. (1988a). *Relational concepts in psychoanalysis: an Integration.* Cambridge, Mass.: Harvard University Press.
Mitchell, S.A. (1988b). The intra-psychic and the interpersonal: different theories, different domains or theoretical artifacts? *Psychoanalytic Inquiry*, 8, 472–496.
Mitchell, S.A. (1991). Editorial philosophy. *Psychoanalytic Dialogues*, 1, 1–7.
Neri, C. (1998). *Gruppo.* Roma: Borla.
Nissim Momigliano, L., Robutti, A., eds. (1992). *Shared experience: the psychoanalytic dialogue.* London: Karnac.
Oelsner, R. (in preparation). Heinrich Racker (1910–1961). In M. Conci and W. Mertens, eds., *Psychoanalyse im 20. Jahrhundert.* Stuttgart: Kohlhammer.
Ogden, T.H. (1994). The analytic third: working with intersubjective clinical facts. *International Journal of Psychoanalysis*, 75, 3–19.
Racker, H. (1957). The meaning and uses of countertransference. *Psychoanalytic Quarterly*, 26, 303–357.
Racker, H. (2013). Observations on countertransference as technical instrument: preliminary communication. In R. Oelsner, ed., *Transference and countertransference today*, 18–29. London: Routledge.
Riolo, F. (1997). Il modello di campo in psicoanalisi. In E. Gaburri, ed., *Emozione e interpretazione. Psicoanalisi del campo emotivo*, 53–68. Turin: Bollati Boringhieri.
Stepansky, P.H. (2009). *Psychoanalysis at the margins.* New York: Other Press.
Stern, D.B. (2013a). Field theory in psychoanalysis, part 1: Harry Stack Sullivan and Madeleine Baranger. *Psychoanalytic Dialogues*, 23, 487–501.
Stern, D.B. (2013b). Field theory in psychoanalysis, part 2: Bionian field theory and contemporary interpersonal/relational psychoanalysis. *Psychoanalytic Dialogues*, 23, 630–645.
Sullivan, H.S. (1962). *Schizophrenia as a human process.* New York: Norton.
Swick Perry, H. (1982). *Psychiatrist of America: the life of Harry Stack Sullivan.* Cambridge, Mass.: The Belknap Press of Harvard University Press.
Tubert-Oklander, J. (2013). *Theory of psychoanalytic practice: a relational process approach.* London: Karnac.
Wallerstein, R.S. (1988). One psychoanalysis or many? *International Journal of Psychoanalysis*, 69, 5–21.

There are three different field theory approaches. Common to the three is thinking that the patient and analyst are working together. But the approaches are otherwise very different. The Barangers' and Ferro's models are the closest.

Elsa Rappoport de Aisemberg

Chapter 10

The third model of contemporary psychoanalytic field theory

S. Montana Katz

There is always a third in psychoanalysis. In this paper I am going to discuss a third in psychoanalytic theory. This is the third model of contemporary psychoanalytic field theory. Two psychoanalytic models, one based on the work of Madeleine and Willy Baranger and the other on the work on Antonino Ferro, are well recognized as field theories. The substantial differences between these two models are not widely understood. This leads some to think of "psychoanalytic field theory" as one model. As I will subsequently note, these two field theory models are distinct and have unique developmental histories.

There is yet a third model. This one is not often acknowledged as a form of psychoanalytic field theory. The third model derives from a family of psychoanalytic models that developed primarily in the United States. The most salient members of this family are the interpersonal, intersubjective, motivational systems, and relational models of psychoanalysis. The early developmental histories of the models in this family were at times painful. This perhaps led to overemphasis and overstatement of what was new in and what was rejected by these models.

In this family of models in the United States there was an appearance of uninterest in dreams and dreaming. Even more radically there was a perceived indifference to unconscious processes themselves. Unconscious processes are of course the baseline of psychoanalytic work. Dreams and dreaming are fundamental processes in the other two field theory models. These salient perceptions of contemporary psychoanalytic work in the United States, taken together with other factors I will discuss subsequently, have resulted in a lack of recognition that this family of psychoanalytic models bear a resemblance to the other forms of psychoanalytic field theory. I hope to alter this perception.

I envision three waves in the development of psychoanalytic field theory. The initial development of field theory in the middle of the twentieth century was the first wave. The field theory of Baranger and Baranger as well as the American models were initiated in this first wave. Contemporary psychoanalytic field theory is the second wave. Ferro's model belongs in this second wave. The third wave lies in the future. In order for psychoanalytic field theory to move into the future it is useful to delineate the principal forms of field theory. In this way the assumptions, operating principles, and techniques specific to each model can be clarified, considered, and compared alongside those of the other models of field theory. This sort of clarification may also lead to situating psychoanalytic field theory within the broader context of psychoanalysis.

For reasons I will explain later in this paper, I give new names to each of the three models of field theory. I call the model of psychoanalytic field theory based on the Barangers' work the "mythopoeic model." I call the model developed by Ferro the "oneiric model." I call the model of psychoanalytic field theory that is based on the work of American psychoanalysts the "plasmic model."

The history of the development of the models of psychoanalytic field theory: the discoveries of context, interdependence, and relationship

Psychoanalytic field theory has its seeds in events and developments after the turn of the last century. This was a period in which firmly held beliefs were shattered. The certainty of facts no longer withstood scrutiny. Truth, reality, and values were questioned. This period in the history of Western cultures spawned the birth of several new psychoanalytic perspectives that bear resemblance to one another in their core values.

Events and trends after the turn of the last century led to changes in psychoanalysis. Some of these changes were elaborations or extensions of Freud's original formulations, including some modifications made by Freud himself. Other developments were in response to perceived failings of psychoanalytic theory and technique. These developments contributed to the germination of psychoanalytic field theories across several continents approximately concurrently and relatively independently.

There was a significant period of change between the two world wars. During these years there was a questioning of meaning, of human existence, and of certainty. There was a movement away from positivist and foundationalist social and scientific models. These models posited absolute, certain, objective grounding in basic objects of reality and basic, incontrovertible truths. What arose in their place were models based on gestalts and interrelationship.

Discoveries and conceptions in the first third of the last century shook up previously held models. Belief in scientific objectivity and the separation of observer and observed could no longer be entertained. Einstein's theories of relativity changed not only physics but all modern scientific understanding. In these two theories the concept of relationship was introduced into measurement. For example, the theories stated that space and time must be considered together, as a working unit. Measurement was shown to be a function of the object of measurement together with the relative motion of the observer.

Heisenberg's Uncertainty Principle also demonstrated the salience of relationship to measurement. The Uncertainty Principle determines the degree of uncertainty in measurement as a result of the observer's act of measurement. The Observer Effect specifically addresses the impact of the tools and act of observation on the observed. It solidifies the understanding that observation is not an inert activity. This had wide application beyond the natural sciences to all fields of study in which observation plays a role. In particular, the Observer Effect was relevant to psychoanalysis and conceptions of the role of the analyst in the analytic process.

These and many other co-temporal formulations emphasized interdependence and an understanding of individuals and of human experience as fundamentally embedded in complex wholes or environments. With the discoveries in this period an emphasis on relationship and interdependence was consolidated.

Bridging the middle portion of the last century, the work of the social psychologist Kurt Lewin was influential in the development of psychoanalytic field theory. Lewin devised a model of human behavior and experience that made fundamental use of contextual concepts of gestalts and environments. He created the concept of a force field in which the individual and the environment are interdependent. The individual and the environment were considered as variables intelligible and predictable only as a constellation. Lewin's field concepts became the foundation of psychoanalytic field theory.

In the following sections I will briefly discuss some salient features of the models of the Barangers and Ferro. This will then afford a comparison with the core aspects of the family of field theories in the United States I will finally offer a description of a resulting model for inclusion as the as-yet-unformulated third model of contemporary psychoanalytic field theory.

The psychoanalytic field theory model of Madeleine and Willy Baranger

In South America a psychoanalytic field theory was developed by Baranger and Baranger (1961–1962/2008, 2009). This model was influenced by Gestalt psychology and the field theory of Lewin. Placing Lewin's field concept at the basis of their psychoanalytic theory together with Melanie Klein's work on projective identification and other influences, Baranger and Baranger offered a reformulation of the structural model. The impetus for their work can be understood as thinking through the consequences of psychoanalytic concepts and principles for clinical work. Their psychoanalytic field theory is an extension of the structural model and not a departure from it. This is in contrast with the American field theories whose motivations were to provide alternatives to drive theory and to the mechanical clinical approach of the structural model.

On the surface, Baranger and Baranger retained much of the structural model, including the objectives of psychoanalytic process, the frame, free association, and interpretation. The objective of a process which uses the analytic field theory of Baranger and Baranger is for the analysand to gain insight. The Barangers describe the goals of psychoanalytic processes as the resolution of the analysand's conflicts through interpretation and insight.

The concepts of projective identification and counter-transference contributed to the Barangers developing a field concept to describe what unfolds in an analytic process. With the emphasis on the interdependence of the participants in the process, Baranger and Baranger described the relationship of the analytic couple as "bi-personal." The Barangers' field is bi-personal. The analyst is viewed as a full participant in the process. The roles of the participants are asymmetrical, however, and the analyst's observing ego is considered to be ever active. The factor of the bi-personality of the field sets it apart from the structural model. The interdependence of the couple in an analytic process occurs within a constellation of a field. This kind of dynamic field is what Baranger and Baranger described as a "psychoanalytic field." In keeping with the heuristics of this field model, developments in the analytic process cannot be exclusively ascribed to either one of the participants.

In this model the principal object of interest and observation within a therapeutic process is the analytic field. Because the field is the object of study, while there are two individuals involved in an analytic process, each participant is understood as constituted by the process in the field. Neither member of the analytic couple can be understood without the other. Both are immersed in the process of the field. By means of interpretation, it is the job of the analyst to extricate both participants from the pathological processes that emerge in the field. Unlike the structural and ego psychology models, and similar to the other American models from the first wave of field theory, each analytic couple and each analytic process are understood as necessarily unique.

The divergence of this model from the structural and ego psychology models enters in the understanding and the consequences of the bi-personality of the analytic situation. This sharply distinguishes the Barangers' psychoanalytic field theory. Baranger and Baranger articulate the emerging understanding in the middle of the last century of the role of the analyst and of counter-transference, and their implications. Given the time period in which it was originally formulated, this model constituted a radical departure. Baranger and Baranger describe analytic process in Kleinian terms as crucially involving projective identification. Lewin's influence additionally gave this model a different dimension. These differences affected clinical technique. In order to explore the modifications and divergences from the structural model, Baranger and Baranger devised a number of new technical terms, including: "the psychoanalytic field," "the point of urgency," "nodal fantasy," "essential ambiguity," "bastion," and "second look."

An example of changes in technique derives from an emphasis on what Baranger and Baranger called the "essential ambiguity" of the psychoanalytic situation. This led to understanding the quality of sessions as of dream material. This was not an entirely new clinical concept. Bertram Lewin (1955) had written in this period about extending dream analysis to clinical sessions. The manner in which Baranger and Baranger applied the essential ambiguity to clinical work as within a dream-like situation was novel. The pervasive use made of the oneiric quality of sessions by the Barangers impacted on future developments of field theory in significant ways.

Baranger and Baranger understood the essential ambiguity of the session as that the psychoanalytic process takes on an altered temporality, like that in fairy tales or dreams. The experience of time of sessions is spiraling and contains past, present, and future simultaneously. The ambiguity in the analytic situation for Baranger and Baranger takes on what they call a "mythopoeic" quality. It is here that their emphasis on Freud's metaphor of psychoanalytic process as like a chess game rather than an archeological expedition assumes specific importance. There is an essential element of an emergent creative process to analytic work rather than pursuit of genetic material.

Following the heuristic of a session as like a chess game, a session has two participants engaged in a structured, creative process. The meanings of the moves in the session, communications, are understood as mythopoeic, indicating the essential ambiguity feature. This gives rise to a dream-like quality to sessions. In this model a field is a dreamscape that is asymmetrically constructed by the participants. It is the job of the analyst to determine the salient unconscious fantasy of a session or sessions and to interpret. The fantasies that emerge in the field belong to the field, not to either participant separately.

Unconscious processes and fantasies are understood in this model as bi-personal and as belonging to the field. In this model, the field itself has its own unconscious process. The unconscious process of the field is described as a unique creative product of the analytic process. A result of the emergence of fantasies of the field is the creation of the unconscious process of the field. This is considered to be not only different from the unconscious processes of the participants and not a sum of their two unconscious processes, but something else. The unconscious of the field is a creative product of the psychoanalytic process. The fantasies and unconscious processes of the field are fundamentally different from those of either participant. The unconscious processes of the field could not have been predicted prior to their moment-by-moment unfolding in the analytic process. According to Baranger and Baranger, it is the unconscious process and fantasies of the field that are the specific objects of interest in a therapeutic process, not those of the analysand.

The quality of the experience of the sessions is that of a dream space, in which every element of the field is at the same time something else. The analyst listens to the communications of the analysand as if listening to a story. Baranger and Baranger call this the "mythopoetic circuit" of the analytic process. This form of analytic listening and bi-personal interaction understands all communications as infused with metaphoric and fantasy elements.

Therapeutic tools of this model are free association, interpretation, the mythopoetic circuit, and what Baranger and Baranger call "bastions" and "the second look." This latter set of dual techniques is introduced to describe blockages or impasses in the work and their dissolution. A bastion evolves in the field through an unconscious collusion of the participants. When the analyst recognizes that there is a block to the work, she must take a step back and try to evaluate the situation, taking what the Barangers call a "second look."

The psychoanalytic field theory model of Antonino Ferro

A few decades later, primarily in Italy, another field theory developed. It was influenced by the Barangers' model and strongly influenced by the work of Wilfred Bion. This has recently been called Bionian Field Theory and has been developed by Antonino Ferro (2006/2009, 2007/2011), latterly joined by Giuseppe Civitarese (2008/2010, 2013).

Ferro drew upon the work of Baranger and Baranger, Bion, Klein, Langs, and Ogden, and was additionally influenced by narratology. He introduced a new model of psychoanalytic field theory. I designate a field theory based on this model the "oneiric model" of psychoanalytic field theory. Ferro's work led to a significant departure from the previous field theory model of Baranger and Baranger. It also contains radical changes in clinical technique.

Ferro's model picks up and accentuates the oneiric quality of the fields of Baranger and Baranger. The psychoanalytic fields of this model are dreamscapes in which the oneiric quality of the sessions is essential and omnipresent. Ferro describes the analyst as listening to all communications from the analysand as communications in and also about a dream. This kind of analytic field, like that of Baranger and Baranger, has its own co-created and independent unconscious process. And here also it is the field—its movements, stagnations, and perturbations—that is the object of interest of the analytic process. The field is considered heuristically to be a living, breathing organism. A difference with the Barangers' model is that here the participants are considered to be in a dream in sessions. In contrast, the Barangers emphasized analyzing the bi-personal story that emerges in the field.

Ferro's form of field theory makes use of Bion's model of mental functioning. This model makes use of Bion's concepts including alpha function, alpha and beta elements, waking dream thoughts, and reverie. Bion's notion of waking dream thought is used and expands upon the Barangers' oneiric quality of sessions. Waking dream thought is emphasized in this field theory model as a way of describing ongoing aspects of mental processes. Bi-personal interaction in an analytic process includes the evacuation and projection of beta elements of the analysand. The model employs the assumption that thinking requires two minds. Beta elements, the unmetabolized protosensory elements, are idiosyncratic, as is an individual's alpha function, which transforms the beta elements into pictograms. The beta elements of the analysand are considered to be processed by the alpha function of the analyst. The resulting alpha elements may then be projected back to the analysand for metabolization and used in waking dream thought.

The transformation into alpha elements affords waking dream thinking. A principal aspect of the role of the analyst in this model is to lend a relatively stronger alpha function to the field for use in creating the alpha function of the field and—derivatively and progressively—of the analysand. In this way the alpha function of the analysand develops through the analytic process. In this field theory model a principal objective of psychoanalytic processes is to mobilize the alpha function of the field and ultimately of the analysand. The goal of an analytic process in this field theory model is alternatively described as expanding the thinking, dreaming, and feeling of the analysand. The goals of this form of field theory have technical implications.

One consequence of the focus of this model is that contents and history are de-emphasized. The dream function of sessions is made use of to analyze all communications between analysand and analyst as about the field and the dyad. This leads to differences from other field theory models in terms of theory and also in technique. The influence of narratology on this field theory model contributes to shaping clinical technique. In the clinical setting one way this influence is understood is as attending to the characters introduced into the field through communications from the analysand in terms of the role they play in the story being told. A session is understood as a virtual reality, a moving dreamscape.

Part of the role of the analyst in this model is to listen to the narrative elements of the bi-personal interactions in the field and think about them as functional holographic images. A point of emphasis in the work of Civitarese is that the oneiric quality of sessions can be understood as like a play. The relative reality of the sessions is compared with the relative reality of a play for the audience immersed in a performance. In the case of analytic sessions each participant—analyst and analysand—is at the same time author and actor in the play. The casting of characters—also a co-creation of both participants—populates the field and gives it shape.

The focus of the process is on what is in the field. This is the case in this model in a more radical way than in other field theory models. There is less of an interest in discerning the objects, structures, or ongoing and historical patterns of the analysand. What is available for use in the analytic process is what is in the field. The field is a creative product of the work of the analytic couple. This model offers the analyst a broader range of clinical options. In a fundamental sense, it is what is in the field as experienced by the analyst that is the subject of the analytic work.

Contemporary psychoanalytic field theory models in the United States

The field theories that began to evolve in the middle of the last century in the United States, contemporaneously with the work of Baranger and Baranger, had several different instantiations. All of these were distinct from the model developed in South America. Unlike the motivations for the development of the Baranger and Baranger model, the field theories that developed in the United States were reactions to perceived problems with the structural model and with American ego psychology in particular. This is notwithstanding the work of Hartmann and Kris (1945) commenting on the compatibility of field theory and ego psychology. The work of Bertram Lewin in the middle of the last century on a version of the dream paradigm of analytic process is another indication of aspects of the clinical application of contemporary field theory's presence within the American ego psychological movement.

Objections to drive theory and Freudian concepts of drive were a major force in the development of field theories in the United States. Other related motivations derived from the rethinking of psychoanalytic concepts of neutrality, the interchangeability of the analyst, the role of the analyst, and counter-transference. The trend of questioning basic concepts of psychoanalysis led to several different ways of replacing the intrapsychic and genetic models. This resulted in new models which involved a psychoanalytic field that includes the analytic couple as a unit. The field theories in the United States were also influenced by postmodernism and hermeneutics in addition to Kurt Lewin's work. This meant that an emphasis on language, meaning, and narrative infused the new models in the United States.

There are different broad strands of field theories in the United States. These include a dominant strand from Harry Stack Sullivan through Edgar Levenson and Donnel Stern. Another runs from British Object Relations through Stephen Mitchell and from Heinz Kohut to George Atwood and Robert Stolorow. Yet another makes use of systems theories primarily in the work of Joseph Lichtenberg and his collaborations with Frank Lachmann and James L. Fosshage. The result has been different forms of psychoanalytic field theories called interpersonal, intersubjective, relational psychoanalysis, and motivational systems theories. While distinct, these field theories have core elements in common, such as emphases on human development, language, and including in the goals of psychoanalytic process the freeing of the analysand from ossified experiential structures and patterns.

Levenson (2005) emphasized the importance of attention to language and was the first psychoanalyst in the United States to demonstrate the importance of making use of postmodern concepts in psychoanalysis. In this regard he emphasized narrative description over objective truth. The past is understood as reflected through the experience of and the understanding in the present. The past is considered as a construct in the present without independent and objective existence in itself. The analytic process is focused on the interactions live in the present between analyst and analysand.

Patterns that emerge in the interpersonal analytic relationship have contributions from both participants with a weighting towards the analysand's emerging patterns. In Levenson's work the concept of mind was articulated in a radical way as a field phenomenon. He wrote, "brain is individual but mind is a field phenomenon . . . à la Winnicott there is no such thing as a mind" (Levenson, 2001, p. 250).

Levenson locates therapeutic change as arising within and from the present situation in which the analyst and analysand find themselves.

Ultimately they explore and come to understand their interactional patterns and situations. Embedded in the patterns that emerge in their dialogue will be some of what Levenson calls the "personal myths" of the analysand. According to Levenson, the interpersonal field contracts the "disease" of the analysand. The analyst becomes involved in and a part of the problem to be understood. Such field phenomena are creations that emerge by means of unconscious communication of the participants. It is the job of the analyst to recognize the experiential configuration of the analytic couple.

A crucial step in this kind of analytic process is for the analyst to understand her own involvement. Following this the analyst may engage the analysand in a joint understanding of a response to Levenson's clinical question "What is going on around here?" The objective is to extricate the analytic couple from the diseased field. The goal of an analytic process is progressively to bring the elements of the unconscious personal myths of the analysand to the light of exploration in the interpersonal field. This is understood as what will afford the analysand greater freedom from the constrictions of the personal myths and with that greater choice and spontaneity in life. In this process the analyst is immersed in the field and participates in it. It is also the analyst's job to be an observer of her experience in the field.

The following is a clinical example from Levenson (1978, p. 10) that demonstrates aspects of this way of working.

> Let me use another dream as an example of this. This is a patient who dreams of eating his hat. I'll omit most of the details, but the point of the dream is that he is eating a hat which he describes as made of "polymer urethane." In the dream he thinks, "Funny it doesn't taste like rubber." I've chosen this dream because it illustrates the different parameters of metaphor and metonymy and their overlap. There are many associative links: for example, he works for a chemical firm. There are even associations to chewing on his hat. But one need not know anything about this man to know that the metaphor for eating one's hat is some kind of act of contrition, or losing a bet and paying off. Yet there are other metaphoric issues. Anybody old enough to remember the 30s remembers it was a very common visual theme in the comic strips and movies. This man is visually oriented, he is old enough and quite witty. So one might think either the reference is somewhat anachronistic, it is not a term which people use much

anymore, or perhaps it sets the time period of the relevant historical experience. But still more, examine the logic of the dream. He eats the hat, he tastes the hat and says to himself, "Funny, it doesn't taste like rubber." This is precisely the logic of the mad-Hatter's tea party when the mad-Hatter is trying to repair a watch with butter and Alice says to him, "You can't fix a watch with butter" and he dips it in the tea and comments wistfully, "But it was the very best butter."

Now those are not free associations nor are they even associations particularly relevant to the patient's private experience. But they are the kind of play I think most therapists do. Once one catches the zany Alice-in-Wonderland logic of the dream the therapist suddenly realizes that he and the patient have been having exactly this kind of exchange; that it goes on all the time when one speaks with this man. He goes off in this funny kind of oblique, paralogical negativism. The metaphor of the dream then has meaning not just for the dream, but for its carrying over of its patterning into the transference, to the other areas of the patient's life. In other words, they are transforms of each other. The metaphor "carries over" which is what metaphors are supposed to do. Moreover once one has heard the metaphor and extended it with the metonymic associations the patient never seems the same again and one never hears what he is saying exactly the way one heard it before. And what's more, one has absolutely no choice in the matter. Something has occurred in the therapy.

Another American model is intersubjective psychoanalysis. This grew out of self psychology. It was developed by George Atwood and Robert Stolorow (2014). Intersubjectivity theory was influenced by structuralism, phenomenology, existentialism, and hermeneutics in addition to self psychology. In this theory developmental structures are emphasized. A focus of therapeutic processes is to discern unconscious developmental patterns and structures of the analysand as they emerge in the intersubjective interaction between analyst and analysand. The theory locates personality as constructed from the organizing principles that underlie developmental structures. And the organizing principles and structures are understood as evolving out of early and ongoing intersubjective interactions with caregivers and others. Psychoanalytic process is described as proceeding in a psychological, intersubjective field.

Motivational systems theory was developed by Lichtenberg (1989) and

Lichtenberg, Lachmann and Fosshage (2011). It was informed by infant research. In this theory human motivation arises from intersubjective experience. The motivational systems approach of Lichtenberg, Lachmann and Fosshage is a developmental model which emphasizes intrapsychic experience within an intersubjective context. Seven motivational systems are described as operative in each person from the beginning of life. Each system consists of a need, evolves over the life of an individual, and can be more or less salient relative to the other six motivational systems at any given moment in the experience of the person. Motives are understood as the basic elements of human experience.

Each motivational system operates within the immediate context of all seven motivational systems in an individual. The individual operates within the larger context of interaction with the motivational systems of others. Together, the analyst and analysand form an interactive system. The empathic mode of the analyst is described as situating the analyst within the experience of the analysand. In an analytic process, the analyst and analysand construct and are immersed in model scenes which capture and organize the experience and unconscious developmental structures of the analysand. In so doing, the analytic couple develops an understanding of the relative roles of the motivational systems in the model scenes and the embedded metaphors therein. Motivational systems theory took a radical stance in opposition to the concept of drives. In the latter's place motivational systems theory developed and articulated a novel notion of human motivation. Motivation is here described in terms of the systems theory concepts of emergence and creative generation. This paves the way for and emphasizes the creative element in human experience and in therapeutic process.

A final and prominent development of field theories in the United States is the relational theory of Jay Greenberg and Stephen Mitchell (1983). Relational psychoanalysis is a bi-personal developmental model. It was influenced by object relations, Fairbairn and the interpersonal model. Clinical work takes place in a relational field from which the understanding of the analysand is constructed as a result of the analytic process. The relational analytic process seeks to make use of history and genetics, understood as unconscious developmental structures that arise for the analysand within relational experience. The approach uses object relations to model early experience and development. The understanding of these elements is contextual. The relational field is also called an interactive matrix and it is considered as unique to the analytic couple. It is there in the matrix that communication and embedded threads of experiential sequences in the analytic process have meaning.

Meaning is constructed in the interactive field and is not something preexisting to be discovered or uncovered. The object of interest in a therapeutic process in relational psychoanalysis is the interactional relational field. The individual, and in particular the analysand, is described as arising out of the field. The concept of mind is described as consisting of the unconscious patterns and structures derived from the relational field. The goals of a relational therapeutic process are for the relational patterns and structures of the analysand to emerge between the analytic couple, and to be explored and understood. As a result the analysand becomes capable of new relational experience.

The following is an abbreviated clinical example from Mitchell (1991, pp. 165f.):

> He asked about the possibility of my reducing the fee somewhat. We agreed that if he came three times a week, I would reduce the fee for all three sessions by $15 . . . In his associations to the dream he recalled several scenes from his childhood involving "sweet" moments between himself and his father, the latter's returning home from work with special presents for him, both of them overjoyed at seeing each other again . . . As the son grew to manhood, the father was constantly trying to give him money, both larger amounts and also subway tokens, which he would try to smuggle into his son's pockets when his son wasn't looking. The son sometimes refused his aid, sometimes accepted it. He sensed that to finally and definitively turn down his father's money would have been to somehow shatter their relationship; his saintly father would never be able to understand, and there would not be much else between them . . . The lowered fee felt to him like his father's tokens, in some way meaningless, yet a powerful, two-sided symbolic statement both about my protectiveness toward him and my efforts to cripple him with my kindness. It became clear that the reduced fee had been laden with meaning for him all along. It had made him feel special and cared for, yet also reduced and infantilized . . . I began to wonder why I had been so quick to tell him I wouldn't raise the fee. How invested was I in being his saintly protector? Was it at my own expense? Did I really not need the extra

money? ... We seemed trapped in the closed world of these two relational configurations in which he was either cruelly deprived or lovingly crippled. This was, in my view, precisely the sort of trap in which we needed to be caught.

In working in and about the present, the clinical emphasis of these models that developed in the United States is opposed to the idea of searching for truths about the past. Instead, the focus is on the bi-personal narrative of the sessions. Exploring this narrative in its broadest sense to include all forms of communication and affect was modeled as leading to unconscious developmental structures of the analysand as they are instantiated in the analytic setting. These themes led some psychoanalysts in this period to attend closely to language. The emphasis on language and language meaning fostered an interest in the uniqueness of the communication in each analytic process.

A way to demarcate the end of the first wave of field theory and the beginning of the second is by means of a shift in the psychoanalytic understanding of basic concepts, such as the unconscious as processes. This was a gradual shift. It occurred during a period in which the terms of the exploration of mental processes were being reformulated in other disciplines too, including linguistics, philosophy, psychology, and biology. The movement included a shift toward a general emphasis on processes.

The work of ego psychologist Jacob Arlow (1969) from the late 1960s onwards concerning the concept of unconscious fantasy was central to the beginning of this shift. Arlow brought the American ego psychology movement forward. He understood unconscious fantasy as a process. His formulation stood in distinction to how fantasy had previously been understood as something more akin to a static snapshot. Arlow understood the process of unconscious fantasy as a mental function. He described fantasy as a continuously present aspect of waking and sleeping mental processes.

Arlow described the process of unconscious fantasy of an individual as containing the "mental set" with which the individual experiences the world. Some elements of an individual's mental set may be shared by others by virtue of physiological, cultural, and other similarities between individuals. Other elements may be highly idiosyncratic, having been developed over time and in particular as a result of developments in early experience.

Arlow's understanding of mental functioning was continued in a relational theory context by Arnold Modell (2005). The concept of unconscious fantasy was closely identified with an intrapsychic approach. The concept of metaphor was not claimed by any specific psychoanalytic perspective. In Modell's work metaphoric processes themselves were considered unconscious and the "currency of the mind." The concepts of unconscious fantasy in Arlow's work and unconscious metaphoric processes in Modell's work are similar in many crucial respects. What separates the concepts are the models in which each is embedded—the former in an intrapsychic structural model based on drives and the latter in a version of a bi-personal model.

The field theory models in the United States agree in terms of clinical technique that the analytic couple is working in and about the present moment of the session, that the work is experience near and in the here and now. Understanding the analysand and the analysand's experience as shaped by developmentally evolving unconscious organizing structures is considered a central analytic task. A core common focus of the models is to construct and discern metaphors, patterns, and structures in the analytic relationship that arise from the analysand's experience in the present and of the past, including fossilized narratives of the self. These concepts fall together under the category of unconscious metaphoric processes. Levenson (1978) understood therapeutic work as consisting of deconstructing and modifying the metaphors of the analysand. Once the metaphors are discerned, the possibility emerges to deconstruct the rigidified patterns and personal narratives of the analysand within the psychoanalytic relationship. This is understood in each of the models as opening the potential for the analysand to have new self, other, and relational experience.

The models developed in this period in the United States could be understood as responses and challenges to the structural model but also specifically to American ego psychology. All models include significant emphasis on a bi-personal dimension to human experience that is modeled in the use of two-person interactive fields. In my descriptions of these models I have tried to draw out the strong resemblances borne by them. There are several different kinds of fields used in them: interpersonal fields, intersubjective fields, and relational fields.

The bi-personal psychoanalytic field models in the United States have a core of commonly held themes. There are at least five dominant, centrally shared themes. These include the essential use of a bi-personal field in analytic process and in understanding human experience generally. Stern (2006, p. 569) describes the field as "the smallest unit of human living." The models also make essential use of research concerning human development; and they include a focus on unconscious metaphoric processes, developmental structures, and patterns. These are understood as having evolved within bi-personal experience. Another theme is the replacement of Freudian drives with conceptions of motivation that are developmentally bi-personally created. There is an understanding in common to these theories of the goals of psychoanalytic therapeutic processes as including the exploration of the metaphors, structures, and patterns of the analysand as they emerge in the analytic exchange. Finally, there is also a core interest in the nature of the language and communication of psychoanalytic processes.

Taken together, these common themes form a specific model and clinical technique of a psychoanalytic field theory that is distinctly American. I call this model the "plasmic model." The term "plasmic" is taken from the name of the fourth and most common state of matter, plasma. There are many aspects of this term from physics that capture the guiding principles of field theories in the United States. For example, plasma has a fundamentally interactive nature. It has complex behavior that is neither rule bound nor random. And plasma forms spatially in fractal configurations, which Lichtenberg, Lachmann and Fosshage (2011) discuss as a way of conceptualizing emotional structures.

The mind in the plasmic model includes and operates by means of unconscious organizing principles, templates, or interactive configurations. These concepts can be captured together in the concept of unconscious metaphoric processes. Metaphoric processes are formed in an individual from early and repeating experience with others. These experiences are internalized with an idiosyncratic structure. In turn, the experience of an individual is the result of what emerges through the filters of the metaphoric processes that are operative in the mind. Mental processes in this field theory consist of the activation, ongoing modification, and development of the metaphoric processes of an individual in interaction with others. The metaphoric processes of an individual are unique. The organizing metaphoric processes also have the potential to share similar developmental patterns with others. Patterns of human development rather than relatively rigid developmental stages are emphasized in this model of mental processes.

Three principles of technique of contemporary psychoanalytic field theory

I shall now draw out a guiding heuristic, clinical principle for each of the three field theory paradigms. These principles are all mutually distinct and each has implications for clinical work.

The principle of mythopoesis

Baranger and Baranger propose the clinical heuristic principle of attending to the mythopoeic elaborations of communications of the analysand. A way they have described applying the principle of mythopoesis is by listening to the communications of the analysand as one would listen to a story—to listen by inserting "Once upon a time . . ." at the beginning of each communication. A way of conceptualizing this is to think of "Once upon a time" as a modal operator that acts on emotional communications in an analytic process.

The operator "Once upon a time" emphasizes the nature of the temporality of analysands' communications and can serve to highlight the fantasy involved in all communications of the analysand.

"Once upon a time" places the statement made by the analysand in at least one cluster of meaning contexts to be played with in the analytic process in order to make, add to, or reconfigure a construction. This operator puts in relief the relative reality of the session. This brings out the fantasy and metaphoric levels of the communications of the analysand. At the same time, it infuses the sessions and the analytic process with a quality of heightened reality. In so doing, the ever-changing nature of the ongoing affective and oral history of the analytic process is emphasized. This way of addressing the therapeutic process brings out the relative reality of sessions and the psychoanalytic process and, more specifically, the relative reality of the present moment. It also displays the plastic nature of memory, genetics, and history. This way of exploring the levels of meaning of utterances within an analytic context indicates the diminished relevance of truth value and of assessing truth value.

The oneiric principle

The oneiric model, based on Ferro's work, employs an oneiric clinical heuristic principle. A way of applying this principle for analytic listening is to attend to the communications of the patient by inserting the prefix

"I had a dream that . . ." in front of them (Ferro, 2007/2011, 2009). Since in this model there is less emphasis on the individual participant's contributions to the dream, fantasies and currents in and of the field, the oneiric modal operator might be thought of as "the field is dreaming that . . ."

The operator "the field is dreaming that . . ." highlights the oneiric and multifaceted quality of all communications in an analytic process and the unconscious communications therein. In this way, thinking in terms of prefixing all communications of an analysand with the modal operator "the field is dreaming that . . .," the analyst is drawn to reflect on the different levels of meaning of the communication, privileging what emerges from the unconscious of the field. Ferro indicates that using the prefix expands and deconstructs the analyst's thinking. In taking the analysand's communications as of a dream, the dream space and quality of the analytic process are salient and comprise the realm in which the analyst works. This in turn leads to interpretation and the co-construction of an emotional reality in the field which fosters the analysand's ability to feel, dream, and think. This dream space, also known as the analytic field, is the arena in which, according to Ferro, change for the patient is possible.

Both the mythopoeic and the oneiric psychoanalytic modal operators are indexical. This means that they are context dependent and context sensitive. They are dependent on several variables; the minimal set includes each member of the analytic couple, a designated utterer, and the space–time location.

The plasmic principle

The field theories in the United States emphasize the contextual nature of the communications within an analytic process. The clinical heuristic principle for these field theories might be called plasmic. The plasmic operator places an emphasis on the relationship between analyst and analysand and on analytic listening as attending to the timbre of the moment-to-moment and ambient relational venture that unfolds in the field. The operator could be expressed as the prefix "I am here now doing this with you." This operator has at least five indexical variables. The clinical models that could be understood as making use of the plasmic operator are not listening to the communications of the analysand like a dream. Rather, the emphasis is on the relationship and what is happening in it at the moment. The analysand emerges from the exploration of what is happening in the moment between and amongst the analytic couple. Attention is focused on the creation and understanding of the unconscious metaphoric processes embedded in the doing in that particular now in that particular relationship. In order to answer Levenson's question the field itself is understood as an object of study.

In the mythopoeic and the oneiric paradigms there is a clear indication of a dominant emphasis on unconscious processes and unconscious-to-unconscious communication. In the plasmic paradigm unconscious processes arise and are attended to through the emergence of metaphoric processes that are involved in the present moment of the relationship. The exploration of these metaphoric processes gives rise to the potential for understanding the unconscious self-systems or personal myths through which the analysand has experience.

Concluding remarks

I hope to have convincingly shown that there are three principal models of contemporary psychoanalytic field theory. In particular I hope to have shown that there is a unique field theory in the United States—the one I call the plasmic model. All three models of field theory are mutually distinct with different heuristic descriptions of the mind and mental processes. Yet all include the core factor of the essential bi-personal nature of mental functioning. Following from the respective descriptions of mental functioning, each model affords different clinical techniques and therapeutic goals. Yet all agree that it is the unconscious processes that evolve in the bi-personal field of the analytic process that are the loci of analytic attention and of therapeutic change.

The three field theory models differ from one another in several important respects. The fields of the oneiric model are different from those of the mythopoeic model. Unlike a game of chess in which each participant makes discrete moves, in this kind of field it is not considered always either ascertainable or of relevance from whom (which participant) something evolved or emerged. This is also unlike the fields of the plasmic model in which part of the therapeutic process is articulating who is doing what to and with whom (Fosshage, 2011).

The mythopoeic and oneiric field theory models place an emphasis on specifying what conception of psychoanalytic field is being employed in the theoretical model and in clinical technique. Field theories related to the development of the plasmic model have not focused on an articulation of the field. Rather the emphasis has been on clarification of the analytic relationship and the structures embedded there. In the other two models the reverse is true.

This discrepancy of focus of attention has led to misunderstandings of each model from the perspectives of the others. These different emphases are consistent with the forms each of the three models has taken. They also point to relative strengths and weaknesses in each model. In particular, the lack of emphasis in the oneiric model on the forms of the relationship of the participants is consistent with the lack of focus on development and the force of unconscious developmental structures. The lack of emphasis in the plasmic model on the field concept indicates insufficient attention to the creative aspect of expanding the symbolization and dreaming capacities of the analysand.

Careful attention to similarities and differences of technique, theory, and heuristics of the three models may afford developments, enrichments and improvements in psychoanalytic field theories in the future. It may also clarify the role and potential future roles of the psychoanalytic field theories within the broader context of psychoanalysis.

References

Arlow, J. (1969) "Unconscious fantasy and disturbances of conscious experience." *Psychoanalytic Quarterly* 38: 1–27.
Atwood, G. and Stolorow, R. (2014) *Structures of Subjectivity*. London: Routledge.
Baranger, M. and Baranger, W. (1961–1962/2008) "The analytic situation as a dynamic field." *International Journal of Psychoanalysis* 89: 795–826.
Baranger, M. and Baranger, W. (2009) *The Work of Confluence*. London: Karnac.
Civitarese, G. (2008/2010) *The Intimate Room*. New York: Routledge.
Civitarese, G. (2013) *The Violence of Emotions*. New York: Routledge.
Ferro, A. (2006/2009) *Mind Works*. New York: Routledge.
Ferro, A. (2007/2011) *Avoiding Emotions, Living Emotions*. New York: Routledge.
Ferro, A. (2009) "Transformations in dreaming and characters in the psychoanalytic field." *International Journal of Psychoanalysis* 90: 209–230.
Fosshage, J. (2011) "The use and impact of the analyst's subjectivity with the empathic and other listening/experiencing perspectives." *Psychoanalytic Quarterly* 80: 139–160.
Greenberg, J. and Mitchell, S. (1983) *Object Relations in Psychoanalytic Theory*. Cambridge, MA: Harvard University Press.
Hartmann, H. and Kris, A. (1945) "The genetic approach in psychoanalysis." *Psychoanalytic Study of the Child* 1: 11–30.

Levenson, E. (1978) "Two essays in psychoanalytical psychology." *Contemporary Psychoanalysis* 14: 1–17.

Levenson, E. (2001) "The enigma of the unconscious." *Contemporary Psychoanalysis* 37: 239–252.

Levenson, E. (2005) *The Fallacy of Understanding and the Ambiguity of Change*. Hillsdale, NJ: The Analytic Press.

Lewin, B. (1955) "Dream psychology and the analytic situation." *Psychoanalytic Quarterly* 24: 169–199.

Lichtenberg, J. (1989) *Psychoanalysis and Motivation*. Hillsdale, NJ: The Analytic Press.

Lichtenberg, J., Lachmann, F. and Fosshage, J. (2011) *Psychoanalysis and Motivational Systems*. New York: Routledge.

Mitchell, S. (1991) "Wishes, needs and interpersonal negotiations." *Psychoanalytic Inquiry* 11: 147–170.

Modell, A. (2005) "Emotional memory, metaphor and meaning." *Psychoanalytic Inquiry* 25: 555–568.

Stern, D. (2006) "States of relatedness." *Contemporary Psychoanalysis* 42(4): 565–576.

We have to observe all kinds of things at once. Unconscious thought is holistic and this is what is creative. You pick out a pattern without knowing how you do it. The second look of the Barangers to understand the way the analyst has been involved by stepping back reminds me of the long tradition in America of what Harry Stack Sullivan called "participant observation." It is very much like what the Barangers call the second look, but for him it is more a continuous part of the process than something you do when there's a problem.

Donnel Stern

Chapter 11

The analytic field as a resonator and instrument for revealing the presence of other fields[1]

Claudio Neri

In his paper on beginning the treatment, Freud (1913) uses the analogy of a train journey, comparing the patient to a passenger sitting in a carriage and the analyst to a railway expert. Associating freely, the patient-as-passenger describes his[2] states of mind, thoughts and emotions as if they were the changing scenes he sees through the window. However, he is unaware of the meaning of what he is describing – and still less of that of the entire sequence of his associative descriptions. Both meanings are unconscious and can be brought to light only through the analyst's work of decoding and interpretation.

For his part, the analyst-as-railway-expert, while not having direct access to the scenes observed by the patient-as-passenger (the source of his associations), can follow the course of those associations and uncover their meaning.

An analyst who espouses psychoanalytic field theory would accept this analogy only in part; he would consider that he does indeed have direct access to certain aspects of the unfolding scenery – namely, the tensions, sensations, emotions and proto-thoughts present in the analytic field he has co-created and shares with the patient. Furthermore, he would point out that the analytic field does not coincide with the "railway-carriage-as-analyst's-consulting-room." This is because, in his view, the analytic field also includes other elements, which are sometimes remote in terms of time, space and representability even if they have parallels in what is happening and is perceived in the analyst's consulting room.

The possibility or impossibility of direct access to at least some aspects of the scenery distinguishes the field theory approach from the classical technique. However, this conception would be embraced not only by analysts who use psychoanalytic field theory but also by others whose allegiance is to a range of different contemporary schools of psychoanalysis.

Can the concept of the psychoanalytic field be applied in a more specific and characterizing manner?

My response

In answering this question, I shall touch upon a number of points.

The analytic field is not the only one to be considered: a patient's life also includes other fields in which he is involved, while other fields also influence his mind, such as the field of an institution or association to which he belongs, or those of his close and extended family.

While the effects of these fields, where present and active, may be favorable, they can also be disturbing. The transition from a configuration in which a benign field holds sway in a patient's mind to one dominated by an oppressive field may be likened to a change in the weather pattern from – in the Italian situation – a cool maestrale wind to a hot, moist sirocco that makes for torpidity of mind and body.

If the therapeutic process is to develop appropriately, it is important to devise a strategy for coping analytically with the oppressive, annihilating fields that may be present and active in a patient's mind. It is, however, difficult to identify these, for all the phenomena concerned are not localized and well defined, but instead diffuse and pervasive. Again, the fields of the psyche are often camouflaged in and indeed *as* the environment.

The psychoanalytic field – that co-created by and shared between patient and analyst – may also be pervaded and clogged up by these other fields. Yet the psychoanalytic field is able to resonate with and reveal the presence of its pathological counterparts, thus potentially marking the commencement of an interesting phase of analytic work. New and important resources for clinical work can therefore accrue from familiarity with and the application of psychoanalytic field theory and in particular from the idea of the analytic field as a resonator and instrument for revealing the presence of other fields.

Context

Before addressing in greater depth the matters outlined above, I should like to introduce some concepts and observations put forward by Italian and American colleagues, which will help me to construct a context for my principal subject, and enable me to set forth my personal views on a number of important issues. These concepts are as follows:

- The idea of the field as a "significant other."
- The concepts of the "modal operator" and "exploration of the field."
- The observation that the work of patient and analyst will be boosted and receive additional support when they become aware of the existence of a shared analytic field.

These ideas and concepts are presented and abundantly illustrated by Marco Conci, Stephanie Montana Katz and Donnel Stern in their respective chapters of this book, so I can be brief here.

The significant other

Sullivan holds that the analyst is a "significant other," by which he means in particular that the patient uses the analyst (the significant other) as an instrument through which to get to know himself.

Marco Conci (2015, p. 1) supplements Sullivan's idea with the original suggestion that not only an analyst but also a field (i.e., the psychoanalytic field) can serve as a "significant other":

> The field concept can ... allow us to reformulate the way in which Freud connected the knowledge we can gain of ourselves to the dialogue with the Other, the "significant other" represented – at the time of his self-analysis of the 1890s – by Wilhelm Fliess. Here is my reformulation: we know ourselves, only if we become aware of the field which we come from and/or [which] has shaped us, as such an awareness becomes possible through the dialogue with a significant other [which will, however, not necessarily be a person, but can also be a field], i.e. with a "significant field" [a new cultural and social environment] with which we come in touch.

Conci's idea is borne out not only in the psychoanalytic situation, but also in other spheres. For example, a new country may be a "significant other" that allows someone to acquaint himself with certain characteristics of his country of origin or facilitates self-knowledge. Many Italians who have emigrated to distant lands, such as the United States or Argentina, have succeeded in using their relationship with and immersion in their new environment to discover in themselves hitherto unimagined qualities of inventiveness, perseverance and dynamism.

Let me add an observation of my own to Conci's conception. In the light of his remarks, the proposition that the analytic field is a co-creation of patient and analyst can be expanded by pointing out that this co-creation does not come about on a basis of equality. The analyst is the member of the couple or group who makes fundamental choices because he assumes and upholds the aspects that enable him to serve as a "significant other." Certain possible aspects of the analytic field are prevented from developing or are at any rate kept under control. For instance, if the members of my therapy group tend to exaggerate the friendship aspect of the group analytic field by constantly calling or texting each other, I usually intervene by suggesting that these communications might deprive our work of fuel by removing it from the context of the sessions when we are all present.

Modal operators and exploration of the field

I now come to the concepts of the "modal operator" and "exploration of the field."

According to Stephanie Montana Katz (2015, pp. 15 and 26), the characteristic mental attitude of a psychoanalyst who espouses field theory (and in particular its developments in the United States) comprises the use of a specific modal operator; in other words, the analyst tacitly prefixes all of his communications with the sentence "I am here now doing this with you."[3]

The principal activity undertaken by the analyst together with the patient is exploration of the shared field. The field becomes the focus of their attention because they are seeking to answer a number of questions, such as "What is happening here?"; "What is going on around here (now, between us)?"; "What has caused the heightened anxiety perceptible in the session right now?"; and "Why has our faith in the possibility of achieving something good and useful lessened or (as the case may be) increased?" These questions arise following a reference by the patient to an important person or as a result of his remembering some significant event. However, they may also be posed because the analytic field has come to resonate with a field present in the patient's mind or with a variation in the configuration of that field.

Awareness of the existence of a shared field

I shall continue my discussion of exploration of the field later. First, however, I shall present the final component of the context for my main subject. It follows from a comment by Donnel Stern to the effect that patient and analyst, as it were, receive a reward that facilitates the progress of their work when they become aware that a shared field exists. This awareness can on no account be taken for granted. Not only the patient but also the analyst may notice the effects on them of the tensions and pressures exerted by the field they share. They may register and take note of the effects of changes and fluctuations in that field. Finally, they may explore the field, attempting to locate and understand what has given rise to the effects they are noticing. However, they may also persist in not being clearly aware of the existence of a shared field.

As it happens, a similar point could be made about the earth's gravitational field. We all notice its effects. We may also feel its variations, for instance high in the mountains. Yet we may remain unaware of its existence.

Stern makes an interesting comment about what happens upon the emergence of awareness that the analytic field exists – namely, that the evidence of its existence is accompanied by a sense of vibrancy and spontaneity, which, in effect, provides patient and analyst with a staunch ally. When they realize that a field has been created between them, there "is the remarkable experience of being carried along by something larger than both therapist and patient" (Stern, 2015, p. 14).

Group psychotherapy and psychoanalysis

In my work as a group psychotherapist, I have often had the experience described by Stern – more precisely, that of benefiting from a field wider than that of the individual psyche, which supports me and the other group members in the work of thinking and understanding. In individual psychoanalysis, on the other hand, I have not experienced the sense of vibrancy and spontaneity mentioned by Stern, but only similar feelings. For example, my experience has been that a relationship has been forged and that it can be trusted. On other occasions, I have experienced comforting and positive evidence that psychoanalysis (as a method and as treatment) exists and corresponds to what the patient and I are doing. On still other occasions, my experience has been that I, as a member of a couple, am making a useful contribution – a contribution that bears the stamp of my unique, personal way of being in and entering into a relationship with another person.

Setting aside the experiences of relationship, of psychoanalysis and of the work of the couple, and thus considering only the field, I must say that the evidence of its existence has presented itself to me not as an experience of vibrancy and spontaneity, but, on the contrary, as an entity independent of both myself and the patient, which, however, constitutes a powerful obstacle to our efforts to make progress. In other words, it is not a breeze that fills the sails and lightens the vessel of our relationship, but a strong headwind or even a storm that bears down on us as soon as we attempt to abandon the safety of the harbor or bay and explore new waters.

I cannot be certain whether this difference between Stern's experiences and my own has to do with my personal and professional characteristics as a group and individual therapist or with more general aspects of the differences between our two settings, but I can put forward some hypotheses. It may be that in individual analysis I tend to make a very clear distinction between the concepts of relationship and the field and am inclined to attribute the more positive experiences to the former rather than the latter. Another possibility is that I am accustomed to connect the experience of evidence of the existence of a shared field with the creation of a wide-ranging psychic space and that this experience is powerful in a group but much more tenuous in the couple relationship. Alternatively, the field concept may predominate in group psychotherapy, while those of relationship and transference hold sway in individual psychoanalysis.

Individuals, relationship and the field

Although it would be interesting to consider all these points in greater depth, that would take us too far from my principal subject here. Again, I do not wish my remark about the difference between group psychotherapy and psychoanalysis to divert attention from the reason for my adducing Donnel Stern's observation. My reason is that I feel it is important to be able to distinguish the existence of the field from that of the patient, that of the analyst and also that of their relationship – whether the evidence of its existence is accompanied by an experience of "being carried along by something larger than both therapist and patient" or instead that of "a storm bearing down on patient and analyst." After all, awareness of the existence of a shared field is vital if the field is to be used as a resonator and instrument for revealing the presence of other fields. It is also essential for regulating the analytic field so that it can serve as a "significant other." Finally, it is necessary for purposive exploration of the field, as discussed by Katz.

An umbral cone

It is now time for me to turn to the main subject of this chapter, which will be illustrated by a case history.

I have written earlier about situations where I was able to identify the presence of other fields within the analytic field. In my contribution on the analysis of Isabel (Neri, 2013), the field concerned was the patient's workplace. In that text I also referred to the effects on another patient and on the shared field of a "kryptonite field" generated by the mind of a mother afflicted with hallucinations and thought disturbances. In an earlier paper I discussed the analysis of Maria, which involved a remote "field comprising a style of nobility and suffering" that had been tacitly transmitted from generation to generation (Neri, 1993, p. 49). In both contributions I also illustrated my opinion on the best approach for addressing and resolving the negative interference of these fields.

I shall now consider another type of field, which is quite idiosyncratic – namely, the umbral cone that may be projected over vast distances by anything bearing a relation to the element of the sacred and by institutions connected with religion. Entering into a relationship with the sacred entails concomitant experiences of fear, wonder and falling under a spell. The institutions that preside over religious life, for their part, arouse in those who aspire to belong to them or indeed who merely come under their sphere of influence a tendency to impose high standards of purity and correctness on their thoughts, fantasies and actions. Although psychoanalysis certainly has little in common with the sacred and with religion, approaching a psychoanalytic institution such as the Italian Psychoanalytical Society with a view to training as an analyst may sometimes be tantamount to entering into an umbral cone with similar characteristics to those of the sacred and of religion.

Manfredi

When we first meet, Manfredi is twenty-four years old, a medical student who is already well advanced in his training. He is intelligent, lively and a keen sportsman. For some years he has been engaged to a pleasant young woman with a positive attitude to the world. Their relationship is intense and rests on firm foundations.

He requests my help for a problem that concerns certain well-defined aspects of his life experience. Thus far, this has not prevented him from leading an active, effectively full life. Sometimes, however, Manfredi's symptoms have become very alarming and he is afraid that they might overwhelm him.

After two and a half years, the symptoms have disappeared; the problem that brought Manfredi into psychotherapy has been substantially solved. However, he decides to continue with his sessions. The psychotherapy helps him to clarify the tangled situation of his family of origin and to get to know himself on a deeper level. In addition, he has a professional ambition: he would like to become a psychoanalyst.

Over the ensuing two years, Manfredi graduates, passes the qualifying examination and opts to specialize in psychiatry. The university accepts his application and he embarks on his specialty.

The next step is to apply to become a candidate at the Italian Psychoanalytical Society, to which I also belong. Manfredi prepares his application, attaches his CV to it and receives a letter naming the psychoanalysts who will conduct his evaluation interviews.

There are two months to go before these interviews are due to take place. Then, all of a sudden, *Quod non fecerunt barbari, fecerunt Barberini!*[4] What the institution of the university did not do, the institution of psychoanalysis has done. An umbral cone of conventionality descends on the analytic field and the sessions. Manfredi's behavior, thoughts and dreams change, now unfailingly exhibiting normality, seriousness, good will, honesty and efficiency. Manfredi brings a dream to each session. He diligently associates to every aspect of it. He speaks with great commitment about his future life and expectations. In a nutshell, everything he says and does is absolutely *comme il faut*.

His behavior can be explained in a number of ways. He is confronted with interviews that, for him, are tantamount to a crucial examination. He has faced plenty of exams in the past without undergoing such a transformation. However, *this* exam is special; it is different from its predecessors because it will lead to his embracing the same profession as his psychoanalyst. Furthermore, his psychoanalyst is a training analyst, like his future examiners.

What surprises me is not Manfredi's behavior in itself; I am in fact particularly struck by the way this attitude – disciplined, exuding good will and conformism – extends to every gesture and thought he expresses in the sessions. It is as if the fourth fairy's magic wand in the tale of Sleeping Beauty – the fairy who commutes into prolonged sleep the death sentence passed by the third fairy with her curse – has transformed everything and everyone, whether men, women, horses, dogs or even inanimate objects.

Interestingly, Manfredi is unaware of this change and of the forces underlying it. I succeed in comprehending its power and extent not so much by observing his behavior and the course of the sessions, as by way of the strange effect it has on me. I notice an intense pressure to behave like a "proper" psychoanalyst; for instance, I feel the need to interpret in detail the dreams Manfredi presents, which contain many clear indications of their meaning. In a word, I myself am at risk of turning into a character from *The Truman Show*.

The spell is easily broken. In a friendly tone, I tell Manfredi: "It seems to me that you have switched into autopilot mode. I cannot make contact with you any more, the way you used to be. I know you are about to have your interviews for admission to the Psychoanalytic Society. But maybe there's also a little too much fear and reverence."

Manfredi is very relieved. He replies: "You're right! I made myself all stiff, like wearing a suit of armor ... But you should make more of an effort to understand how important this project is for me."

This exchange enables us to find each other again, and in the ensuing sessions Manfredi's associations, as well as his dreams, become more varied and, in particular, more free and spontaneous. The analytic field regains its earlier seriousness and commitment, as well as the intimate and agreeable climate that previously characterized it.[5]

Conclusion: the Geiger counter

We must try to imagine the analytic field as (among other things) a sensitive instrument for revealing the presence of something, rather like a Geiger counter. When a shared analytic field has become established, our ability to imagine it as such an instrument permits the identification of areas that bear the baneful stamp of a traumatic event in the patient's life, or the transformation of the entire field under the influence of "other fields" that have been activated in his mind.

Acknowledgment

I wish to express my thanks to Mercedes Lugones, whose careful reading and valuable suggestions have enabled me to make this contribution more relevant to the practice of psychoanalysis.

Notes

1 Translated by Philip Slotkin (MA Cantab).
2 Translator's note: For convenience, the masculine form is used for both sexes throughout this chapter.
3 In grammatical terms, "modal operators" are modal and phrasal verbs, such as "want," "can," "must" or "know" – that is, verbs to which is added a particular modality denoting volition, possibility, requirement or competence in relation to the action described.
4 This Latin tag – meaning "What the barbarians failed to do, the Barberinis did" – was attached to the Pasquino statue near Rome's Piazza Navona as a lampoon directed at Pope Urban VIII (Maffeo Barberini), who had removed some bronze beams from the Pantheon for use in his cannon foundry and to decorate the columns and baldachin of the high altar of St Peter's Cathedral. In Italy, the phrase subsequently passed into common parlance to signify that one's theoretically well-bred neighbors are sometimes more dangerous than uncivilized foreigners.
5 Manfredi's case history can be read with reference to many other psychoanalytic concepts than those I have chosen. For example, it lends itself readily to interpretation in terms of a couple fantasy that has assumed the form of a bastion and has then been resolved (Baranger and Baranger, 1961–1962/2008). However, I remain faithful to my own reading, which I believe is convincing and has given good results in my clinical work.

References

Baranger, M. and Baranger, W. (1961–1962/2008). The analytic situation as a dynamic field. *International Journal of Psychoanalysis*, 89: 795–826.

Conci, M. (2015). Field theory: a dialogical approach, a pluralistic perspective, an equifinalistic vision. Paper presented at the Panel on Field Theory, Cambridge, MA, July 21.

Freud, S. (1913). On beginning the treatment (Further recommendations on the technique of psycho-analysis I). In *The Standard Edition of the Complete Psychological Works of Sigmund Freud*, London: Hogarth Press, 1953–1974, Vol. 12, pp. 121–144.

Katz, S. M. (2015). The third model of contemporary psychoanalytic field theory. Paper presented at the Panel on Field Theory, Cambridge, MA, July 21.

Neri, C. (1993). Field theory and trans-generational phantasies. *Rivista Psicoanalisi*, 39: 43–62 (reprinted in F. Borgogno, A. Luchetti and L. Marino Coe (eds.), *Reading Italian Psychoanalysis*, London: Routledge, 2016, pp. 406–416).

Neri, C. (2013). Isabel: social field, psychological field, and narrative field. *Psychoanalytic Inquiry*, 33: 267–271.

Stern, D.B. (2015). Emergent properties of the interpersonal field. Paper presented at the Panel on Field Theory, Cambridge, MA, July 21.

It is a reasonable project to think about trying to use a general concept of field to define something that is substantial and underlies different psychoanalytic field concepts. It is however difficult enough to try to think about defining the three basic models of field theory, look for commonalities amongst them, and use that for a platform to think about branching out to other psychoanalytic perspectives. It would be to bring a way of speaking across psychoanalytic perspectives without trying to impose agreement or hierarchy.

S. Montana Katz

Chapter 12

Emergent properties of the interpersonal field[1]

Donnel Stern

I remember feeling, even as a graduate student seeing my first patients in the early 1970s, that the clinical process took place *between* the patient and me, and that my experience and the patient's were not only our own, but also parts of a larger whole. In my first book (Stern, 1997), I recently reread a description of the interpersonal field. It brought back to me those first experiences of that sense of the clinical situation and reminded me of how long the interpersonal field has been central in my mind—longer, even, than I have known it by its name. Here is the passage:

> A fully interpersonal conception of treatment is a field theory. The psychoanalytic relationship, like any relationship, takes place in a field that is defined and ceaselessly redefined by its participants. It is not only the intrapsychic dynamics patient and analyst bring to their relationship that determine their experience with one another. The field is a unique creation, not a simple additive combination of individual dynamics; it is ultimately the field that determines which experiences the people who are in the process of co-creating that field can have in one another's presence. It is the field that determines what will be dissociated and what will be articulated, when imagination will be possible and when the participants will be locked into stereotypic descriptions of their mutual experience. Each time one participant changes the nature of his or her involvement in the field, the possibilities for the other person's experience change as well ... The field is the only relevant context.
>
> (Stern, 1997, p. 110)

Emergence in the third person

One characteristic of the field has always held a particular fascination for me: its emergent properties. The field comes into being between two or more people in a way that cannot be predicted or controlled. It can only be accepted or rejected. To the extent that we can accept it, we sense and understand (and these are not necessarily the same thing at all) something of how this emergent quality informs and shapes the clinical process.

There is a link in psychoanalysis between the unconscious and the quality of emergence. This is not a very well-theorized link; in fact, it is not at all clear exactly what we are referring to when we invoke it, as indubitable as I think its existence is to most psychoanalysts. The quality of emergence is itself no better defined than the link that connects it to the unconscious. So, before going on to discuss the link to the unconscious, which I do later in this paper, I begin by trying to explain what I mean by emergence.

In psychoanalysis, we often experience the phenomena that we understand to "emerge" to be separate from us. That is, we think of emergence in the third person—some "it" emerges, so that the quality of emergence exists apart from subjectivity. Consider, for instance, the frequent appearance of the concept of emergence and the descriptor "emergent" in recent applications of nonlinear dynamic systems theory to the clinical situation (e.g., Seligman, 2005; Boston Change Process Study Group, 2010; Coburn, 2013). The emphasis in this work is not phenomenological—the primary emphasis is not the experience of the analyst or the patient, but on their interaction as a self-organizing system. Emergence in this frame of reference is not really part of our "felt sense" of things, but a characteristic of clinical process itself—clinical process as an object of observation. When the word "emergence" is used in this way, it describes attributes that are *experienced* as if they exist apart from the one who perceives them (even if, as in this case, we must also grant that the observer is part of the phenomenon in question).

Most of the time, psychoanalysts use the word in this third-person sense. We use it to describe aspects of treatment and characteristics of mind. Most of us, including me, continue to write and speak this way more or less routinely.

Emergence in the first person: the "felt sense" of emergence

But the way I intend to use the word "emergence" in this paper, and the way I generally find emergence to be most compelling in my daily clinical work, is not as a reference to attributes of things that feel as if they exist apart from me, but as a way of representing certain parts of my *first-person* experience, and the patient's, in the consulting room. This is emergence in the phenomenological sense. I have learned from my patients that they and I often have a simultaneous sense of the emergent quality of our experience, although sometimes I have that sense myself without knowing if the patient shares it. In either case, I have learned to value such moments highly, because they herald the appearance of something unexpected.

I have observed for many years that all experience is unbidden. It comes *to* us, we never plan it, and in that sense it is always a surprise (Stern, 1990, 2013). Most of the time we are unaware of this unbiddenness. It simply escapes notice.

But the moments when I have a *felt sense of emergence* are different in this respect. At those times I *feel* the unbiddenness of experience. I have a felt sense of the *arrival* of experience in my mind, of how little my conscious intentions seem to have to do with the whole process. I feel myself as a conduit for experience that comes into being through me. Paradoxically, this kind of experience, more than any other part of my experience—and precisely, I think, because it seems to come to me from elsewhere—feels most thoroughly of my own making. I feel it firmly as *mine*. My patients' sense of this kind of experience is similar, to the extent to which they have been able to articulate it to me.

A mild sense of emergence is common—an everyday event in my clinical experience. The more intense and gripping experience of emergence is rare. *Any* sense of emergence, though, whether mild or gripping, is vital, alive. It is often emotionally powerful, but even when it is not, it is arresting. It carries a sense of mystery, ranging from a feeling of surprise that merely raises the eyebrows, to sudden, intense curiosity, to awe and wonder, and every once in a long while to the numinous or magical.

"Emergence" in this frame of reference describes a certain affective state of things. It is the felt sense of moments that portend the unexpected, or are themselves unexpected. In moments of emergence I am connected to unseen things that feel, despite their invisibility, greatly important to matters at hand. There is a sense of nascence, of budding, of coming-to-be.

Foehl (2014, p. 295), in describing the quality of "depth" in clinical work, articulates what I am trying to express: in moments of emergence, we are suddenly privy to "a sense of the boundless reaches of what we do not yet know."

I have had experiences of emergence that were private. In these instances I was generally alone, and aware of my aloneness. In other words, I was not only physically by myself but also felt alone, although not necessarily lonely. Many of these experiences were in dreams; others took place while I was in nature, or overlooking the city from an elevated position. They have also occurred as I watched a film, read a novel, stood looking at a painting—or indeed as I wrote a paper, finding myself amazed at the appearance in my mind of some expression that captured what I wanted to say in a way that carried me beyond what I had understood in the previous moment.

But most of the emergent experiences I have had in the consulting room have not been private in this way. The unseen things I feel connected to in my office, whatever else they may be, are part of the context of my relationship with the particular person who is with me. That much I can tell, even though I cannot determine what those things are. It is a feeling of opening-into, of possibility, so it is generally welcome even when whatever will come next does not necessarily feel pleasant or fulfilling.

Now let me come full circle to my primary subject—the field. The experience of emergence is, to my mind, one of the most important ways in which any clinician can experience the interpersonal field. Conditions are not always right for it to take place, because it usually (but not always) requires a certain synergy of purpose between patient and analyst, a clinical collaboration that is not always available.[2] (Enactment, as I describe below, is one of the primary obstacles in this regard.) No doubt there are more prerequisites than a collaborative clinical atmosphere, but those other conditions are always unknown to us. We do not know why we have this kind of experience when we do. But in any moment in which my patient and I are working collaboratively, an experience of emergence is possible.

Is "depth" exclusively associated with the internal world?

Like emergence, the idea of depth is both closely associated with unconscious process and only infrequently theorized. Wachtel (2003,

2014), who wrote about the phenomenon in the third-person sense I have already described (i.e., some "it" has depth), concluded that psychoanalysts often lose sight of the fact that the idea of depth is a metaphor, mistaking it for a feature of the natural world and thereby creating some unfortunate effects on psychoanalytic understanding. Depth, Wachtel (2003) observed, is equated with profundity: the "farther down" something lies, the closer to the beginning, the more profound it is. Wachtel's primary objection to this equation is that it leads us to accept unthinkingly the view that earlier, "deeper" events in a person's history are therefore more profoundly influential than later events. For my present purpose, while I appreciate Wachtel's point, my primary objection is the equation of depth with internality. We take for granted that the internal is more profound than the external, and therefore more important in the creation of experience and living. Social interaction, wrote Wachtel (2003, pp. 20–21), "enter[s] into the psychological equation from the direction of the senses, that is, from the 'surface' rather than the 'depths.' From the vantage point of the depth metaphor, social influences are therefore at risk of appearing 'superficial.'"

Wachtel also quotes Greenberg and Mitchell (1983, p. 80), who, in their description of "drive/structure" models in psychoanalysis, make the point that in these models,

> social reality constitutes an overlay, a veneer superimposed upon the deeper, more "natural" fundaments of the psyche constituted by the drives. Any theory omitting or replacing the drives as the underlying motivational principle and, in addition, emphasizing the importance of personal and social relations with others is, from this point of view, superficial by definition, concerned with the "surface" areas of the personality, lacking "depth."

While today many—perhaps most—psychoanalysts are not adherents of drive/structure models, we are all nevertheless prisoners, to a certain degree, of assumptions contributed by those models. They are our history, and the wide acceptance that the internal life is profound and the social is superficial—and the interpersonal field is certainly social—is one of the artifacts of that history.

None of this is meant to deny the profundity of the internal; the clinical illustration I offer later in this paper should be enough to excise any impression that I feel that way. Instead, what I mean to argue is that profundity is not *exclusively* associated with the internal. As Wachtel points out, social influences can also be unconscious. One might say, in fact, that this was the great insight of Harry Stack Sullivan (e.g., 1956), who understood problems in living as the outcome of our dissociation, on the basis of anxiety, of significant parts of social living. We simply do not see, feel, or understand those parts of interactions with others that would call out too much anxiety if we were to grasp them. Just as social phenomena can be unconscious, they can also be emergent. That, as I have said, is my understanding of the interpersonal field. I hope that this point, too, will take on more substance in the clinical illustration.

The felt sense of emergence and the phenomenology of depth: depth as a field concept

Foehl (2014) brings the philosophy of Merleau-Ponty and the thinking of Bion to bear on the phenomenology of depth in psychoanalysis. Foehl's focus on experience—depth in the first person—and his revision of the idea of depth in terms of a contemporary epistemological perspective suitable for grasping the idea as a field concept make his work especially relevant to my consideration of the felt sense of emergence. In his essay, Foehl replaces the vertical, internal-world metaphor of depth with one rooted in relationships: between figure and ground ("form to field"), self to world, and subject to other. It is the relationship between our explicit experience of the foreground (for example, figure, self, or subject) and our less articulated sense of the background (ground, world, or other) that gives us the feeling of depth.[3] The vaguely perceived presence of the background—it is "there" but its meaning is unrealized in this moment— adds a dimension to our explicitly grasped experience.[4] In this way experience gains "an affective resonance and fullness . . . that would otherwise be flattened into either an univocal regularity of 'it is how I see it' or an undifferentiated haze of not specifying what might be experienced" (Foehl, 2014, p. 298).

I imagine "flattened" experience to be like a painting without perspective: its two dimensions allow no movement from the surface of the picture into its background; everything in the picture exists on the same plane. Add perspective, though, as European painters in the Renaissance learned to do, and the eye is free to travel from the painting's surface into any level of the background, and we can in that way discover spatial relations between elements existing at any layer of depth. But we do not need to formulate every one of those relations explicitly to be affected by their presence. Even to view for a moment a painting made with perspective awakens a recognition of the possibilities it offers. Depth is our awareness of the possibility that relations we have not yet imagined will emerge, and it appears only when those possibilities, like three-dimensional perspective, are already present and alive in our experience.

I think this feeling of possibility is closely related to Foehl's "affective resonance and fullness," and the felt sense of emergence, it seems to me, grows from both. The felt sense of emergence, we might say, is a manifestation of depth.

We can use the phenomenon of enactment to lend this point substance. Enactment is an example of a part of clinical process that we can certainly describe as emergent in the third-person sense, because it arises from unconscious sources; there is no sense of conscious volition. Because the unconscious root of enactment is, by definition, missing from its conscious experience, that experience is typically constricted and often rigid. Enactment feels as if it is just the way things are. One's own involvement with the other—that is, one's motivation to create and maintain the very state of affairs that is later revealed to have been problematic—is invisible. It often feels as if the enactment is the other's fault, as if one is being provoked into an uncomfortable affective state that one would be able to avoid if it were not for the troublesome behavior of the other; or as if one is reacting to the other in a way that is entirely reasonable.

And so enactment, despite being emergent in the third-person sense, is perhaps the epitome of the kind of clinical process that, in Foehl's words, is "flattened into . . . univocal regularity." Could any experience be a better illustration of what it means to say (again in Foehl's words) that "It is how I see it"?[5] Enactment is defined precisely by that taken-for-granted attitude, that feeling that what is happening in the clinical relatedness means what I think it means, and nothing more. Depth and ambiguity collapse. This point is recognized by analysts everywhere. The Barangers (1961–1962/2008, p. 799), for instance, write:

> It could be said that every event in the analytic field is experienced in the "as-if" category . . . [It is crucial that] each thing or event in the field be at the same time something else. If this essential ambiguity is lost, the analysis also disappears.

Now consider the new, spontaneous perceptions of oneself and the other that, when they become available, resolve enactments (Stern, 2004, 2010).[6] These new perceptions reveal, often quite suddenly, a new and different meaning in what has been transpiring in the clinical relatedness. Sometimes it is the analyst whose perception changes first, sometimes the patient (Stern, 2003, 2004). It does not really matter which participant initiates the new perception, because in either scenario the new perception leads the one who develops it to treat the other differently, and that new and different treatment, and the new affective atmosphere that accompanies it, generally awakens in the other participant an awareness of the same new perception. This new grasp of the relationship often arrives with a felt sense of emergence. Simultaneously a new feeling of depth appears in the interpersonal situation or, in a phrase of Foehl's that I like, a "synchronic experience of multiply layered conscious and unconscious processes" (2014, p. 298).

During an enactment, we can say, the foreground and background of experience, or conscious and unconscious, are broken off from each other. Or we can say that they are fused. Either metaphor works, because both portray a consciousness that no longer exists against a background.[7] Things are flattened; there is no depth. There is a sense of certainty about things that are perhaps better left uncertain, because uncertainty allows possibility. The possibility of new meaning is shut down. Things are what they are, nothing more.

But as the new perception of oneself and the other resolves the enactment, conscious and unconscious come back into communication with each other (see Ogden, 1992). Foreground disembeds from background, once again existing in relation to it. The possibility that things could be otherwise, or *also* otherwise, returns and the picture deepens.

In the cellar: a clinical illustration

I turn now to a clinical illustration of what I mean by the felt sense of emergence. This example is not the report of an enactment and its resolution. It is instead a less difficult kind of moment, the kind of clinical interaction in which the analyst feels basically good about his or her participation and that I have elsewhere called "continuous productive unfolding" (Stern, 2009a).

First, a word of caution. To select a moment, or a case, that describes the quality of emergence is liable to suggest that the material selected is worthy of special note, thereby drawing attention from the fact that the state of affairs it describes is part of everyday analytic work. That is a risk I will have to take to make my point. I have chosen to write about a portion of one clinical session, but in order to underline the ordinariness of the phenomenon I will also say something about the many other moments of this kind that took place during that treatment.

The illustration comes from the treatment of George, a married artist in his seventies with grown children, who continued to spend most of his time in the studio creating art. George was capable and intelligent, and obviously creative. He attended treatment three times per week. On the day in question, about four years into his treatment, he walked into my consulting room and, as usual, sat down in the reclining chair, leaned all the way back, and closed his eyes. It had never seemed necessary to discuss using the couch, because George evolved this posture naturally, and it always seemed to me to serve the same purpose: it allowed him a more intimate kind of contact with his internal world.

On this day, George began telling me about Ted Hughes's English translation of Ovid's *Metamorphoses*, which he was reading that week. (He was an avid reader, especially of poetry.) In particular, he was taken with a tale about a nymph who, raped by a river god, turned into water and flowed into her attacker, becoming part of him. George thought there was something both intriguing and sexy about this. By "sexy," he said, he meant that turning into water and flowing into the attacker was sensually appealing and would feel good. He said that he also felt that the feeling of becoming part of someone else was similar to something he sometimes experienced with me, as if I were the river god and he were the nymph.

At the time, I was already familiar with the theme in the transference to which George was referring—the characterization of me as powerful and arbitrary, sometimes sadistic, sometimes loving, and him as smaller, weaker, always loving, and deeply attached to me, resulting in his vulnerability to feeling rejected and hurt. On this day he added the element of sensual pleasure and outright eroticism, not to mention rape—themes that continued to be developed in many of our future sessions.

I had been through a great many sessions with George in which most or all of the content concerned "the cellar"—our shorthand for a faceless older man's sexual abuse of George, events that may have taken place in the basement of George's parents' house when he was very young, perhaps four or five years old. George had been in analysis once before, thirty years earlier, but the cellar events, whatever they were, had barely come up then, and had not been explored. Despite his introspective proclivity, George himself had never really thought about these memories or fantasies—a fact that, by this point, given our immersion in these matters, was startling to him. Despite his current interest, however, there was really nothing in George's mind at this point that he felt he could count on to be a literal memory of such events, so the scenarios of the abuse that he recounted in great detail could not be taken as factual. They were creations, or re-creations. But they were still highly significant to George, and therefore to me. Moreover, George felt as if he were not their author. During our many sessions together, what he related to me arrived unbidden in his mind.

George and I were "in the cellar" over and over again. Sometimes I was a misty kind of observer or witness, barely there at all; sometimes I was simply absent. But my presence, as significant as it was (I will have more to say about this), was not the main event. In the cellar, the focus was on George, who was vivid, and the faceless man, who was shadowy. As the nature of the relationship between these two changed during a session, George's self-states shifted. I could feel it. No doubt I responded with my own self-state shifts. Sometimes George was a helpless, frightened boy who was being abused; sometimes there was pleasure and perhaps something like love between him and the faceless man; and sometimes George was ferocious—a big, dangerous cat, a predator with long, sharp claws. When he was a cat, or at least in the cat-state, George might feel rage, and he often imagined himself at those moments on the threshold of a mysterious, darkened room within which, he thought, there might be a lot of blood. While the atmosphere at such times could be chilling, I was never particularly uncomfortable. George certainly could be angry with me, sometimes very angry; and there were times, sometimes extending over several weeks, when this was the focus of our sessions. But he was never angry with me in the cellar. His cellar rage was not directed toward me. Instead, I was a facilitating witness (see Stern, 2009a, 2009b, 2012, 2013) to events that generally seemed to me to be self-affirming on George's part, even the rageful ones. George's fantasies gave shape to affect states—states of self—that I think he needed to be able to experience more explicitly than he had in the past. To do that, he needed me to be there to know these things with him. My witnessing presence, I believe, contributed to his capacity to formulate what he told me, and then, eventually, to step back and think about these things for the first time in his life.

The actual physical events that took place in the cellar were seldom clearly discernible to George, although they were clearly sexual in nature. His visual images of these events were vague. What I can say about his feelings and fantasized bodily experience was that he could be terrified, sexually aroused, in physical pain, loved and loving, and worried and sad about the possibility of losing the faceless man's interest. Unsurprisingly, there was a good deal of fantasy about penises and long, penis-like objects in his mouth, throat, and anus. George identifies as heterosexual. The idea of sex with men used to intrigue him, but when he tried it he did not feel aroused. Perhaps he would have been interested in both men and women with or without whatever took place in the cellar; or perhaps he was drawn to sex with men because of what took place in the cellar. Perhaps both alternatives are true. It did not really matter, to me or to him.

Consider all of this as background for what happened on the day when George told me the story about the nymph and the river god. I listened to his thoughts after he told me about the tale, and after he had related the story to his feelings about me. After a while, I said something very simple, more or less spontaneously, and from deep within my involvement in the moment and with him: "It reminds me of the cellar." I imagined we were both probably thinking the same thing. Despite that feeling of mystery that comes with the sense of emergence, which I did feel, what I said seemed uncontroversial to me.

George was silent for maybe ten or fifteen seconds. Then he said in a low voice, "I'm stunned."

It seemed we had not been thinking the same thing at all. But George's response conveyed to me that, in response to my remark, an emergent experience had come about in his mind, too. I may have offered him the idea, but his intense affective reaction was the shock of recognition. You experience that only when you are suddenly faced with something that summons an answering, involuntary, emergent, and immediate sense in your own mind that this thing belongs to you.

My remark and the experience that gave rise to it were the outcome of a jointly created interactive and affective process that had formative properties. I did not *figure out* my way into the connection between the cellar and Ovid's tale; I *felt* my way into it. Even that way of putting it makes what I did sound more consciously volitional than it was, however.

What I said to George grew from living under the spell that he and I, without conscious intention, had cast together on our mutual history, the story of the nymph and the river god, and ourselves in that room, in that moment. My experience was the manifestation of the interpersonal field, in other words, not just of my individual capacity to think, know, or understand. Or, to put it another way, we should *always* understand the analyst's capacity to think, know, and understand in the clinical situation as a phenomenon of the field, not as the creation of the analyst's solitary mind. The analyst does not stand back and observe. She does her best work when living under the kind of spell George and I had cast. My thought grew from what was happening between us. It would have been impossible without it.

When George and I are in the cellar, the outside world retreats. It is quiet, the office is dim, and I have noticed that colors tend to darken. There is the illusion that I am right there in that cellar. I know something about how it looks, because George has told me all the details, and I imagine a version of those details for myself and inhabit them. (I am an onlooker to this process of imagining.) The ends of our sessions can be startling. It can be wrenching to return ourselves to the everyday world. That shock testifies to the depth of our involvement, our mutual absorption in the matters at hand. We are thoroughly immersed in a joint fantasy. What comes to exist between us is woven from the strands of George's inner life, from my fantasy of his fantasy life, from George's fantasy of my fantasy, and on and on. *Someone* is weaving this experience between us, but it does not feel to George or me that it is either one of us. We can say that our mutual experience is the invention of the third (Ogden, 1994, 2004; Benjamin, 2004), or that it constitutes the third. Of course that is true, but as illuminating as that concept is in many clinical contexts, it sheds no light on the phenomenon of emergence.

I hope I have managed to explain that the process of emergence in this case is not unique, even though the events between George and myself were particularly dramatic and moving. I could probably use as an example of emergence any other treatment of real depth. In fact, the quality of emergence has always been so central to me that I suspect that any one of the many case examples I have published in articles and books could serve as an illustration. Any collaborative treatment contains emergent moments, usually (but not always) during the periods of collaboration themselves (see note 2, below).

It is impossible to know for sure whether George's apparent sexual abuse actually took place. However, for various reasons, gleaned from his history and symptoms, I strongly suspect that some kind of traumatic sexual contact *did* occur. I believe that that sexual contact, the betrayal it represented, and especially the terrible rejection that seemed to bring it to an end (which limitations of space prevent me from discussing here)—or, rather, the means George devised to live with those things—shaped his life in various damaging and distressing ways. The images, fantasies, quasi-memories, and bodily sensations that George described almost continuously during many sessions, over several years, came to him without volition. Their flow, therefore, was itself emergent, and it felt that way to him.

I am convinced that all these things came to George when they did, in the forms that they did and in the order that they did, because he was *telling them to me*. It was the field we shaped between us, not just George's intention to free-associate (although he did indeed intend to do that), that was responsible for the emergence of this material. Just as the analyst's capacity to think, know, and understand is rooted in the field, so is the patient's freedom (or lack thereof) to formulate his experience (Stern, 2013).

More often than not, rather than trying to interpret George's cellar experiences by converting them into some other frame of reference, I accepted them at face value. If I imagined they had symbolic import, I usually kept that thought to myself (my comment that "It reminds me of the cellar" was an immediate exception to this observation); and if the cellar experiences were vague and hard to understand, I usually did not encourage George to clarify them. He knew perfectly well that I was wondering about what all this might mean, beyond what it signified literally; and, of course, he wondered, too. But despite sharing that attitude, we usually allowed the material to take us wherever it was going. We were leaves on the stream. It seemed important for the meanings in George's experience to have a chance to emerge by themselves. The atmosphere between us during the sessions when George was in the cellar was not flattened and univocal. I sensed depth and possibilities for the growth of meaning. It usually felt to me that offering interpretations of our time in that awful cellar would have been heavy-handed, risking intellectualization.

I do not wish to claim that proceeding in this way is always best. With other patients, at moments when it seems to further the work, I go about things differently, querying and offering interpretive interventions. But with George, most of the time, at least while he was in the cellar, it seemed best to proceed in the way that I did. When I did have something to say, my comments were generally intended to expand the material along the narrative lines it already seemed to be following. My interventions, in other words, were frequently—to borrow a useful term from another frame of reference—*unsaturated*.

I hope that I have communicated in this illustration the quality of felt emergence that frequently characterized this treatment. I hope that this material conveys what Edgar Levenson (1982, pp. 11–12; original emphasis) writes in one of my favorite passages from his work: patient and analyst feel that

> *some* process is going on which they have not initiated or energized. There is the remarkable experience of being carried along by something larger than both therapist and patient: A true sense of an interpersonal field results. *The therapist learns to ride the process rather than to carry the patient.*

Notes

1 This is a briefer version of a chapter that previously appeared as "Introduction: emergent properties of the interpersonal field," in Stern (2015, pp. 1–34). It is reprinted with kind permission from Taylor & Francis, LLC.
2 Sometimes, as Stuart Pizer (personal communication, 2014) points out, an episode of felt emergence takes place at a moment when a clinical collaboration is not particularly notable—although even at those times the episode seems to depend on *previous* collaboration. He writes, "I have experienced certain moments of emergence as the yield of a *preceding* period of collaboration. This happened with one patient, for example, after a weekend that followed weeks of collaborative process. On that particular day, though, the collaboration was not particularly foregrounded or explicitly experienced. The immediate impetus for the sense of emergence we both experienced was that she took a step based on the earlier work . . . and we were there."
3 See also Hoffman (1998), whose "dialectical-constructivist" presentation of conscious experience as the outcome of the relation of an explicit foreground to an implicit background is similar in certain respects to what Foehl has to say.
4 This vaguely experienced background is what phenomenological and existential philosophers such as Merleau-Ponty and Gadamer mean by "being." Being is never fully manifest. It is always *more* than consciousness, but "more" in a way that has no explicit meaning as yet. So we can think of the experience of depth as the impression created by our awareness of the contextualization of consciousness in being. Gadamer (1960, pp. 443–444) calls being "the infinity of the unsaid" (phrase translated and quoted by D.E. Linge, 1976). He writes that the shape of the unsaid, which changes with the content being expressed in words, plays an important role in establishing the meaning of whatever *is* said.

5   In my frame of reference, what is missing in the experience of enactment is dissociated. Dissociated subjectivity is a significant portion of what I refer to as unformulated experience (Stern, 1997). Remember that Foehl (2014, p. 298) suggests if experience loses the "affective resonance and fullness" of depth, it becomes either "flattened into an univocal regularity" (see the text) or dispersed into "an undifferentiated haze of not specifying what might be experienced." The latter phrase is a good description of what I mean by unformulated experience. What I would say, then, in Foehl's terms, is that enactment leads to a flattening of conscious experience and the maintenance of the dissociated portion in a kind of undifferentiated, unsymbolized haze (see Stern, 1997, 2010).
6   For clinical illustrations of enactment and its resolution, see Stern (1997, 2010, 2013).
7   To offer an account of multiple self theory here would distract from my primary argument. But I do think of enactment in those terms. For presentations of that view, see Stern (2004, 2010).

References

Baranger, M. and Baranger, W. (1961–1962/2008). The analytic situation as a dynamic field. *International Journal of Psychoanalysis*, 89:795–826 (originally published in Spanish; this is a translation of the 1969 revision of the original article).
Benjamin, J. (2004). Beyond doer and done to: an intersubjective view of thirdness. *Psychoanalytic Quarterly*, 73:5–46.
Boston Change Process Study Group (2010). *Change in Psychotherapy: A Unifying Paradigm*. New York: W.W. Norton & Co.
Coburn, W. (2013). *Psychoanalytic Complexity: Clinical Attitudes for Therapeutic Change*. Hove: Routledge.
Foehl, J. (2014). A phenomenology of depth. *Psychoanalytic Dialogues*, 24:289–303.
Gadamer, H.-G. (1960). *Wahrheit und Methode: Grundzüge Einer Philosophische Hermeneutik* [*Truth and Method: Fundamentals of Philosophical Hermeneutics*]. Tübingen: Mohr.
Greenberg, J.R. and Mitchell, S.A. (1983). *Object Relations in Psychoanalytic Theory*. Cambridge, MA: Harvard University Press.
Hoffman, I.Z. (1998). *Ritual and Spontaneity in the Psychoanalytic Process: A Dialectical-Constructivist View*. Hillsdale, NJ: The Analytic Press.
Levenson, E.A. (1982). Follow the fox: an inquiry into the vicissitudes of psychoanalytic supervision. *Contemporary Psychoanalysis*, 18:1–15.
Linge, D.E. (1976). Editor's introduction. In H.-G. Gadamer, *Philosophical Hermeneutics*, trans. D.E. Linge. Berkeley: University of California Press, pp. xi–lviii.
Ogden, T.H. (1992). The dialectically constituted/decentred subject of psychoanalysis, I: The Freudian subject. *International Journal of Psychoanalysis*, 73:517–526.
Ogden, T.H. (1994). The analytic third: working with intersubjective facts. *International Journal of Psychoanalysis*, 75:3–19.

Ogden, T.H. (2004). The analytic third: implications for psychoanalytic theory and technique. *Psychoanalytic Quarterly*, 73:167–195.

Pizer, S. (2014). Personal communication.

Seligman, S. (2005). Nonlinear dynamic systems theory as a metatheory for psychoanalysis. *Psychoanalytic Dialogues*, 24:648–662.

Stern, D.B. (1990). Courting surprise: unbidden perceptions in clinical practice. *Contemporary Psychoanalysis*, 26:452–478.

Stern, D.B. (1997). *Unformulated Experience: From Dissociation to Imagination in Psychoanalysis*. New York: Routledge.

Stern, D.B. (2003). The fusion of horizons: dissociation, enactment, and understanding. *Psychoanalytic Dialogues*, 13:843–873.

Stern, D.B. (2004). The eye sees itself: dissociation, enactment, and the achievement of conflict. *Contemporary Psychoanalysis*, 40:197–237.

Stern, D.B. (2009a). Partners in thought: a clinical process theory of narrative. *Psychoanalytic Quarterly*, 78:701–731.

Stern, D.B. (2009b). Shall the twain meet? Metaphor, dissociation, and co-occurrence. *Psychoanalytic Inquiry*, 29:79–90.

Stern, D.B. (2010). *Partners in Thought: Working with Unformulated Experience, Dissociation, and Enactment*. New York and London: Routledge.

Stern, D.B. (2012). Witnessing across time: accessing the present from the past and the past from the present. *Psychoanalytic Quarterly*, 81:53–81.

Stern, D.B. (2013). Relational freedom and therapeutic action. *Journal of the American Psychoanalytic Association*, 61:227–255.

Stern, D.B. (2015). *Relational Freedom: Emergent Properties of the Interpersonal Field*. New York: Routledge.

Sullivan, H.S. (1956). Selective inattention. In *Clinical Studies in Psychiatry*. New York: Norton, pp. 38–76.

Wachtel, P.L. (2003). The surface and the depths: the metaphor of depth in psychoanalysis and the ways in which it can mislead. *Contemporary Psychoanalysis*, 39:5–26.

Wachtel, P.L. (2014). Depth, perception, and action: past, present, and future. *Psychoanalytic Dialogues*, 24:332–340.

Chapter 13

Field theories and process theories

Juan Tubert-Oklander

I would like to start with an overtly categorical statement: *there is no such thing as psychoanalytical field theory*. There are rather quite a few psychoanalytical field *theories*, a whole family of related approaches to psychoanalysis, and as such they all show a family resemblance, although they are by no means equal (as the members of a family usually are). Or, perhaps, we should talk about psychoanalytical field *theorizing*, meaning a whole new way of constructing not only psychoanalytical theories, but also our very experience of what transpires in our analytic offices during the sessions, and the way in which we think, talk, write or discuss it.

Field theories emerged in physics when it was discovered that certain phenomena, such as magnetism and gravitation, could not be accounted for in terms of the traditional chains of cause and effect, but rather required a description of what was happening simultaneously in every point of the event space under consideration. The limits of such space are only pragmatic, since the field continues to expand far beyond our capacity to detect it, and is theoretically infinite. This is *classical field theory* in physics, which differs from contemporary quantum field theory, which we are not going to discuss now. *A classical field is a function defined over some region of space and time.*

These concepts were imported into psychology by Gestalt theorists, who were particularly interested in the study of "wholes," as opposed to that of "parts" (Koffka, 1935; Merleau-Ponty, 1942/1963; Katz, 1943/1979). This represented a rupture from the traditional analytic approach of natural science of breaking up the objects of inquiry into parts and studying them, with the conviction that knowing their properties would automatically bring about a full understanding of the whole. This kind of research does wonders in explaining the functioning of clockwork, but it fails when dealing with living beings, persons, relations, groups, or societies.

Hence a new perspective was needed, one that started from the study of wholes, before considering the parts. This was called "holism." From such perspective, *the whole was considered to be more than, prior to, and more elementary than the sum of its parts.* In other words, the relationship between the whole and the parts constituted a field (Tubert-Oklander, 2013a).

Kurt Lewin, a German psychologist who migrated to the US in 1933, introduced this concept in the socio-psychological study of behavior in the 1940s. His original studies had been in biology, so he had a solid foundation in natural sciences, which was bound to influence his theoretical approach. When he turned to psychology, he studied and worked with the founders of the Gestalt school, such as Max Wertheimer and Wolfgang Kohler. Consequently, he was clearly interested in the total situation in which human events take place, and the essential confluence of individuals and their environment. This led him to resort to physical fields as a metaphor, in order to describe and account for the interactions between the individual and his/her total environment. His maps of the individual's life space are rather schematic—but highly suggestive—attempts to describe and account for the highly complex individual–environment interaction that gives birth to all human experience, thought, behavior, and relations (Lewin, 1948, 1951).

It should be noted that Lewin and Harry Stack Sullivan had a close relationship and a mutual influence. Sullivan's field theory, which focused on interpersonal relations and their insertion in the social context, was the first to introduce the field concept in the realm of psychoanalysis (Sullivan, 1953).

During that same decade of the 1940s in which Lewin and Sullivan were working on this approach, the French philosopher Maurice Merleau-Ponty (1945/1962) developed his own field concept, also derived from Gestalt psychology. However, unlike the other two theoreticians, he did not base it on physics, but rather on Heidegger's existential conception of human experience. Indeed, he issued a stern criticism of Gestalt psychology's attempt to find causal explanations for psychological phenomena, akin to those of the natural sciences. On the contrary, his conception of the field was both phenomenological (in Husserl's terms) and existential (in Heidegger's).

Interestingly enough, these three authors all died in their fifties. Merleau-Ponty, who was born eighteen years after Lewin and sixteen after Sullivan, outlived the other two by more than a decade and left a highly pregnant set of philosophical and psychological writings, in spite of his untimely death at the age of fifty-three.

Enrique Pichon-Rivière, founder of psychoanalysis and group analysis in Argentina, who had a major influence on Madeleine and especially Willy Baranger, was also deeply interested in the essential unity of the intrapsychic and social realms. He was clearly influenced by Lewin, whom he often quoted; and, even though he does not mention Sullivan in his published writings, the striking similarity of their approaches and the testimony of those who knew and worked with Pichon-Rivière strongly suggest that he read and was influenced by Sullivan.

Pichon-Rivière uses the field concept in order to depict and explain the perpetual dialectic of the inner and the outer, which is the very stuff of human existence. Thus, he writes,

> The most important field in psychiatry is the intrapsychic field, what we call the inner field of an interpersonal and group nature, meaning that it is the psychological field made of a certain number of people who act in a particular dynamic relationship.
> (Pichon-Rivière, 1979, p. 36; my translation)

But he not only poses this essential unity of individual and environment but also introduces the temporal dimension of a process. His concept of an interpersonal bond fuses the inner (intrapsychic) and outer (interpersonal) dimensions of relationships in terms of their dynamics and evolution. The internal bonds and the external bonds are integrated in a dialectic spiral process, by means of which what was originally external becomes internal, then external again, and so on. There is a fluid interchange between the two fields, which helps to establish the differentiation between the inside and the outside, while at the same time keeping a deep continuity between them. Hence, individual and society form an indissoluble unit, a single dynamic field, because we all carry society within us: "One cannot think in terms of a distinction between the individual and society. It is an abstraction, a reductionism that we cannot accept" (Pichon-Rivière, 1979, p. 57; my translation).

Pichon-Rivière felt that orthodox psychoanalysis, centered on the intrapersonal concept of instinctual drives, excluded the most important social and political dimensions. Hence, in his later years he preferred to speak of "social psychology" rather than "psychoanalysis." His particular brand of social psychology was a highly complex admixture of Lewinian theory, Marxist sociological theory, his particular understanding of psychoanalysis and group analysis, and his own theoretical, technical, and clinical developments.

Willy and Madeleine Baranger, who had studied and worked with Pichon-Rivière—indeed, Willy had been analyzed by him—developed a more strictly psychoanalytic concept of the analytic field. In their seminal paper "The Analytic Situation as a Dynamic Field" (Baranger and Baranger, 1961–1962/2008) they introduced the idea that the analytic situation should be understood in terms of the total situation. It is a field, in which a change in any of its elements affects all the others, and any new occurrence is the result of the combined effect of all the elements, their structural organization, and their dynamics.

One curious detail is that the Barangers mention Lewin in their original article when introducing the field concept (perhaps as a result of Pichon-Rivière's influence). However, when the same article appeared in their 1969 book *Problems of the Analytic Field*, Lewin's name had disappeared, to be replaced with that of Merleau-Ponty (Churcher, 2008). Surely the French philosopher's work was much nearer to their humanistic upbringing, as philosophers, than Lewin's physical analogy.

This certainly reminds us both of Sullivan's interpersonal theory and the bipersonal psychology introduced by the members of the British Independent group, such as John Rickman, Donald Winnicott, and Michael Balint, but it is much more than that. The analytic field is not only the emergent result of the conscious and unconscious interaction between two human beings, starting from their explicit contract and developing along the lines of transference–countertransference phenomena. It also includes all sorts of elements that are not usually taken into account, such as the arrangements and other characteristics of the analytic room, the house or building in which it is placed, and the part of town in which all this happens, the personal demeanor, history, personality, values, and beliefs of both parties (including the analyst's theoretical and technical persuasion), and the whole social, historical, cultural, and political context (Zac, 1968).

Nonetheless, the Barangers, unlike their teacher and mentor Pichon-Rivière, did not extend their field concept beyond the limits of the office to include the socio-political dimension. This was done by José Bleger (1967), David Liberman (1976), and Joel Zac (1968, 1971), also disciples and continuators of the work of Pichon-Rivière, who described and analyzed the much wider implicit, and often invisible, frame that surrounds, determines, contains, and gives meaning to the more visible interactions between analyst and patient that constitute the analytic process.

It is in this sense that it may be said that the analytic field is not created by the bipersonal interaction, both conscious and unconscious, but that *a significant part of it is already there before the two parties meet for the first time*. Of course, the peculiar organization of any given analytic field is determined and modulated by the distinctive characteristics of both members of the pair and their mutual relation, but it is also largely a consequence and expression of their shared social, political, cultural, historical, geographical, and ecological context, which usually remains in the background, until some turn in the evolution of the field forces us to analyze it. It is also determined by the initial definition of the nature of the work they are going to carry out together, and their respective participation and contribution to it, which was established in the contract and later expanded, developed, and reinforced by their mutual interactions (Tubert-Oklander, 2013b).

This raises a new point of discussion. The field conception of the analytic situation gives us a simultaneous description of all the significant factors and their mutual influence. This is an atemporal or synchronic view and analysis of what happens in the treatment, which is in sharp contrast to the sequential, temporal, or diachronic descriptions that characterized classical psychoanalysis. But of course the analytic dialogue and relation have much to do with history, and they also evolve in time. How, then, is this temporal dimension included in our field theories?

In the first place, history is an essential part of the *content* of the analytic dialogue, of what analyst and patient discuss. The temporal dimension is then a symbolic element in the *hic et nunc* of the atemporal analytic field. But it is also true that the field is not at all static, but dynamic, and evolves over time. The problem is that field theories, on account of their observational and theoretical strategy of constructing a view based on a simultaneous description of all the significant factors in the situation, are at a loss when they have to incorporate and account for the temporal phenomenon of *change*.

It is not the case of the analytic field theoreticians ignoring the unquestionable fact that change is not only a part but also the *raison d'être* of an analytic treatment. On the contrary, all of them stress that the field is inherently dynamic and try to account for its positive evolution, which is the very stuff of therapeutic change. The Barangers, for example, faithful to their Kleinian upbringing, attribute such changes only to the power of the analyst's interpretations. The problem is that such explanations are far from satisfactory. Moreover, they reintroduce the outdated cause-and-effect model that field theories set out to transcend in the first place.

This is where we sorely require the introduction of a *process theory* (or theories). The concept of the analytic process is by no means new—it has been with us from the very beginning of psychoanalysis—but classical psychoanalytic theory has traditionally described it as a sequence of events that takes place within the patient, and which is initiated by the introduction of the analytic frame and fueled by the analyst's interpretations. Hence, from this perspective, the analyst as a person is not a part of the analytic process, albeit his professional interventions act as a cause for it.

This is a far cry from the holistic view provided by analytic field theories, which necessarily includes the analyst as an intrinsic part of the field. So, what we need in order to complement field theories is *a holistic process theory*.

Such a theory was developed in Buenos Aires by Enrique Pichon-Rivière and a close group of co-workers and disciples, including Bleger, Liberman, Jorge Mom, Edgardo Rolla, and the Barangers, between 1954 and 1958 (Baranger, 1979/2009). It centered on the concept of a *spiral dialectic process*, characteristic of the analytic situation and treatment (Pichon-Rivière, 1971a, 1971b; Zito Lema, 1976).

The spiral has traditionally been a symbol for evolution and change. A bi-dimensional spiral looks somewhat like a circle, but not quite, since every circular turn comes back to the beginning a little further from its center, so we end up with an unlimited series of continuous, ever-widening circles. This is indeed an apt metaphor for the analytic process, which returns over and over again to the same subjects and themes, but each time with a wider and deeper understanding of their meaning.

But Pichon-Rivière's spiral was three-dimensional, since it included not only the circular and widening dimensions, but also an advance on each turn. Thus, the resulting image was that of an ever-widening and forward-moving, funnel-shaped cone—something like a whirlwind. There are in it, therefore, three simultaneous movements: a *circular* one that repeatedly returns to the same point, which represents the essential themes of an analysis; a *widening* one, which determines that each turn makes a larger circle, representing the increasing depth and subtlety of understanding; and a *forward* one, which resembles the lead of a screw thread and corresponds to the progress of an analysis.

To these, I would add a fourth movement of *displacement*—a lateral movement of the whole spiral, pretty much like the advance of a tornado, which moves into new areas. This would represent sea-changes in the evolution of a whole analysis, which approaches new problematics, and the growing shared understanding that provides both parties with new views on the nature of the work they are doing together and new opportunities for exploration. But this requires that the analytic dialogue turn upon itself in order to question its underlying assumptions and analyze their implications. Hence, the analytic process must be *reflective*.

Pichon-Rivière's conception of the spiral process is *dialectical*, not in the Hegelian tradition, but in that of Socrates' *maieutics*—the intellectual midwifery of helping someone give birth to an idea. His focus was on the *cognitive* aspects of the treatment—the development of understanding—but the analytic process also necessarily includes an *affective* and a *conative* (interactional) evolution of the analytic relationship, which have come to the fore in recent years, with the development of the relational trend in psychoanalysis. These three dimensions—cognitive, affective, and conative—may be conceived as the "Golden Braid" of the analytic process, which always blends thought, feeling, and action (Tubert-Oklander, 2013b).

One of the most important aspects of the process concept is that, even though it may be initiated, fueled, and modulated by both parties' purposive actions, it has its own course and momentum, much as winds and tides do, which are independent of the will and thought of analyst and patient alike, so that they can only be accepted, observed, and analyzed.

Processes should be clearly differentiated from the kind of causal chains that are traditionally described by the natural sciences. *A process is an evolution in time that has an organization, a direction, and an intentionality of its own.* It is self-regulated and its organization and dynamics steer its course toward some goals, which are unconscious for both parties, although they can be partially identified and analyzed by means of their interpretative dialogue. Hence, process theories reintroduce the temporal dimension into the atemporal field theories by means of a holistic conception that is akin and complementary to them.

Even though Pichon-Rivière's process theory came about a few years before the Barangers' field theory, they both emerged from a similar intellectual climate and their shared theoretical and technical interests. It is true that the field theory came after that of the spiral process and is fully compatible with the latter, but it does not directly derive from it. The two theories are different, but they share a family resemblance—as might be expected on account of the close and intense relation between their creators. Neither is meant to replace the other and they are truly complementary, since they both approach a single human phenomenon—the psychoanalytic treatment—but do so from different vantage points and try to answer a different set of questions about it.

Of course, there are other possible field or process theories. The two theoretical strategies—namely, to study the analytic situation in either structural and simultaneous or temporal and evolutionary terms—generate two distinct but mutually related families of theories. I have focused on Pichon-Rivière's and the Barangers' concepts because I know them best, and they have had the greatest influence on my own thought and practice, but I have also briefly added my own development of the process concept, on which I expound extensively in *Theory of Psychoanalytical Practice: A Relational Process Approach* (Tubert-Oklander, 2013b).

What I want to emphasize here is that we need to have both field and process theories in order to construct a holistic, relational, and fully dynamic approach to psychoanalytical practice and thinking. The comparative assets and liabilities of the various field and process theories are still to be established (Donnel Stern (2013a, 2013b) has already made one such approach in the case of field theory), but I am inclined to think that it is not a case of winnowing out bad theories in order to keep only the good ones. Rather, I believe that the various theories are the outcome of different trainings, traditions, and assumptions, and that they may well function as alternative theories and coexist in a conceptual space as part of the ongoing dialogue between those of us who share this holistic perspective.

Leaving behind the narcissism of little differences, the real opposition is that between those who still adhere to a naturalistic, linear, mechanistic, and atomistic explanation of human events and those of us who conceive mind, relationships, and the analytic treatment as intrinsically dynamic organic wholes that have both a synchronic structure and a diachronic evolution.

References

Baranger, M. and Baranger, W. (1961–1962/2008). The analytic situation as a dynamic field. *International Journal of Psycho-Analysis*, 89: 795–826 (originally published in Spanish as La situación analítica como campo dinámico. *Revista Uruguaya de Psicoanálisis*, 4(1): 3–54; reprinted with small revisions in Baranger, W. and Baranger, M., *Problemas del campo psicoanalítico*. Buenos Aires: Kargieman, 1969, pp. 129–164).

Baranger, W. (1979/2009). "Spiral process" and "dynamic field." In Baranger, M. and Baranger, W., *The Work of Confluence: Listening and Interpreting in the Psychoanalytic Field*. Ed. E.L. Glocer Fiorini. London: International Psychoanalytic Association/Karnac, pp. 45–61 (originally published in Spanish as "Proceso en espiral" y "campo dinámico." *Revista Uruguaya de Psicoanálisis*, 59: 17–32).

Bleger, J. (1967). Psycho-analysis of the psycho-analytic frame. *International Journal of Psycho-Analysis*, 48: 511–519.

Churcher, J. (2008). Some notes on the English translation of *The Analytic Situation as a Dynamic Field* by Willy and Madeleine Baranger. *International Journal of Psycho-Analysis*, 89: 785–793.

Katz, D. (1943/1979). *Gestalt Psychology*. Westport, CT: Greenwood Publishing Group.

Koffka, K. (1935). *Principles of Gestalt Psychology*. New York: Harcourt, Brace & Co.

Lewin, K. (1948). *Resolving Social Conflicts*. New York: Harper.

Lewin, K. (1951). *Field Theory in Social Science*. New York: Harper.

Liberman, D. (1976). *Comunicación y psicoanálisis [Communication and Psychoanalysis]*. Buenos Aires: Alex.

Merleau-Ponty, M. (1942/1963). *The Structure of Behavior*. Trans. Alden L. Fisher. Boston, MA: Beacon Press.

Merleau-Ponty, M. (1945/1962). *Phenomenology of Perception*. Trans. C. Smith. London: Routledge (originally published in French as *Phénoménologie de la perception*. Paris: Gallimard).

Pichon-Rivière, E. (1971a). *El proceso grupal. Del psicoanálisis a la psicología social (1) [The Group Process: From Psychoanalysis to Social Psychology (1)]*. Buenos Aires: Nueva Visión.

Pichon-Rivière, E. (1971b). *La psiquiatría, una nueva problemática. Del psicoanálisis a la psicología social (2) [A New Problematic for Psychiatry: From Psychoanalysis to Social Psychology (2)]*. Buenos Aires: Nueva Visión.

Pichon-Rivière, E. (1979). *Teoría del vínculo [Theory of the Bond]*. Buenos Aires: Nueva Visión.

Stern, D.B. (2013a). Field theory in psychoanalysis, Part I: Harry Stack Sullivan and Madeleine and Willy Baranger. *Psychoanalytic Dialogues*, 23: 487–501.

Stern, D.B. (2013b). Field theory in psychoanalysis, Part 2: Bionian field theory and contemporary interpersonal/relational psychoanalysis. *Psychoanalytic Dialogues*, 23: 630–645.

Sullivan, H.S. (1953). *The Interpersonal Theory of Psychiatry*. Ed. H.S. Perry and M.L. Gawel. New York: Norton.

Tubert-Oklander, J. (2013a). Field, process, and metaphor. In S.M. Katz (Ed.), *Metaphor and Fields: Common Ground, Common Language, and the Future of Psychoanalysis*. New York: Routledge, pp. 162–181.

Tubert-Oklander, J. (2013b). *Theory of Psychoanalytical Practice: A Relational Process Approach*. London: International Psychoanalytical Association/Karnac.

Zac, J. (1968). Relación semana–fin de semana. Encuadre y acting out [The week–weekend relation: the setting and acting-out]. *Revista de Psicoanálisis*, 25(1): 27–91 (includes comments by N. Rascovsky de Bisi, D. Liberman, and E. H. Rolla, as well as the author's response).

Zac, J. (1971). Un enfoque metodológico del establecimiento del encuadre [A methodological approach to the establishment of the setting]. *Revista de Psicoanálisis*, 28(3): 593–610.

Zito Lema, V. (1976). *Conversaciones con Enrique Pichon-Rivière. Sobre el arte y la locura* [*Conversations with Enrique Pichon-Rivière: On Art and Madness*]. Buenos Aires: Timerman Editores.

Chapter 14

Commentary on field theory presentations

Joseph Lichtenberg

What is the scope or range of field theory?

One view is that field theory is a designator that covers the entire psychoanalytic endeavor – "the field of psychoanalysis." Another view is that field theory is a way to conceptualize any specific moment in a particular analysis. In this usage analyst and analysand are viewed as co-creating an emergent, flexibly changing field. Analyst and analysand individually and jointly influence the field. And, once emergent, the field influences the lived experience of both analyst and analysand.

What perspectives are emphasized in field theory?

One perspective emphasizes the role of reflection by analyst and analysand in creating the field. The analysand provides the principal source of information upon which he and the analyst reflect. The analysand begins with whatever reflective capacities he brings to the developing field and gradually moves along with the analyst toward increasing exploratory reflection. The analyst reflects on the analysand's narrative and her parallel narrative. When the analyst's reflection is more conceptually based, she focuses on emotion-centered patterns of intentions and goals; when her reflection is more reverie based, she focuses on fantasy and dream imagery. The experience and reflections of both analyst and analysand are impacted by non-specific aspects of the ambience of the emergent field. Permutations in the field result from whether analyst's and analysand's recognition of patterns of motivation and dream imagery is sequential, disparate, or simultaneous.

Another perspective is euphemistically referred to as "the field seen by a fly on the wall." This broad overview takes in the activity of the entire field both at a moment in time, like a photograph, or over a period of time, like a video. The emphasis is on the interplay of experience – analyst and analysand each affecting the other – co-creating new contexts and affective ambience. This view is a construct about two people's experience in a dyadic field rather than each person's perception of the ongoing experience. Each participant is too constrained by the power of his or her subjectivity fully to experience or conceptualize the entire dyadic field. Nonetheless, this overview provides field theory with an extension of interpersonal and intersubjective theories and acts as a counter to a strictly intrapsychic focus on what Stolorow has called the myth of the isolated mind (Stolorow and Atwood, 1992).

Is there – or can there be – one field theory?

Since the beginning of psychoanalysis a search for common ground has been impeded by the tyranny of words. Adherence to theories centering on constructs like dual drives, Oedipal conflicts, tripartite model, defense interpretation, projective identification, selfobject, and separation-individuation have been used as litmus tests for adherents – a form of entrapment by allegiance. For example, one group drawn to field theory emphasizes a listening perspective based on reverie and aims to dream the dream for the patient or for patient and analyst to dream the dream together. Another group treats dreaming and the dream in a traditional manner, tracking day residue, past experiences, and current associations in order to reveal the implicit and explicit meanings represented in the dream. Is field theory more or less associated with perspectives that are more poetic and exquisitely sensitive to unconscious mentation? As compared to reverie-centered listening, others propose sensing into or empathy. Here the immediate goal is to apprehend the state of mind of the analysand, her perspective, affects, intentions, and goals as she experiences them – a surface-down approach. Another perspective emphasizes neither the dream as dreamed together nor the message apprehended via empathy but a constant search for what is not in the message as revealed – that is, what the narrative is designed to avoid, hide, protectively obscure. So analysts who might espouse field theory might see the work as dreaming deep together, or going from the surface down, or deeply resonating and attuning. One group describes sensing meanings and inferring intentions from what is communicatively accessible, another by drawing inferences about conflicts involving mechanisms of defense and dissociation. Are we describing different *styles* that all field theories recognize or are we describing different field theories with no essential commonality?

If analysts of different theoretical schools were asked to describe what went on in a clinical session – reporting the "he said, I said" and the atmosphere in the room – I believe there would be many similarities. Then, if the presenter were asked "How do you understand and explain what transpired?" there would be great variance. Our explanations – the metatheories and their sources – differ greatly. For many Americans, the "field" includes infant research and a wide range of neuroscience as well as concepts based on non-linear relational systems and self-states. Terms like transference–countertransference have very different meanings in the different theories and sensibilities of followers of ego psychology, Kohut, Klein, Bion, and the Barangers. We can ask how much a theory of an analytic field – a clinical field of analyst and analysand – is affected by the variance in each and all of these approaches.

Besides sharp differences in theories of how the mind works, and how pathology develops, psychoanalysts of different schools provide varying accounts of therapeutic action. What brings about positive change? Is it when analyst and analysand share a dream? Or when analyst and analysand track the sources of stress and/or acute trauma in early life? Or when they work through defenses that obscure access to conflicts? Or when they repair disruptions in communication and restore a safe, trusting relationship? Or when they stand together in spaces open to reflection or on a shared observational platform open to mutual observation? What brings about a sense of authenticity and a feeling of recognition of the analysand's (and often the analyst's) core being? Finally, does field theory help to give priority to one or more therapeutic effect or does it argue for greater inclusion of all and a reduced significance of the differences?

I will end with a clinical vignette. Mrs. G, a thirty-five-year-old, attractive woman, was referred to me by her previous analyst when she moved from New York to Washington. She described her previous analysis with a recently graduated analyst trained in a classical institute in terms of long silences, Oedipal interpretations of envy and urges to castrate, and an argumentative ambience. For many months, every effort I made to offer empathic understanding of her feelings or to interpret her strivings led to a provocative rejection. Finally, after one particularly striking rebuff, I said, "You know we are not getting along at all well."

She shouted, in her angriest voice, "*We?* We! There is no 'we' here. There is only a you and a me!"

The next day she came in, stood by the couch, and said, "I refuse to get on the couch unless you answer my question. Can analysis help me?"

I took a moment to regain my composure and answered, "I believe you can be helped by analysis. I am far less certain that it should be with me."

She said, "Thank you," then, after a pause, "I will be back tomorrow."

Paraphrasing our statements, I was saying we had evolved a field in which "*we* are not getting along" – a field characterized by opposition. She was saying she had experienced no shared "field" – only the absoluteness of separate selves, "no 'we' . . . only a you and a me." The fly on the wall clearly observed a field comprising an analyst who acknowledged the existence and spirit of a field, albeit a troubled one, and an analysand who denied that field's existence.

To complete the clinical narrative, Mrs. G returned the next day and – to my surprise and delight – became a friendly, cooperative, co-explorer of the dynamics of her antagonistic relationships with her previous analyst and with me. She had an expectation that she and I would repeat that mode of intimacy that based on her past experience was a form of attachment she had come to value. The dramatic shift in our working alliance meant that the field, our analytic relationship, remained intact while the core ambience of the field shifted radically.

It is difficult fully to explain the powerful leverage that resulted from her question and my answer. I believe an important component was Mrs. G hearing me taking responsibility for contributing a negative influence to the field and/or at least being ineffectual in lessening or altering the enactment. In my answer I was saying, "The field consists of mutual interactive influences. Take me out of it and create another field with someone else and you will benefit." As it turned out, the someone else was a me with her and a cooperative her with me that she allowed us to bring to life.

Reference

Stolorow, R. and Atwood, G. (1992). *Contexts of Being*. Hillsdale, NJ: The Analytic Press.

Index

absolute certainty 71
acute enactments 102–3
adventure of the analysis 94
affective patterns 197
"affective resonance and fullness" (Foehl) 181
Agieren (Freud) 102
Aisemberg, Elsa Rappoport de 138
alpha elements (Bion) 10, 73
alpha function (Bion) 73, 95, 146
ambience 56
ambiguity 181
ambivalence 82
American ego psychology models 142–3, 147, 153, 154
analysands: beta elements 146; dreams 95–6; as "an other" to analysts 16 *see also* patients
analyst-as-railway-expert 163
"analyst at work" 7
analysts 13; alpha function 146; body 48–9, 51–2; critical capacity 106; dreams 76, 96; functions 105–6; patient dependence on 59; self perspective 18, 26; transference 68; trusted safe person 23; unconscious communication 49
analysts and analysands: conjoined mental activity 81; dialectic dynamisms 35–6; emotional involvement 94, 97–8; interaction 24–7; interpersonal field 13; intersubjective interaction 87; plasmic model 157–8; as real people 98; role in field theory 201–2; shared field 166; unconscious collusion 74 *see also* analytic relationships
analytic bond 32
analytic consulting rooms 77
analytic dyad 94

analytic fields: and analytic third 81; creation before bi-personal interaction 195; definitions 131–3; Madeline Baranger and Willy Baranger 194; resonator and instrument 163–72; theories 113–33, 196; transference 98; unconscious communication 46
analytic listening 16
analytic processes 92, 143, 149
analytic relationships: affective evolution 197; asymmetrical relationships 72; conative evolution 197; counter-transference 47–8; dialectical process 32; transference 20, 21–3 *see also* analysts and analysands
"Analytic Situation as a Dynamic Field" (Baranger & Baranger) 194
analytic third (Ogden) 47, 80–1, 86, 125
"anything goes" approaches 76–7
Argelander, Hermann 129–31
Argentine Psychoanalytic Association 46
Aristotle 35
Arlow, Jacob 130, 153–4
arrival of experience 177
asymmetrical relationships 72
atemporal field theories 195, 198
"atmospheric" factors 6, 8
Atwood, George 148, 150
autobiographical self 83

babies 73, 80–1, 95
Bacal, H. A. 86
Balint, Michael 124
Balter, Leon 130
Baranger, Madeleine, "Intrapsychic and the intersubjective in contemporary psychoanalysis" 121–4

Baranger, Madeleine, and Baranger, Willy,: analytic field theory 47; "Analytic Situation as a Dynamic Field" 194; analytic/total situation 194; bastion of the analytic field 39, 129, 145; bi-personal field 74, 121–4, 131, 142; counter-transference 143; depth and ambiguity 181; dreamscapes 145–6; "essential ambiguity" 143–4; field concept 195; field theory 72, 73–5, 140; "field turn" 122; holistic process theory 196; influences 46; mythopoesis 156; "mythopoetic circuit" 144–5; point of urgency 74; *princeps* statement 45, 49; *Problems of the Analytic Field* 194; "psychoanalytic field theory" 140, 142–5; "second look" 145; transferential interpretation 33; *Work of Confluence* 122
Baranger, Willy, "Contradictions between theory and technique in psychoanalysis" 124
Basile, Roberto 75
"bastions" (Baranger & Baranger) 145
"beam of darkness" (Freud) 64
Benedetti, Gaetano 124–6
beta elements (Bion) 5, 10, 47, 73, 146
Bezoari, Michele 75
bi-dimensional spiral 196
Bionian Field Theory 77, 145
Bion, Parthenope 127
Bion, Wilfred Ruprecht: analytic third 80–1; beta-elements 47; dreaming 94–6; hallucinosis 57; ideas as facts 69; mental functioning model 10, 146; mother/baby communications 73, 81; "negative capacity" of suspending thought 34; reception in Italy 127–8; waking dream thought 63
bi-personal developmental models 151
Bipersonal Field (Ferro) 126
bi-personal fields: Madeleine Baranger and Willy Baranger 74, 121–4, 131, 142; United States 154–5
bi-personal interactions 146, 147
bi-personal narratives 153
bi-personal psychology (British Independent group) 194
"bi-personal unconscious fantasy" (Baranger & Baranger) 132
Bleger, José 31–2, 33, 39, 46, 195
Bleuler, Eugen 115
Bleuler, Manfred 125

bodily counter-transference 48–9
bodily needs 83
bodily perception 50
Boehlich, W. 120
Bohleber, Werner 129–31, 132
Bolognini, S: *Psychoanalytic Empathy* 47–8; *Secret Passageways* 47–8
Borbely, A. F. 34
Boringhieri, Paolo 126
Botella, César 45, 47, 50
Botella, Sara 45, 47, 50
brain stem 82–4
breakup, unconscious defenses 34
British Object Relations 148
Bromberg, P. 16
Buenos Aires 46
Busch, Fred 77

"*caccia*" (hunting/death) 9
Care 83
Cassorla, Roosevelt 66
cellar events 183–8
censorship 63
Centro di Ricerche Psicoanalitiche di Gruppo "Il Pollaiolo" 127
change 195–6
character function 105
chess-game model (Freud) 92
chiacco (noose) 6–7
child abuse patients 37
child analysts 87
chronic enactments 97, 102
Civitarese, Giuseppe 12, 75–6, 78, 145, 147
classical field theory 191
classical model 21, 23
clinical techniques 154
co-author function 105
cognitive evolution 197
cognitive/psychomotor development 14
collusion of mutual idealization 99–102
collusion of persecution 104
communication 49–50, 69
communication field 120
complementary countertransference (Racker) 195
complementary identification (Racker) 74
complexity theory 14
Conci, Marco 30, 165–6
concordant identification (Racker) 74
conjoined mental activity 81
conscious and unconscious dialectics 31
constructivist perspectives 16

contemporary psychoanalytic field theory 47–8, 118, 140, 147–55
"continuous productive unfolding" (Stern) 182
"Contradictions between theory and technique in psychoanalysis" (W. Baranger) 124
"Conversation with a Stone" (Szymborska) 8
Corrao, Francesco 75, 127
counter-transference: Elsa Rappoport de Aisemberg 48–9, 51–2; Heinrich Racker 132; S. Bolognini 47–8
"created between the two" 124
Cremerius, Johannes 120
Cristina, María 33
critical capacity 106

Damasio, Antonio 82–3
Darwin, Charles 130
Davidson, D. 35, 38
dealienation 39
deformed memories 103
de León de Bernardi, Beatriz 44
"delusional production" 61
"dementia praecox" (Kraepelin) 115
de M'Uzan, Michel 46, 47, 50
depth 178–82
"dialectical spiral" (Pichon-Rivière) 33–4, 193, 196–7
dialectics, transferential interpretation 31–40
dialogical approaches 133
di Chiara, Giuseppe 127, 129
Diderot, D., *Jacques the Fatalist* 5
"*die szenische Funktion des Ichs*" ("scenic function of the ego" Argelander) 130
director function 105
displacement model 21, 23
dissociated subjectivity 181n5
distortions of reality 19
domains 86
Dora (patient) 68
"double field theory" (Conci) 115
dreaming: Antonino Ferro 156–7; capacity to 99; fields 93–6; function 146; for patients 7, 9–10, 202; repression/expression 63
see also hallucinosis; non-dreams
dream language 90
dreamscapes 144, 145
dreams-for-two 96

dream work/thought (Freud) 63
drive/structure models 179
drive theory 147–8
dyadic fields 202 *see also* analysts and analysands

ego psychology models 142–3, 147, 153, 154
Einstein, Albert 141
emergence 176–8, 185
emotional experience 84
emotional involvement 94, 97–8
empathic listening 16–17, 25
empathic modes of observation (Kohut) 15–16
enactments 181, 182
environment, and bodily needs 83
"essential ambiguity" (Baranger & Baranger) 143–4
Etchegoyen, H. 32
experiential perspectives 15–18, 26
"exploration of the field" 166
extratransference 20

false connections 20–1
see also transferences
false dreams 102
fantasies 40, 156, 186
see also unconscious fantasies
Fear 83
felt sense of emergence 177–8
fencing 4, 7
Ferro, Antonino: analytic interaction 4; *Bipersonal Field* 126; contemporary psychoanalysis 48, 140; instinctual drives 85; oneiric model 140, 157; post-Bionian field theory 75–8, 127–8; psychoanalytic field theory 145–7
Feynman, Richard, *QED: The Strange Theory of Light and Matter* 71
field concept: Gaetano Benedetti 125–6; Hermann Argelander 130; Madeleine Baranger and Willy Baranger 129, 195; Maurice Merleau-Ponty 192; socio-political dimension 195
field of dreaming 106
fields: analyst–patient relationships 168–9; as a dreamscape 144; observer's capacity to observe 91–2; patient's life 164; as significant other 165; as smallest unit of human living 155
field theories: approaches 138; background 140–2; constructing 70; definition 68–9,

86; development 147–8; one or more theories 202–4; perspectives 201–2; spiral processes 198 *see also* named psychoanalysts
"field turn" (Baranger & Baranger) 122
figurability field (Botella & Botella) 47, 50
first-person experience 177–8
first wave of field theories 140
first wave of field theory 153
"flattened" experience 180–1
Fliess, Wilhelm 113
Foehl, J. 180, 181, 182
"For an Amorous Lady" (Roethke) 84–5
Foresti, Giovanni 75
Fornari, Franco 128
Fosshage, James, L. 22, 112, 148, 150–1, 155
foundationalist social model 140–1
Freud, Sigmund: *Agieren* 102; analytic interaction 4; analytic process 92; "beam of darkness" 64; chess-game model 92, 144; dream work 63, 95; drives 117, 155; dynamic approach 115; foundation of psychoanalysis 133; "free floating attention" 120–1; implicit field theory 119–21; intra-psychic fantasy 117; knowledge (K) 94; mythical caricature 81–2; perceptions 13; peremptory drives 83; personal reconstruction of mine 120; "significant other" 113; *Standard Edition* 126; *Studies of Hysteria* 20; train analogy 163; transference 19, 21, 68; unconscious communication 49
Fromm-Reichmann, Frieda 125
functional holographic images 147

Gaddini, Eugenio 128
game of oppositions 33
Geneva congress 1955 (IPA) 127
genuine unconscious 49–50
George (patient) 183–8
Gestalt psychology 13, 142, 191–2
Gill, M. 21–2
Giulia (patient) 62
"Golden Braid" of analytic processes 197
Gove, P. B. 68–9
gratifying imperative needs 82–3
Green, Andre 47, 80, 81
Greenberg, Jay 115, 151, 179
Grotstein, Jim 8, 10
group integration 36
group psychotherapy 167–8

"hallucination" 58
hallucinosis 57–64, 96 *see also* dreaming; non-dreams
Hartmann, H. 147
hate (H) 82, 85, 94
Heath, Sheldon 69
Heidegger, M. 192
Heisenberg, W. 13, 141
Herzog, B. 86
history, and analytic dialogue 195
holism (study of wholes) 192
holistic perspectives 198
holistic process theory 196
hormones 83
hostile humor 17

ideas, as facts 69
impasses 74–5
implicit field theory (Freud) 119–21
incompleteness 91
individual analysis 168–9
Inhelder, Barbel 70
inner field (Pichon-Rivière) 193
instinctual drives 85
intentions 17
interactional relational field 152
interaction patterns 16–17, 148–9
intermediate field model 6
internal/external bonds, dialectic spiral process 193
International Bion Conference (1997) 128
International Field Theory Association (IFTA) 1
International Psychoanalytical Association (IPA) 127, 128
interpersonal bond 193
interpersonal field 175–88
interpersonal relationships 117–18, 148–9
Interpersonal Theory of Psychiatry (Sullivan) 115
interpersonal theory (Sullivan) 13, 115–16, 194
interpretation 6
intersubjective interactions 46, 87 *see also* relational theories
intersubjectivity theory 150
interventions 74
inter world wars period 140–1
"Intra-psychic and the interpersonal" (Mitchell) 117–18
"Intrapsychic and the intersubjective in contemporary psychoanalysis" (M. Baranger) 121–2

intrapsychic approaches 117–18, 154, 193–4
intrapsychic field (Pichon-Rivière) 193
introjective identification (Klein) 87
Isaacs, Susan 39–40, 132
Isabel (patient) 169
Italy 126–9

Jacques the Fatalist (Diderot) 5
Johnson, M. 35
Juan (patient) 36
judgemental dimensions 60

Katz, S. Montana: analytical groups 53; field theory models 174; *Metaphor and Fields* 14–15, 45, 133; mythopoeic and oneiric models 140; psychoanalyst mental attitude 166
Keats, John 73, 76
Klein, M. 32, 87, 94, 102
knowledge (K) 94
Kohler, Wolfgang 192
Kohut, Heinz 15, 148
Kraepelin, Emil 115
Kris, A. 147
"kryptonite field" 169

Lacan, J. 34
Lachmann, Frank 148, 150–1, 155
La escritura o la vida (Semprún) 52
Lakoff, G. 35
language 69
lapsus (fall, tumble) 63
Le libere donne di Magliano (Tobino) 9
Les Clients d'Avrenos (Simenon) 5
Levenson, Edgar 148–50, 154, 158, 188
Lewin, Bertram 143, 147
Lewin, Kurt 13, 74, 141–2, 192–3
Liberman, David 46, 195
Lichtenberg, Joseph 56, 148, 150–1, 155
light and sound technician function 105–6
"lion" metaphor 36, 38
listening perspectives 15–18, 26, 202 *see also* dreaming
Litowitz, Bonnie 69
"little bug" metaphor 36, 38
Lorand, Sandor 82
losing perspective 82
love (L) 82, 85, 94
Luigi (Librarian) 9
Lust 83

Maclean, Paul 83–4
Manfredi (patient) 169–71

Manfredi, Stefania 121
mayeutic process of interpretation 39
meaning, relational theory 152
"Medea" function 61
Meltzer, Donald 80
memory in feelings (Klein) 102
mental creativity 5
mental functioning (Arlow/Modell) 154
mental functioning model (Bion) 146
mental setting 97–8
Merleau-Ponty, Maurice 34, 74, 180, 192–3
Metamorphoses (Ovid) 183, 185–6
Metaphor and Fields (Katz) 14–15, 45, 133
metaphors 34–6, 37–8, 94–5, 154–5
metapsychology 45
mind, concept of 152
Mitchell, Stephen: clinical example 152–3; drive/structure models 179; field theories 148; and H. S. Sullivan 115; interpretation 123–4; "Intra-psychic and the interpersonal" 117; "Penelope's loom" 118–19; *Psychoanalytic Dialogues* 133; *Relational Concepts in Psychoanalysis* 117, 118; relational theory 151; "relational turn" 116–19
mobilization, unconscious defenses 34
modal operators 166
Modell, Arnold 154
model of human behavior (Lewin) 141
mothers 73, 80–1
motivation 17
motivational systems theory 150–1
Musatti, Cesare 126
mutual idealization 100
mutual seduction 104
mythopoeic model 140, 156 *see also* subjective mythopoiesis
"mythopoetic circuit" (Baranger & Baranger) 144–5

narrative description 148
narratology 145, 146
"negative capability" (Keats) 73, 76
Neri, Claudio 127
new ideas 71
new models 131–2
Night and Day exhibition (Ofili) 63
nightmares 98–9, 103
Nissim Momigliano, Luciana, *Shared Experience: The Psychoanalytic Dialogue* 128

non-dreams 96–7 *see also* dreaming; hallucinosis
non-dreams-for-two 97, 102
nonlinear dynamic systems theory 14
non-neurotic fields 47, 48
North America 13–14 *see also* United States

objective observation 13, 91
objectivist epistemology 19
object-relational orientation (Balint) 124
object relations 151
observer effect 13, 141
Oelsner, Robert 122
Ofili, Chris 63
Ogden, Thomas 7, 10, 31, 46, 47, 80–1, 125
"once upon a time" mythopoesis 156
oneiric models 140, 145, 156–7
"Onset of schizophrenia" (Sullivan) 116
organizing model of transference 20, 22–3 *see also* transferences
other-centered perspectives 16, 17, 25
O (ultimate reality) 8, 94
overadaptation 50–1
overprotection 79
Ovid, *Metamorphoses* 183, 185–6

Pablo (patient) 51–2
palimpsest models 106–7
Panksepp, Jaak 83, 84
parapraxis 57–8, 60–1, 63
parasympathetic control, visceral organs 84
"participant observation" (Sullivan) 117, 131–2
past, as construct of the present 148
patient-as-passenger 163
patients: deeper events in history 179; dependence 59; dreams 76; fields 164 *see also* analysands
patterns 16–17, 148–9
"Penelope's loom" (Mitchell) 118–19
perceptions 13, 74
peremptory drives (Freud) 83
permission 62 *see also* hallucinosis
perpetual inner-outer dialectics 193
personality 150
"personal myths" (Levenson) 149
personal-perceptual experience 74
personal reconstruction of mine 120
phenomenological approaches 34
"phenomenological–existential" philosophy (Merleau-Ponty) 74

physics 191
Piaget, Jean 22, 70, 86
Pichon-Rivière, Enrique 33–4, 122, 193, 196–8
plasmic models 140, 155, 157–8
Play 83
pluralistic perspectives 113–33
point of urgency (Baranger & Baranger) 74
Pope, Alexander 71–2
Porges, Stephen 84
positivist model 140–1
post-Bionian field theories 77–8
"post-Bionian psychoanalysis" (Ferro & Civitarese) 75–6
postmodernism 148
princeps statement (Baranger & Baranger) 45, 49
Problems of the Analytic Field (Baranger & Baranger) 194
process-based observations 14
process theory (Pichon-Rivière) 196–8
profundity of the internal 179–80
projective identification (Klein) 87
proper unconscious 49–50
protection 79
Psychiatric Interview (Sullivan) 115
psychic mourning 50–1
Psychoanalytic Dialogues (Mitchell) 133
Psychoanalytic Empathy (Bolognini) 47–8
"psychoanalytic field theory" (Baranger & Baranger) 72, 142–5 *see also* field theories
psychoanalytic treatment 72, 86
"psychological symbiosis" 123
psychoneurotic field 48
psychosomatics 48

QED: The Strange Theory of Light and Matter (Feynman) 71

Racker, Heinrich 17, 33, 74, 122–3, 132; *Studi sulla tecnica psicoanalitica* 127
Rage 83
Razinsky, Liran 68
reality 19, 91
real person (analysts/analysands) 98
recognition 75
reductionism 69–70
regional concept 133
relational analysts 18
Relational Concepts in Psychoanalysis (Mitchell) 117, 118

relational field theories 14, 19
relational theories: Arnold Modell 154; intersubjective interaction 87; Jay Greenberg and Stephen Mitchell 151–3
"relational turn" (Mitchell) 116–19
relationships 168–9
relativistic epistemology 19
Renik, Owen 49
repressed unconscious 49–50
Resnik, Salomon 122
resonances 18, 44
reverie 47, 202
reveries 95
Ricoeur, P. 35
Riolo, Fernando 128–9
rituals 9
Roethke, Theodore, "For an Amorous Lady" 84–5
Rolland, J. C. 46
Rosenberg, B. 48
Rosenfeld, Herbert 127
Roussillon, René 45–6, 47

"scenic function of the ego" (Argelander) 130
"scenic understanding" (Argelander) 130
Schizophrenia as a Human Process (Sullivan) 115–16, 195
"schizophrenia" (Bleuler) 115
scientific model 140–1
Searles, Harold 125
"second look" (Baranger & Baranger) 145
second wave of field theories 140
second wave of field theory 153
Secret Passageways (Bolognini) 47–8
self perspectives 18, 26
self psychology 87
Semprún, Jorge, *La escritura o la vida* 52
sexual abuse 104, 183–8
shame of not-being 61
Shared Experience: The Psychoanalytic Dialogue (Nissim Momigliano) 128
shared field 166, 167
Shulevitz, Judith 79
"significant other" (Conci) 165–6
Silberstein, Eduard 120
Silverman, Martin A. 90
Silvio (patient) 50–1
Simenon, G., *Les Clients d'Avrenos* 5
Smith, L. 14
"social psychology" (Pichon-Rivière) 194
socio-political dimensions 195
somatic protoself (Damasio) 83

Sonia (patient) 98–105
South America 32, 147
spectator function 105
SPI National Congress (1994) 128
spiral processes (Pichon-Rivière) 33–4, 193, 196–7
stagnation 74–5
Standard Edition (Freud) 126
Stefania (patient) 62
Stepansky, Paul 133
Stern, Donnel B.: "continuous productive unfolding" 182; emergence 4; field definition 155; and Harry Stack Sullivan 13; interpersonal field 175; American field theories 148; shared field 167–8; unconscious thought 162
Stolorow, Robert 148, 150
structural models 142–3, 179
Studies of Hysteria (Freud) 20
Studi sulla tecnica psicoanalitica (Racker) 127
subjective mythopoesis 8 *see also* mythopoeic model
subjectivity 14, 18, 21, 26
"subjugating intersubjectivity" (Ogden) 81
Sullivan, Harry Stack: death 193; "epistemological revolution" 116; field theory 115–19, 148, 192; interpersonal theory 13, 194; *Interpersonal Theory of Psychiatry* 115; "The onset of schizophrenia" 116; "participant observation" 15, 117, 131–2; *Psychiatric Interview* 115; *Schizophrenia as a Human Process* 115–16; significant others 165; social influences 180; unconscious fantasy 123–4
surface-down approaches 202
Swick Perry, Helen 115
symbolic network of thought 93
symbolic paternal function 61
symbols, as metaphors 94–5
systems theories 14, 148
"szenisches Verstehen" ("scenic understanding," Argelander) 130
Szpilka, J. L. 34
Szymborska, Wisława 8

Taormina congress 1980 (IPA) 128
temporal dimensions 195
tertiary process in analysis (Green) 80
theater critic function 105
theater model 102, 105

Thelan, E. 14
theoretical constructs 71
theoretical schools 203 *see also* Italy; named psychoanalysts; North America; South America; United States
theories of relativity (Einstein) 141
theory of interpersonal relations (Sullivan) 13
theory of intersubjectivity (Renik) 49
Theory of Psychoanalytical Practice (Tubert-Oklander) 198
therapeutic action theory 19
therapeutic change (Levenson) 148–9
"therapeutic field" (Benedetti) 125–6
third entity (child's and mother's mind) 81
third model 139–40, 158
third person 176, 181
third wave of field theories 140
Tobino, Mario, *Le libere donne di Magliano* 9
Tomasi di Lampedusa, Alessandra 127
total analytic situation 194
totalist model (Gill) 21–2
transference–countertransference 68–73, 74, 98, 203
transference neurosis (Freud) 21
transferences 19–23, 183
transferential interpretation 31–40
transformation in hallucinosis (TH) 57–64
transitional phenomena (Winnicott) 47
transitional subject (Benedetti) 124–6
triune brains 84
Tubert-Oklander, Juan 4; *Theory of Psychoanalytical Practice* 198
Tuckett, David 77

ultimate reality (O) 8, 94
umbral cone 169–71
uncertainty principle 91
Uncertainty Principle (Heisenberg) 13, 141
unconscious collusion 74
unconscious communication 49–50
unconscious fantasies 46, 74, 130, 144, 153–4 *see also* fantasies
"unconscious fantasy of the couple" 122–3
unconscious motivations 17
unconscious necessary 66
unconscious personal myths 149
unconscious primitive fantasies (Isaacs) 39–40
unconscious processes 31, 139, 144, 178–80
unconscious root of enactment 181
unconscious, the, and emergence 176
United States 139, 140, 147–55
  see also North America
unsaturated interventions 188
Uruguayan Psychoanalytic Society 46

vagus nerves 84
vertex of observation 93, 106
virtual/actual reality 77
visions of the unconscious 63

Wachtel, P. L. 20, 179, 180
waking dream thought (Bion) 63, 146
Wallerstein, R. S. 34–5
Webster's Third New International Dictionary 68–9
Wertheimer, Max 192
White, William Alanson 115
whole (holism) 192
windows, staring out of 26
Winnicott, D. W. 47, 82
Work of Confluence (Baranger & Baranger) 122

Zac, Joel 195